Bloodshed at Little Bighorn

WITNESS TO HISTORY

Peter Charles Hoffer and Williamjames Hull Hoffer, *Series Editors*

BLOODSHED AT LITTLE BIGHORN

SITTING BULL, CUSTER, AND THE DESTINIES OF NATIONS

TIM LEHMAN

The Johns Hopkins University Press | *Baltimore*

The Johns Hopkins University Press
2715 North Charles Street
Baltimore, Maryland 21218-4363
www.press.jhu.edu

Library of Congress Cataloging-in-Publication Data
Lehman, Tim.
   Bloodshed at Little Bighorn : Sitting Bull, Custer, and the destinies of
nations / Tim Lehman.
      p.   cm.— (Witness to history)
   Includes bibliographical references and index.
   ISBN-13: 978-0-8018-9500-5 (hardcover : alk. paper)
   ISBN-10: 0-8018-9500-6 (hardcover : alk. paper)
   ISBN-13: 978-0-8018-9501-2 (pbk. : alk. paper)
   ISBN-10: 0-8018-9501-4 (pbk. : alk. paper)
   1. Little Bighorn, Battle of the, Mont., 1876. 2. Sitting Bull, 1831–1890.
3. Custer, George A. (George Armstrong), 1839–1876. 4. Indians of North
America—Great Plains—History. 5. Indians of North America—Great
Plains—Government relations 6. Frontier and pioneer life—Great Plains.
7. United States—Territorial expansion. 8. United States—Race relations—
Political aspects—History. 9. Whites—United States—Attitudes—History.
10. Racism—United States—History. I. Title.
   E83.876.L45 2010
   973.8'2—dc22   2009035576

A catalog record for this book is available from the British Library.

Special discounts are available for bulk purchases of this book. For
more information, please contact Special Sales at 410-516-6936 or
specialsales@press.jhu.edu.

The Johns Hopkins University Press uses environmentally friendly book
materials, including recycled text paper that is composed of at least 30
percent post-consumer waste, whenever possible. All of our book papers
are acid-free, and our jackets and covers are printed on paper with recycled
content.

For my late father, G. Irvin Lehman,
who knew the value of stories;
and for my sons, Tom and Topher,
who carry them into the next generation

CONTENTS

Bloodshed at Little Bighorn

PROLOGUE

It was a terrible, terrible story, so different from the outcome we had
hoped for.   LIEUTENANT JAMES BRADLEY, MONTANA COLUMN, 1876

THE FIRST people to mourn the news of Custer's crushing defeat
at the Little Bighorn were the Apsáalooke, the Children of the Large Beaked
Bird, known to the whites as the Crow Indians. On the morning of June 26,
1876, the day after the battle, a group of Crow scouts traveling with General
Alfred Terry saw fresh pony tracks nearby and a pillar of smoke some 15 miles
in the distance. Fearing that the tracks and the smoke might indicate that
enemy Sioux warriors were close by, the scouts advanced cautiously. They
soon deduced that the tracks belonged to three Indians who were watching
them from a vantage point 2 miles away on the other side of the Little Bighorn
River. After a series of smoke signals indicating friendship, the Crow leader
Little Face met the three riders at the river and talked. The riders, it turned
out, were also Crow scouts. They had ridden with Custer and been among
the last to see him alive. The three scouts, White Man Runs Him, Hairy Moc-
casin, and Goes Ahead, told Little Face how they had guided Custer to find
the large village of Sioux and Cheyenne, how he had attacked the previous
afternoon, and how he had been overwhelmed. As they left the scene of the
battle, the last thing the scouts saw was the bodies of the Seventh Cavalry
"strewn all over the country."

Little Face returned from the river weeping "with a bitterness of anguish
such as I have rarely seen," chief of scouts Lieutenant James Bradley remem-

bered. Addressing the other Crow scouts, Little Face told the story of the previous day's battle "in a choking voice, broken with frequent sobs." These "first listeners to the horrid story of the Custer massacre" then let out a "doleful series of cries and wails" that was "a song of mourning for the dead." One by one they went off alone to weep, chant, and grieve, "rocking their bodies to and fro," mourning for the death of America's most famous Indian fighter.[1]

The next day Bradley, along with General Alfred Terry's column of four hundred infantrymen, advanced farther up the valley of the Little Bighorn, where they discovered the remains of a large Indian camp. Scattered over the valley floor lay robes, pots, kettles, axes, china dishes, saddles, lodgepoles, and other debris that indicated a hastily moved Indian village. Amidst the village leftovers they found the badly burned remains of three severed heads and a few bloody articles of clothing that belonged to officers of the Seventh Cavalry. The worst was yet to come. As they approached the ridge, officers observed what appeared to be white boulders on the distant hillsides shining in the sun. Focusing his field glasses on the far slope, Lieutenant Godfrey nearly dropped them in horror as he realized that the white shapes were the naked bodies of the dead. Captain Thomas Weir stared at the eerie corpses and uttered, "Oh, how white they look! How white!" Weir, who had a bookish sensibility and instinctively grasped how such a compelling image of white bodies against a brown hillside might translate into stories, added, "My, that would be a beautiful sentiment for a poem."[2] Using the few shovels, axes, and picks they had, the soldiers dug shallow graves in the rocky Montana soil and attempted to bury the naked, rotting corpses. It was a scene of "sickening, ghastly horror," one officer remembered, as the putrid bodies received "a scant covering of mother earth" and were left "in that vast wilderness, hundreds of miles from civilization, friends, and home—to the wolves."[3]

Twenty-four hours later and about 25 miles south from where Custer's dead lay buried in their shallow hillside graves, a village of seven thousand Sioux and Cheyenne Indians celebrated their remarkable victory. On the sacred fourth evening after the battle, after mourning their losses and fleeing south to avoid Terry's soldiers, the villagers lit bonfires, danced, recounted stories, and sang. Around the campfire young warriors came of age by telling of their brave deeds and established war leaders added luster to their reputations. Word spread that their victory had come against "Long Hair" Custer, and singers invented kill songs to satirize the famous soldier chief: "Long Hair, guns I hadn't any. You brought me some. I thank you." Another kill song spoke of grief to their enemy's widow: "Long Hair has never returned yet, so his wife is crying all around. Looking over, she cries."[4]

Four hundred miles east of this celebration, Elizabeth Bacon Custer had gathered with a group of women on Sunday afternoon, June 25, 1876, the day of her husband's last battle, to sing hymns. On this Sunday one woman suggested "Nearer, My God, to Thee," but this was immediately vetoed because it was too close to the trepidations of many army wives. Two weeks later, about 2 a.m. on the morning of July 6, Elizabeth Custer woke to a messenger who confirmed her worst fears: her husband and 260 other officers and men of the Seventh Cavalry had been killed by Indians at the Little Bighorn. For a time Libbie Custer wept inconsolably. Then she stepped out into the early morning chill to inform the other soldiers' wives of the fate of their husbands. For the rest of her long life, she remained committed to creating the mythology of her dashing husband's career and interpreting the vital meaning of his early death.

Generals William Tecumseh Sherman and Philip Sheridan, architects of the army's campaign against the Sioux and Cheyenne, first heard the news while attending the nation's centennial celebration in Philadelphia. Building on the theme "A Century of Progress," the festivities featured exhibits of the recently invented telephone, a number of crude internal combustion engines, and a 39-foot-high steam engine. Like many who heard the story, Sherman and Sheridan initially refused to believe it, discounting the newspaper headlines as a fanciful tall tale based on the fertile imaginations of frontier scouts. Yet even as Sherman explained his disbelief to a reporter, an aide handed him Terry's dispatch from the Montana battlefield. Apparently, the most improbable of events, a band of primitive Indians defeating a modern army, was true after all.

Within days of the battle, the story of what happened on June 25, 1876, on the bluffs above the Little Bighorn River in remote southeastern Montana, had the power to make men and women weep in anguish, shout and sing in jubilation, wonder in puzzlement about what actually happened, and argue endlessly about the meaning of it all. Over a century and a quarter later, the story still has that same power.

1 ⟩ THE PEN, THE PIPE, AND THE GUN

> I am no white man! They are the only people that make rules for other people, that say, "If you stay on one side of this line it is peace, but if you go on the other side I will kill you all." I don't hold with deadlines. There is plenty of room; camp where you please. — CRAZY HORSE

IT ALL started with a broken-down cow.

During the hot days of August 1854, some five thousand Lakota Sioux camped along the cool bank of the Platte River, not far from Fort Laramie. They were waiting for the Indian agent to disperse goods that had been promised to them under the terms of the treaty they had signed near that spot only three years earlier. On the nearby Oregon Trail a Mormon wagon train snaked its way through the Wyoming prairie. A worn-out cow, thin, slow, and surely on its last legs, straggled well behind the main party. As he watched the slow-moving wagon train, a young Lakota named High Forehead got the notion to shoot the struggling cow. Afterward, as the Lakota butchered and ate the scrawny beast, its owner, intimidated by the large number of Indians, hurried on to Fort Laramie to report the incident. Believing this shooting to be merely the latest in a series of intolerable offenses, army officers decided it was time to make a point by arresting the shooter. With the aid of twenty-nine men, two howitzers, and one drunken interpreter, Lieutenant John Grattan, fresh from West Point and itching for a fight, set out the next day to arrest High Forehead. Grattan, who had boasted that the Indians were no match for the U.S. Army, said that he wanted to "crack it to the

Sioux."[1] He told his men that he did not expect them "to be compelled to fire a single gun." If shooting started, however, his order was to "fire as much as you damned please."[2]

When they arrived at the Indian camp, Conquering Bear, whom the whites had named chief of all the Lakota in the 1851 treaty, came out to parley with the soldiers. When Grattan demanded the arrest of the cow killer, the Lakota leader Man Afraid of His Horses watched the soldiers load their weapons and tried to calm the waters. "Look, my friend, do you not see a heap of lodges?" he asked Grattan. Refusing to be deterred from his task, Grattan declared, "I have come down here for that man, and I'll have him or die."[3] At the other end of the camp, High Forehead, fearing that his arrest would mean a humiliating death in captivity, prepared himself to die fighting rather than surrender. In accordance with Lakota custom and the terms of the 1851 treaty, Conquering Bear attempted to compensate for the lost cow with a gift of greater value, offering to allow the Mormon to select any horse from his own herd of sixty. Meanwhile, the interpreter, an inveterate Indian hater who had been drinking heavily that day, shouted to the Lakota, "Today you are all women." He promised that the soldiers were going to kill them and he would personally eat their hearts. Other nearby Lakota urged Grattan to silence his interpreter. While women and children sought cover near the riverbanks, warriors prepared their ponies for a fight.

Conquering Bear walked from Grattan to High Forehead, attempting to mediate a solution, but when High Forehead steadfastly refused to surrender, Grattan ordered his infantrymen and howitzers to fire at High Forehead's lodge. Aimed too high, the howitzers did little damage, but the bullets cut down not High Forehead but Conquering Bear, mortally wounding him. Man Afraid of His Horse, hoping to avoid further bloodshed, rode in front of the warriors, urging them not to attack. Ignoring his pleas, several hundred warriors overwhelmed the soldiers and killed all of them. Heady with their success, many of the young warriors wanted to continue the fight by attacking the lightly defended Fort Laramie, but the dying Conquering Bear and other elders restrained them. In the end, a few warriors broke into the American Fur Company's trading post, seized the goods that the Indian agent held there, and then gradually dispersed into small bands for the fall buffalo hunt.

This was the Lakota's first large-scale fight with white soldiers, and the Indians themselves were divided about what their next steps should be. Man

Afraid of His Horse counseled restraint and convinced many of his Oglala to move away from Fort Laramie to avoid further interaction with the whites. Relatives of the dead Conquering Bear, however, sent around a war pipe requesting warriors to join them in avenging their fallen leader. In November a group of warriors, including Conquering Bear's cousin Spotted Tail, attacked a mail train, killing three people and capturing a large amount of gold. Other Lakota warriors harassed wagon trains on the overland trail, taking horses and a few goods. The quarter-century conflict between the Lakota and the United States, sometimes called the Great Sioux War, was off to a sputtering start.

Lakota Rising

For the previous half century the Lakota and the United States had existed in an uneasy peace on the Great Plains. Their first encounter had come during the Lewis and Clark expedition and narrowly avoided bloodshed. As the Corps of Discovery pushed its way up the Missouri River, the Lakota (also known as the Teton or western Sioux) stopped them and demanded tribute. While Lewis described the Sioux as "the vilest miscreants of the Indian race" who "must ever remain the pirates of the Missouri,"[4] in fact they were the most powerful people of the region and at the center of a vast trade network that stretched across the plains and connected peoples for hundreds of miles in every direction. Horses from New Mexico; guns, axes, knives, and mirrors from the Great Lakes; buffalo meat and hides from the Plains tribes; and corn, pumpkins, and tobacco from the Mandan, Omaha, and Arikara, the farming tribes along the river bottoms of the Missouri, all made their way across the plains and up and down the Missouri, where the Lakota had a monopoly on the river traffic. Lewis and Clark thought that the river was a freeway, while the Lakota were used to treating it as their toll road.

The Lakota of the nineteenth century were the classic Plains Indians of the American imagination: mounted nomads, noble warriors with feathers in their hair, living free on the open plains, eating and sleeping in tipis, performing sacred ceremonies, engaging in highly stylized and elaborate rituals of warfare, moving seemingly at will across the open country, and bearing the dignity of free people. During these years, the Lakota were numerous, powerful, and in their full flower as a Great Plains horse-and-bison society. The Lakota, however, did not enter the historical stage in the mid-nineteenth century from a timeless past, but rather were themselves in the process of profound cultural changes. They had lived on the plains west of the Missouri for only a few generations, lured to the region by the abundant buffalo herds that grew fat on the rich prairie grasses. Previously they had hunted deer, gathered wild rice, and trapped beavers in Minnesota, where the French dubbed them "Sioux," a translation of an Algonquian word meaning "enemy." While Sioux came to be used as a widespread and seemingly indispensable collective term for these people, many of them (then and now) preferred to be called Dakota (eastern or Santee) or Lakota (western or Teton), depending on the dialect, a word meaning "the people" or "the allies" and connoting friendship.

During the 1700s, the Sioux moved westward from their Minnesota home and became nomadic buffalo hunters with a warrior culture. Using guns acquired from the fur trade with the French and horses traded from the Southwest, the Lakota by the mid-1800s were the most powerful tribe on the northern plains. What made their migration possible was their successful adaptation to the horse, an animal that increased their mobility and altered the way they obtained their food, fought their enemies, organized their societies, and thought about themselves. A horse could carry four times more weight than and travel twice as fast as a dog, the Lakota's previous beast of burden. A mounted hunter could travel far to find buffalo, which led to an increase in food supply that supported a steady rise in Lakota population. Numbering about eight to ten thousand at the time of Lewis and Clark, the Lakota would grow to sixteen or twenty thousand by the time of the battle of the Little Bighorn. They were the only tribe on the northern plains to grow in population during the tumultuous nineteenth century.

Aided by the horse, the Lakota came to understand their identity as intimately linked with their main food source, the buffalo. Like other Plains peoples, they found uses for many parts of the animal: brains for tanning hides, horns for spoons, shoulder bones to dig, hooves as glue for arrows, hair for ropes, fur for blankets, and skins for clothes of all sorts, bags, bridles, and lodge covers. As the buffalo became central to their material existence, so too did the animal become the source of their most sacred spiritual story, "White Buffalo Calf Woman," which explained the origins of the pipe ceremony, the vision quest, the sweat lodge, and other sacred ceremonies of the Lakota. So thoroughly did the Lakota's fate become entwined with the buffalo that they came to refer to themselves as the *Pte Taoyate*, the Buffalo Nation, a name suggesting power, strength, generosity, and perseverance.

Powerful as they were, the Lakota faced problems during the nineteenth century. Although the American presence on the plains was weak during the first half of the century, American diseases ran ahead of people or armies. Epidemics became commonplace on the plains, and an 1837 smallpox outbreak wiped out nearly half of the native population of the plains. Ironically, the nomadic Lakota suffered lower casualties than the horticultural villages scattered along the Missouri River and probably gained in relative strength as a result of the epidemic. Another problem developed as the apparently inexhaustible resource of buffalo herds was by midcentury becoming scarce enough that Plains Indians and fur traders alike complained about the relative scarcity of this unique source of prosperity. Like other Plains tribes, the Sioux hunted buffalo both for subsistence and for its value as a trade commodity. Every year thousands of buffalo furs went down the Missouri River in exchange for manufactured goods, including guns. As the Plains Sioux displaced the Arikara, the Kiowa, and the Pawnee along the river bottoms and pushed the Crow and the Shoshoni farther westward, they engaged in nearly constant warfare for control of the rich buffalo lands west of the Missouri. Their culture elevated warrior exploits over other activities, and consequently leadership fell increasingly to military chiefs. They also acquired enemies from other tribes—enemies who would prove willing to protect themselves by siding with United States soldiers at the Little Bighorn.

As the Sioux moved west, they chose to ally themselves with another group who were new to the western plains, the Cheyenne. Like the Sioux, the Cheyenne had adopted the horse and moved west in search of buffalo. Calling themselves the *Tsistsistas*, or "our people," the Cheyenne also became full horse-and-buffalo nomads of the plains, marrying into Lakota society and so maintaining a strong alliance with them. By the middle of the nineteenth century, they had settled into an area that held some of the best remaining game herds on the plains, the upper Yellowstone River and its tributaries. Moving into this country put them directly in conflict with the Crow Indians, and it took them to the place where they would fight their most famous battle, the Little Bighorn.

A mix of mountains, prairies, and river bottoms, Crow Territory had sufficient ecological variety to support both wildlife and horses in unusual abundance. Because this land was so desirable, the Crow people had to defend it vigilantly, and the pressure of constant warfare took its toll. The boundaries of their territory shrank steadily during the nineteenth century, and casualties to the male warriors skewed the gender ratio so much that some Crow villages had twice as many women as men. More than one nineteenth-century white observer wondered whether the Crow would survive as an independent tribe or whether they would be conquered and absorbed into the surrounding peoples. By the second half of the century, desperation forced the Crow to accept an alliance with the United States to fight against the advancing Lakota. When warfare erupted on the plains between the United States and the Lakota in 1854, Crow fought with the U.S. Army in the hopes of protecting themselves and maybe even reclaiming some of their old hunting grounds. Their challenge was considerable. The Lakota were a proud and independent people, more accustomed to victory than defeat, more likely to dispossess their neighbors than surrender to them. Perhaps this is why they found in themselves the strength, as well as the audacity, to challenge the U.S. government.

What the Lakota did not know was that in 1854 the United States was poised for a much more aggressive display of power than anything the Lakota had previously experienced. For generations the Plains Indians were affected only by the reverberations of distant European empires—horses, diseases, manufactured goods, guns—but by the mid-nineteenth century, Americans were anxious not simply to travel through the interior of the continent but to possess it, which ultimately meant dispossessing the native populations. Many Americans hoped, in the words of the Northwest Ordinance of 1787, that this could happen with the "utmost good faith" and that Indian "lands and property shall never be taken from them without their consent." At the beginning of the republic, Jefferson called this new kind of expansion an "empire of liberty," one that would spread republican values rather than a coercive colonialism. Believing in the Enlightenment ideal of human equality, Jefferson asserted that American Indians shared the inalienable moral rights of other Americans and would in time assimilate to mainstream society. He imagined that "our settlements and theirs meet and blend together, to intermix, and become one people."[5] This Jeffersonian blending, however, was of peoples rather than cultures. Jefferson, like almost all of his contemporaries, assumed that a society of farmers based on widespread ownership and cultivation of private property was a higher form of civilization than one based on the inefficient system of hunting wild animals. Indians would have to lose their culture in order to join American society. Restricting their area for hunting, that is, dispossessing them of their lands, might hasten the process of assimilation. Those natives who resisted, Jefferson conceded, might have to be pushed westward into what came to be called "permanent" Indian Territory.

Yet not all Americans agreed that Indians could find a place in the expanding American republic. Many settlers, especially those on the bloody edges of the frontier, advocated extermination rather than assimilation. Ironically, it was Jefferson's idealized heroes, the virtuous yeoman farmers, who undermined any chance for Jeffersonian imperialism to proceed in its more benevolent form. Farmers seeking access to land pushed west faster than Jefferson could have possibly expected: Southerners poured into Texas in the 1820s and 1830s, settlers traveled overland to Oregon in the 1840s, Mormons migrated to Utah along the same trail, and finally tens of thousands of Forty-Niners followed the trail heading for the California gold fields. The 1840s proved to be the most expansionist decade in American history as the federal government acquired Texas by annexation, California and the Southwest by war with Mexico, and Oregon by negotiation with Britain. Farmers and miners spilled into the newly opened territories; a trickle of one hundred emigrants on the Oregon Trail in 1841 became a flood of twenty-five hundred by 1845 and a torrent of more than twenty-five thousand emigrants by 1850. Earlier debates about the logical or natural boundaries of the United States were now cast aside as the young nation increased its land area by almost 70 percent and spread to the Pacific Ocean. Even the powerful Lakota, who had doubled their population and increased their land base during the first half of the nineteenth century, might have been impressed by a nation that tripled its land base and whose population mushroomed by 600 percent or more from the age of Jefferson to the age of Sitting Bull.

As emigrants crossed the plains on the way to farming settlements in Oregon and gold claims in California during the 1840s, they adopted an idea particularly suited to this aggressive phase of western expansion: Manifest Destiny. The formulation came from John O'Sullivan, the editor of the expansionist *Democratic Review,* who claimed that Americans had "the right of our manifest destiny to overspread and to possess the whole continent which providence has given us for the development of the great experiment of liberty and federated self-government." As an advocate of Jacksonian democracy, O'Sullivan claimed the mantel of divine inevitability for the expansionist platform of his party in the face of Whig opposition. Phrasing decisions as destiny, the Irish editor claimed, "Already the advance guard of an irresistible army of Anglo-Saxon emigration has begun."[6] O'Sullivan's phrase caught on so quickly because it suggested a destiny that was demographic, racial, and providential. At its most basic, Manifest Destiny simply reflected the fact that the nineteenth-century United States had one of the fastest growing populations on record, thereby fulfilling the divine command to replenish the earth. Repudiating Jefferson's idea of the racial (if not cultural) equality of Indians, O'Sullivan instead claimed that Anglo-Saxons—that is, Europeans—were racially superior because they were inherently more capable of self-government. By extension, then, Anglo-Saxons possessed a divine mandate to rule over inferior "races" such as Mexicans or Indians. Blessing the entire expansion process was divine Providence, which might be interpreted either literally or in a more secular form as inevitable progress. As Missouri senator Thomas Hart Benton told the Senate, any race that resisted this divine law, which stood in the path of Manifest Destiny, faced a choice of civilization or extinction.

Although it was not immediately obvious, this explosive expansion of American society and its imperious rationale of Manifest Destiny created a fundamentally different situation for the natives of the northern plains. Previous generations of Americans, combining Enlightenment universalism and Christian humanitarianism, had hoped that, given enough time, Indians would assimilate into American society. Those who resisted, as Jefferson recognized, could be removed to the western territories where they could live in "permanent" Indian Territory. Separated from the corrupting influences of white society (whiskey, weapons, fighting), the Indians could assimilate at their own pace. This idea of pushing Indians beyond the line of civilization and into vacant western lands permeated United States Indian policy from the first colonies through the 1830s, when Andrew Jackson championed Indian removal as the humane solution to the "Indian problem." The expansion of the 1840s, however, made the idea of an "Indian Frontier" in the western territories obsolete, as there was no longer any line beyond which Indians could be pushed. In 1848 Indian Affairs Commissioner William Medill advanced a solution to this new problem. He wanted "to colonize our Indian tribes beyond the reach, for some years, of our white population; confining each within a small district of country, so that, as the game decreases" the hunters would be "compelled to resort to agriculture."[7] This idea of colonies within national boundaries, later called reservations, developed out of earlier policies as a kind of internal Indian removal, a means of providing a temporary way station for Indians on the path to assimilation. For critics the policy amounted to a fig leaf of morality on what amounted to a land grab, but for some sincere reformers the idea of reservations was a way to combine Christian philanthropy with the reality of American expansion. As far as American policy was concerned, the Plains Indians now faced a choice of extinction or reservation. The Lakota were no longer at the distant reaches of American power; they were now surrounded by it.

Yet none of these changes were obvious in the late summer of 1851 when ten thousand Plains Indians of many tribes gathered at Horse Creek, 40 miles east of Fort Laramie, to meet with representatives of the U.S. government. In one of the largest gatherings of Indians ever known on the plains, the government representatives dispensed twenty-seven wagonloads of goods—clothes, knives, kettles, tobacco, and bright cloth—in a symbol of what many Indians hoped would be a long-term relationship of reciprocity and good will. Looking for stability, the government intended to make a treaty with the Indians that would ensure intertribal peace and guarantee the safety of emigrants along the overland trails. The treaty first established separate regions for each tribe, hoping that setting out tribal boundaries would minimize intertribal warfare and allow the U.S. government to assign responsibility for any depredations against whites in any district. Although not yet reservations as such, these fixed tribal boundaries, the government hoped, would be the first step toward concentrating Indian populations, restricting Indians onto a shrinking land base, and hastening the process of assimilation.

Demonstrating complete ignorance of the decentralized nature of tribal political structure, the government representatives demanded that each tribe appoint one chief who could speak for and exercise control over all of his people. This made little sense to the egalitarian tribal societies of the Sioux, Cheyenne, or Crow, where authority alternated between hereditary chiefs, war leaders, and tribal police, depending on the needs of the situation. Unlike white leaders, none of these leaders had the power to coerce; chiefs had to listen to the people, maintain their confidence by positive example, provide generously for their people, and protect them from outside threats. The whites insisted that Conquering Bear, who had no desire for a position he knew to be impossible, act as chief of all of the Sioux. In an attempt to consolidate what it hoped would be his elevated power with the Sioux, the government showered Conquering Bear with a conspicuously large supply of goods. In a pointed demonstration of Lakota leadership, however, he re-

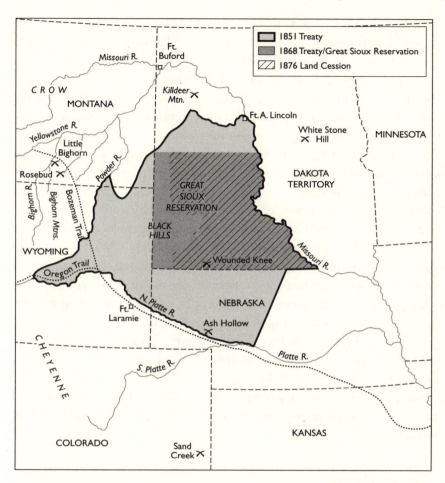

Indian country on the northern plains, surrounded by forts and trails, and growing smaller with each treaty. The Little Bighorn and Rosebud battles occurred on land contested by both the Crow and the Lakota.

distributed it all to his people, keeping nothing for himself or his immediate relatives.

The rest of the treaty was likewise full of misunderstandings. The document promised safe passage for all emigrants on the overland trails, gave the government authority to establish roads and military posts as needed on Indian lands, promised to protect the Indians from depredations by white settlers, and promised compensation to Indians for these concessions in the form of annual provisions of food and goods worth fifty thousand dollars for fifty years. Perhaps because a mere 270 soldiers represented the military might of the U.S. government, the Sioux and other Indians did not feel obliged to agree with the treaty terms. Black Hawk, a leader of the Oglala Sioux, explicitly denounced the territorial limits and the attempted ban on warfare: "You have split the country and I do not like it. These lands once belonged to the Kiowas and the Crows, but we whipped these nations out of them, and in this we did what the white men do when they want the lands of the Indians."[8] Clearly, the Sioux at Fort Laramie had no intention of quitting their raids on other tribes, and by some accounts they were raiding horses from the Crow within weeks of the conclusion of the conference. Only a handful of Sioux "touched the pen" to the written treaty. In fact, it is difficult to know exactly what such a ritual would have meant in the context of the oral culture of the Sioux. The closest comparison for them was probably smoking the sacred pipe, which validated the spirit of truth in all that was spoken at a meeting but did not compel unified action. Besides, for the time being, the Lakota were still the dominant power of the plains. In a dazzling display of military strength, one thousand brightly dressed Sioux warriors paraded through the negotiations on horseback, four abreast, singing and carrying an American flag, followed by several hundred of their Cheyenne allies. The moment represented perhaps the greatest demonstration of Indian military power on the plains, indeed of any military power on the plains, until the Sioux and Cheyenne gathered again in large numbers twenty-five years later in the fateful summer of 1876.

Trigger Happy

Three years after this display of Indian military might, the Lakota were debating how to proceed after the incident between Lakota warriors and Lieutenant Grattan's men. What they did not know was that U.S. military officials had already decided on a course of action. While early reports blamed Grattan for provoking the fight, army officials in Washington, D.C., interpreted his defeat as a "massacre" and demanded that it be avenged. They ordered General William S. Harney to Fort Leavenworth to take command of six hundred soldiers for an expedition designed to punish the Lakota. With a burly physique, a dominating personality, and a neat white beard, Harney impressed all around him as fit for the part of the avenger. One Sioux nickname for him was the "Mad Bear." The next August Harney marched his men up the North Platte River with a determination to fight. "By God," he declared, "I'm for battle—no peace."[9]

Employing a tactic that would be repeated in counterinsurgency campaigns from the Spanish-American War to Vietnam, the new Indian agent at Fort Laramie, Thomas Twiss, attempted to separate the "friendlies" from the "hostiles." He directed all Sioux who wished to remain friendly with the United States to move south of the Platte River, while those who remained on the north side of the river would be considered enemies and subject to retaliation. Oglala and Brulé argued about the appropriate response to this new threat, and eventually the camps divided, some going north and some south. Those who stayed north, confident in their numbers and fighting abilities, sent a message that if Harney "wanted peace he could have it, or if he wanted war he could have that."[10] Conquering Bear's band, now led by Little Thunder, who like his predecessor argued for peace, inexplicably remained north of the river in easy view of the main trail. Although some of those involved in the Grattan fight were in his camp, Little Thunder may have still believed that he could convince Harney of his peaceful intentions.

On September 2, 1855, Harney divided his forces and attacked the 41 lodges of Little Thunder's village as they were camped near Blue Water Creek, only 6 miles from the overland trail along the Platte River. As his soldiers prepared in the early dawn hours, Harney roared orders to his officers: "There are those damned red sons of bitches, who massacred the soldiers near Laramie last year, in time of peace. They killed your own kindred, your own flesh and blood . . . Don't spare one of those damned red sons of bitches."[11] As Harney's forces moved into position for a two-pronged attack at dawn, scouts discovered that the women in camp, anticipating the attack, had already begun to flee. Fearing that the whole camp might disappear before his slow-moving attack force was in place, Harney cleverly asked Little Thunder for a talk under a flag of truce. Thirty minutes later, with his forces surrounding the departing village, Harney ordered the attack to commence. As rifles opened fire on Little Thunder's people, an anonymous newspaper reporter accompanying the expedition wrote, "I never saw a more beautiful thing in my whole life."[12]

Little Thunder's warriors fought desperately to provide cover for their families to escape. Although wounded four times, Spotted Tail fought courageously and killed or wounded several soldiers before stealing an army horse and making his escape. Overall, Harney's forces killed eighty-six people and took seventy women and children as prisoners, a devastating loss for the Lakota. They simply had no expectation that the U.S. military would inflict death and destruction of this magnitude. Of the three to four hundred people in Little Thunder's village, nearly half were killed, wounded, or imprisoned. In addition, most of the camp's horses and household goods were destroyed. On the U.S. side, four soldiers were killed and seven wounded, indicative of their overwhelming superiority in numbers and weaponry. The soldiers salvaged from the wreckage some bags, moccasins, and household artifacts, as well as some uniforms and equipment from Grattan's command and papers from the previous fall's mail robbery, enough evidence for Harney to justify the destruction of the village.

After his victory at Blue Water Creek, Harney marched to Fort Laramie, where he demanded the surrender of those who had raided the mail train and stolen a considerable amount of gold the previous fall. If they refused to surrender, he threatened to attack other Lakota villages and turn the captives from Little Thunder's band over to the Pawnee, their sworn enemies, who would likely ensure that they suffered a painful, ignoble death. The Lakota took Harney's threats seriously, so in order to save their villages Spotted Tail and the other warriors decided to surrender. Spotted Tail may have found extra courage for this decision because his wife and child were among the prisoners. Riding their best ponies and wearing their war shirts, Spotted Tail and his warriors sang their death songs as they rode into Fort Laramie, turning themselves in for what they expected would be certain annihilation.

Harney sent Spotted Tail and the other prisoners to Fort Leavenworth in eastern Kansas, the first time Spotted Tail had been that far east. He was amazed at the towns and agricultural settlements along the way, as well as the strength and numbers of U.S. soldiers at the fort. He may have been more impressed to learn that this was just one of many forts. Throughout his imprisonment, the soldiers generally treated him with respect. To his great surprise, he met a lieutenant who had fought at Blue Water Creek and had rescued a baby from the battlefield. The baby turned out to be Spotted Tail's son. Rather than being hanged as he had anticipated, Spotted Tail and the other prisoners received a presidential pardon, and the next year they were returned to their people. After his experiences in Kansas, Spotted Tail became convinced that the whites were simply too powerful to oppose militarily and that continuing to war against them would mean the destruction of his people. After his imprisonment he became an advocate for accommodation with the whites and pursued diplomacy rather than warfare as the best way to preserve his people and their culture.

In 1855 the Plains tribes were still uncertain as to the exact nature of the new threat from the whites. After intimidating Spotted Tail into surrender, Harney marched his army north, around the Black Hills and through the heart of Lakota country, daring any one to stop him. After this deliberate violation of their sovereignty, Harney called for all of the Lakota to send representatives to a council in Fort Pierre the following spring. In March of 1856 he dictated the terms of a new treaty to the temporarily stunned delegates: each band must appoint a "chief" who would be responsible for all actions of that group, all stolen property must be returned, anyone who had killed a white person must turn himself in for arrest, and Indians must not "lurk" near the overland trails. Lakota leaders understood that this treaty could not be enforced—no chief could require obedience from an entire band, nor could warriors be expected to turn themselves in for judgment by a white judicial system—but only Bear's Rib, the spokesman for the Hunkpapa, spoke out against the treaty. His argument fell on deaf ears. Harney explained that the chiefs must either sign the new treaty or be given the same treatment as Little Thunder's band at Blue Water Creek. If they signed, then he would arrange for goods to be delivered and would release the captives from Little Thunder's band still held prisoner.

Much to Harney's dismay, President Pierce did not approve of the new treaty and refused to send it to the Senate for approval. The House of Representatives denied funding to implement the provisions of the treaty, and the Office of Indian Affairs tried to undermine what they thought of as inappropriate army interference in Indian policy. Harney left the plains the following summer, allowing the Lakota to wonder what the white intrusion meant for their people. Among the Hunkpapa who were probably present at this meeting was the young Sitting Bull, who would have understood this demonstration of army arrogance as a good reason to avoid dealing with soldiers. The lesson for Sitting Bull and many Lakota would seem to be that the "Mad Bear" of the U.S. Army might do much harm when enraged, but eventually the bear would wander off and life could go on unchanged.[13]

Meanwhile, south of the Platte River, some of the younger Cheyenne warriors continued their occasional raids on travelers heading westward on the overland trails. The army, following the advice of General Harney that "the Cheyennes are an unruly race" who would only behave "if they are kept in dread of immediate punishment," became convinced that the trail could only be made safe for white emigrants with a display of force. Thus, in 1857 the army sent Colonel Edwin Summer and eight companies of cavalry and dragoons on an expedition to punish the Cheyenne. "Bull" Summer, as his men called him, had a commanding physical presence and seemed the perfect counterpart to Harney. The Cheyenne, aware of the punishing attack of Harney on their Lakota allies, initially hoped simply to evade the path of Summer's invading army. As the Council of Forty-four, the elders who governed the tribe, debated the best response to Summer's advance, younger warriors grew anxious for a fight, their confidence fortified by the promise of sacred powers. Two young holy men, Ice and Dark, claimed that all warriors who washed their hands in the sacred lake would become bulletproof and that any warrior who used their special white powder in his musket would be guaranteed of a hit with every shot. Bolstered by such assurances, the Cheyenne believed that their fate would be different from that of their friends on Blue Water Creek.

At Summer's approach, the warriors rode out to meet the advancing line of three hundred cavalrymen. To the Cheyenne's great surprise, the soldiers did not shoot but rather drew their sabers as they charged. Realizing that Ice and Dark's powers protected them from bullets but not from blades, the Cheyenne suddenly doubted themselves and made a hasty retreat. Summer's men chased them for miles as they abandoned their village and fled in different directions across the prairie. While many went south, others headed toward the North Platte River and beyond to the safety of the Black Hills.[14] Two days later, when Summer found their abandoned village, he burned 170 lodges, 20,000 pounds of buffalo meat, and all of the blankets, clothes, cooking utensils, and other supplies. Afterward, many members of the Cheyenne Council of Forty-four, especially the respected leader Black Kettle, concluded that the whites were so powerful that it would be disastrous to fight them. For Black Kettle, as for Spotted Tail, making peace with the whites was the only way to escape total destruction.

Soon after the Cheyenne battle, the Lakota in the north called for a great council to discuss how to deal with the white invasion. Many northern Lakota, especially the Hunkpapa, still smarted from Harney's treaty terms of the previous spring and circulated a pipe calling all to come to this meeting near Bear Butte, in present-day South Dakota. Over five thousand attended, perhaps as many as ten thousand, representing all of the bands of the northern Lakota. One participant later reported, "Their hearts felt strong at seeing how numerous they were . . . If they went to war again they would not yield so easily as before."[15] Living to the north of the Oregon Trail and having less experience with the whites, these Lakota came to very different conclusions than their southern relatives. While moderates argued for accepting some annuities and allowing white traders to stay in Lakota country, more militant voices demanded that all whites should be driven out of the country and no treaties should be made with the government. Yet even most militants believed that white traders should be allowed a presence in Lakota Territory because they provided access to guns and munitions that were crucial to defending the homeland.

Coming from an optimistic and unified people, the Bear Butte discussions yielded a consensus on several key points: overland travel along the North Platte River and steamboat traffic up the Missouri River would be allowed to continue, but north and west of these rivers would remain Lakota country, not to be compromised by treaty; the Black Hills region was the heart of Lakota Territory and must remain wholly for themselves; and they would continue war against the Crow to the west in the Powder River country to gain more access to the abundant buffalo herds there. If the Americans respected this definition of Lakota Territory, then there would be no further need to fight them. Among those navigating the complex issues at the Bear Butte council in the summer of 1857 were a young Crazy Horse and the maturing Sitting Bull. In time they would become the two most famous champions of the spirit of the Lakota people as laid out during this high-water mark of Sioux confidence.

Sitting Bull, whose iconographic face came to personify the free spirit of the Lakota, was born about 1830 near Grand River, South Dakota, into a politically influential family in this confident, expanding society. His father and his two uncles were leaders in the Hunkpapa band, one of the seven bands of the Lakota. The Hunkpapa led the tribe's movement west onto the high plains in the decades after 1750, and as a result they were constantly at war with other tribes. However, they had less contact with the *wasichus*, or whites, than the other bands that had experience with emigrants along the overland trails. Sitting Bull grew to manhood in a world of complex kinship networks where he was related, either biologically or by adoption, with nearly everyone around him. He called his uncles "father" and knew many others as cousins, aunts, or grandparents, so that everyone in his *tiospaye* or extended family lodge group, usually between fifty and one hundred people, felt related to one another. Extended kinship networks then spread out to become an *oyate*, a word that can be translated as band, tribe, or nation. For Sitting Bull's people, society was constructed through a series of kin relations extending from the immediate family outward to include all of the *Lakota*, or Allied People. This kinship could even include adopted captives of war, who, if accepted, became members of Hunkpapa society just as fully as any biological connection. Leadership in Lakota society could come through heredity, success in war, or demonstrations of generosity, and Sitting Bull's "fathers"—all three of them—brought him prominence in all of these. Leaders in Lakota society did not rule by command, but rather by example and by seeking the wisdom of the council of elders. Even though the council of chiefs always sought consensus, in practice Lakota society was ripe with disagreement and factionalism. Kinship connections mediated and controlled these differences, but the pressure of the *wasichu* threat would dangerously exaggerate them.

Sitting Bull earned the nickname "Slow" as a boy for his deliberate, thoughtful habits, even though he was usually the winner in running games. Like all Lakota boys, he learned to ride a horse bareback as early as age six, and by age ten he killed his first buffalo. When he was fourteen, Slow joined a Hunkpapa war party heading to Crow country and counted his first coup, or brave war deed, by riding down a Crow warrior and striking him with his tomahawk. Upon their return to camp, his father gave to Slow his own name, Sitting Bull, and a shield of buffalo hide that held sacred power to protect. Because he had counted coup, Sitting Bull was entitled to wear a feather in his hair, a mark of respect and rank among his people. Over the years Sitting Bull fought in enough battles to count coup at least thirty times and earn the right to wear thirty feathers in his headdress, marking him as one of the great war leaders of his people.

In addition to establishing a reputation as a courageous warrior, Sitting Bull was known for his prowess in hunting and for his generosity, highly regarded traits in Lakota society. Because Sitting Bull could often kill more buffalo than his immediate family needed, he was expected to share with anyone in his village who was hungry. He frequently gave meat to those who had been less successful in the hunt; what he gave away in food he gained in prestige. Sitting Bull's special relationship with animals and the spirit world further enhanced his status among his people. He was widely admired for his

Sitting Bull, charismatic chief of the Lakota who led the alliance of northern Indians at the Little Bighorn. This is one of the many portraits taken
after his surrender when he became the most recognized face of the Lakota people. Taken by David Frances Barry in Bismarck, North Dakota,
about 1888. Courtesy Denver Public Library.

special ability to communicate with *Wakan Tanka*, the Great Mystery, and with the many other spirits that animated the natural world. His society did not compartmentalize religion—indeed had no word for it—but believed that everyday actions were intimately involved with spiritual powers, and that the more one understood these powers the more success one would have in warfare, hunting, or any other activity.

Those around him recalled how Sitting Bull talked with buffalo and wolves on different occasions, learning from them and expressing a special kinship with their spirits. Like other Lakota, he communicated with *Wakan Tanka* through the pipe ceremony, smoking his family's replica of the sacred red catlinite pipe. With its carved red bowl, wooden stem, and decorative eagle feathers, the sacred pipe passed thru the generations and represented one form of ceremonial contact with the Great Mystery. Sitting Bull also became known for the many times he performed the Sun Dance, the summer ceremony in which individuals volunteered for great sacrifice and pain in order to have visions that would help the people. Sitting Bull volunteered many times, staring at the sun while dancing, even cutting himself and suspending himself with leather skewers through his chest and back muscles while he danced, in order to seek divine guidance for the Lakota. As a warrior, hunter, and spiritual leader, Sitting Bull was primed for leading his people against the most serious threat to their existence that they had known, the invasion of the *wasichus*.

The other Lakota leader known for his resistance to white invasion was Crazy Horse, born with the name Curly Hair about a decade after Sitting Bull. As a member of the Oglala band, he grew up not far from the overland trails that carried increasing numbers of wagon trains through Lakota Territory, each of which brought more horses eating precious grass, more emigrants cutting valuable timber, and more hunters killing and scaring away wildlife. Curly Hair grew up listening to the increasing complaints of his people against the invasion of the whites and for most of his adult life avoided contact with them. These complaints became especially bitter after 1849 when cholera broke out along the trail, an epidemic that many Oglala suspected was sent by the whites to wipe out the Indians. Curly Hair watched four of his stepsisters, all under the age of five, die from disease. Two years later he attended the treaty negotiations at Fort Laramie, listening to the promises of the U.S. government and to the suspicions of his people. In 1855 he went on a vision quest, a rite of passage for many young Lakota men and one of the most sacred ceremonies for many Plains tribes. For four days he neither ate food nor drank water, each day holding his sacred pipe to the rising and setting sun. When he received a vision, it involved thunder and hawks, symbols of power and protection. Two years later he counted his first coup in an attack against the Pawnee. Later that summer he attended the great council of the Lakota at Bear Butte as they decided how to respond to white intrusions on their land. Here he listened to Sitting Bull and others who urged the Lakota to fight in order to protect their homeland. Unlike Sitting Bull, however, he was intensely shy, not politically inclined, and not much of an orator. Yet as he listened, the young Curly Hair committed himself to defending the Lakota domain from all comers, especially the untrustworthy *wasichus*. This conviction, informed by childhood experiences and shaped by these Bear Butte discussions, shaped his behavior for the rest of his life.

As Curly Hair left Bear Butte that summer, he joined a war party led by his old childhood friend, High Backbone. During the fighting, he distinguished himself with conspicuous bravery by rescuing High Backbone, who had been wounded, and by counting coup at least five times, including taking two scalps. During the celebrations after the war party had returned to camp, Curly Hair's father gave to him a new name in honor of his accomplishments and transferred to his son the power that the older man had received from a vision of a grizzly guardian who promised "powers to conquer all earthly things, including the white men who are coming into our land."[16] The name was Crazy Horse, the name of his father and his father before him, and the name the son would make synonymous with undaunted resistance to the white invasion.

Minnesota Invasion

Meanwhile, in Minnesota trouble was brewing between the Santee Sioux, the Lakota's eastern relatives, and the white settlers who were flooding into the fertile farmland they called home. When Minnesota became a territory in 1849, about five thousand white settlers had made their way to these upper reaches of the Mississippi River, living next to perhaps twelve thousand Indians in the territory. Nine years later when the territory became a state, the white population had mushroomed to nearly 150,000, more than ten times the Indian population. To accommodate this rapid growth, the government had forced the Sioux into accepting two treaties that together required them to give up twenty-eight million acres in exchange for a small patch of land along the Minnesota River and annual payments designed to ease the Sioux's transition to farming. Despite the lingering feeling that they had been cheated by the treaties, many of the Santee began the assimilation process— attending mission schools, cutting their hair short, and taking up farming. Yet the distribution of Indian annuities in Minnesota was rife with frontier corruption. Political leaders appointed friends to jobs in the Indian service, and together they skimmed profits from payments intended for the Indians. Fueled by profits and patronage, the system kept federal dollars flowing to the frontier, where local and state officials maintained their political machines and the Indians remained poor. In 1862, the Santee Sioux starved while provisions languished in the warehouse. In a spectacularly egregious display of contempt, Indian trader Andrew Myrick remarked, "So far as I am concerned, if they are hungry let them eat grass or their own dung."[17]

Only a few days after this remark, the Santee Sioux launched a surprise attack on Minnesota settlers, killing over four hundred people in a 100-mile radius. Overrunning the trading post, they killed Myrick, mutilated his body, and stuffed his mouth with grass, providing a cruel, symbolic rejoinder to his callous remark. Minnesotans quickly regrouped and launched a decisive counteroffensive. Led by former Governor and now Colonel Henry H. Sibley, the militia used superior firepower in a series of pitched battles to subdue the uprising. By fall they had killed hundreds of Sioux, captured two thousand, and sent many more heading west into the newly formed Dakota Territory.

The popular outcry in Minnesota and the nation did not distinguish between innocent and guilty, between the peace faction and the war faction within Sioux society, but demanded revenge against all Sioux. Newspaper editorials fed the flames of vengeance, calling for swift retribution and even extermination of all Indians as the only way to satisfy settlers for their loss of family and friends or to provide security against future Indian wars. In the face of these calls for extermination and even threats of vigilante action against all Indians, Sibley organized military tribunals to try the suspects among the two thousand Sioux prisoners. In the hasty trials the Sioux had no legal representation and their mere presence at the scene of a battle counted as evidence of murder, unless they could prove that they had not killed anyone. In the end, the court found 303 Sioux guilty of murder or other crimes. President Lincoln, influenced by religious and humanitarian appeals for the Sioux and concerned about the legality of the tribunals, reviewed the trial records and reduced the guilty list to thirty-eight, all of whom were hanged in the largest mass execution in American history. According to one eyewitness, as the gallows platform dropped, "there was one, not loud, but prolonged cheer from the soldiery and citizens."[18]

Popular opinion in Minnesota demanded more retribution as settlers grieving from the loss of family and friends poured their hatred out against those who they perceived as savages. The *Saint Paul Press* editorialized: "The war is not over! What the people of Minnesota now demand is . . . that war will now be on the offensive. In God's name let the columns of vengeance move on . . . until the whole accursed race is crushed."[19] One voice against this popular attitude came from Sarah Wakefield, who had been held captive by the Sioux for six weeks. After her release, she spoke and wrote against the dominant mood, arguing that Indians were "God's creatures" who, if they "had been properly fed and otherwise treated like human beings," might not have made war against the settlers and then "how many, very many innocent lives might have been spared." She was especially indebted to Chaska, one of the partially assimilated "farmer Indians" who had cut his hair, lived in a house, and adopted some white ways, who had risked his life to save hers. He was, she testified, a good man who "knew right from wrong" and "although he was not a Christian, he knew there was a God." Wakefield became especially disheartened when Chaska, probably because of mistaken identity, was among those hanged.[20]

The military campaigns that followed the war against the Santee Sioux brought the U.S. Army into the heart of Lakota Territory and escalated into what now became nearly continuous war between the United States and the Sioux. The reaction to the Santee Sioux's desperate defense of their home became an excuse for the conquest of the fertile farmlands of Minnesota and eastern Dakota, which meant war not only against the Santee Sioux but also against all Sioux. In 1863 General Sibley led a large force up the Minnesota River and overland onto the plains, where he attacked several villages. General Alfred Sully, meanwhile, proceeded up the Missouri River and in early September assaulted a large Sioux village at Whitestone Hill, driving the warriors from the field and forcing the village to evacuate. Sully's men spent the next two days burning what the Sioux had left behind, including three hundred lodges and over 400,000 pounds of buffalo meat, the village's winter food supply. One of the Dakota who escaped from this battle was Ink-paduta, a leader of the uprising a year earlier and well known for his hostility to whites. The Minnesota experience confirmed his hatred. He traveled west, was befriended by his Lakota relatives, and found an ally in Sitting Bull. Thirteen years later, in the summer of 1876, he was in Sitting Bull's camp at the Little Bighorn.

The next year General Sully again led a large force into the heart of Lakota Territory, and this time there was no mistaking the bitterness on both sides. Three warriors attacked and killed Captain John Fielmer, a geologist who accompanied the expedition, as he was exploring ahead of the main column. Sully ordered his cavalry to pursue the warriors, and after an 8-mile chase they cornered them and shot over two hundred bullets into their bodies. Sully, not satisfied with this revenge, ordered the three warriors decapitated and placed their heads on poles on the highest hill "as a warning to all Indians who might travel that way."[21] The Sioux, although no strangers to wartime cruelty, were outraged at what they viewed as a sign that Sully intended to exterminate them all.

Later that summer Sully and his 2,200 men attacked a large Lakota village near Killdeer Mountain that stretched for about 4 miles. Sully claimed that the warriors numbered six thousand, so it was no wonder that the Sioux waited for his attack with confidence. Hundreds of warriors rode out 5 miles from the village to meet the soldiers, while women, children, and old men watched the action from a high hill. The warriors had the advantage of being faster and more maneuverable, with individuals and small groups probing weaknesses and attacking the soldier's lines with spontaneous initiative. But the army had the advantage of superior firepower—small howitzers and rifles compared to bows and old muskets—as well as the military discipline to lay down coordinated volleys of fire. After a hard fight, the Sioux were forced to leave the field and hastily abandon their village. Sully again burned all that remained of the village, including 150 lodges, 40 tons of dried meat, brass and copper kettles, and saddles. He even ordered his men to shoot the three thousand dogs left behind in the Sioux camp. Soldiers found two baby boys in the village, and while they were deciding what to do with them, some of Sully's Winnebago scouts, a tribe with long-standing hostilities toward the Sioux, ran up and smashed in the infants' heads, explaining, "Nits make lice."[22]

After destroying the village's supplies, Sully pursued the Lakota into the difficult terrain of the Badlands, which he described as "Hell with the fire out." The fighting was inconclusive, mostly serving to reinforce hatreds building on both sides. Sitting Bull participated in this fight and had a memorable exchange with one of Sully's Indian scouts, who called out, "We are thirsty to death and want to know what Indians you are." Sitting Bull replied, "Hunk-papas, Sans Arc, Minneconjou, and others. Who are you?" The scout shouted a vague response, "Some Indians with the soldiers." Then Sitting Bull made his point, "You have no business with the soldiers. The Indians here have no fight with the whites. Why is it the whites come to fight the Indians? Now we have to kill you, too, and let you thirst to death."[23] As this exchange suggests, Sully's campaign, like many army campaigns in the West, relied extensively on Indian scouts for navigating the terrain and locating the enemy. The army usually had no trouble finding scouts, for the many years of intertribal warfare left no shortage of hatreds among the Plains tribes. The Sioux themselves had even fought with the U.S. Army forty years earlier in a campaign against the Arikara. Some historians characterize these scouts as mercenaries, fighting for pay against their own people, but it is more accurate to see these nineteenth-century Plains natives as they perceived themselves: members of their own bands with strong tribal loyalties that trumped the broader pan-Indian identity that would emerge more fully in the twentieth century.

Sitting Bull took a lead role in another revealing drama during the 1864 campaign. When Sully attacked Sitting Bull's Hunkpapa village, the Sioux were holding a white woman, Fanny Kelly, as their captive. Some Oglala Sioux had captured her in an attack on her family's wagon train along the Platte River in July and carried her north, eventually trading her to the Hunkpapa. During her six-month captivity, she never developed the sympathy for the Sioux that Sarah Wakefield had felt. Kelly wrote that the "greedy, cunning and cruel savages who had so ruthlessly torn me from my friends" were nothing like the "dusky maidens of romance" or "the fearless Philip, the bold Black Hawk, the gentle Pocahontas" of the romanticized history she knew. "The true red man," she insisted, "does not exist between the pages of many volumes." As it turned out, there was plenty of room for cruelty and kindness on both sides of the racial divide. Sitting Bull eventually arranged for Kelly's release, and that winter a group of Lakota brought Kelly, wrapped in buffalo robes, to Fort Sully. As she entered and the gates closed behind her, she murmured, "Am I free, indeed free?" She finally understood, she later wrote, "what freedom meant to one who had tasted the bitterness of bondage and despair." For his part, Sitting Bull noted that she had been sad during her captivity and now was "out of our way."[24] In a curious coincidence, however, twelve years later Lieutenant James Bradley, on his way toward the

Little Bighorn as a scout for Colonel John Gibbon's Montana column, found a note that Kelly had secretly dropped along the trail. Knowing none of the details, Bradley assumed that Kelly had suffered the proverbial "fate worse than death" and recommitted himself to defeating the Sioux in order to make the region safe for white women.[25]

By the end of 1864 Sully was satisfied that his campaigns had decimated the military capabilities of the Sioux. Begun as a way to punish the Santee Sioux for their uprising in Minnesota, whites quickly seized the opportunity to dispossess Indians of land farther west. Charles A. Bryant, who wrote the first history of the war in 1864, boldly stated the premise of the conflict. Reflecting a version of Manifest Destiny, Bryant claimed that Indians who did not follow God's command to cultivate the earth were "in the wrongful possession of a continent" and must yield to "the superior right of the white man."[26] As a result of the Minnesota invasion, there were now a series of military outposts along the Missouri, from Fort Sully on the southern stretch to Fort Union near the mouth of the Yellowstone, 300 miles upriver. Although the Lakota were now hemmed in by the overland trails in the south and these new forts to the east, they still hoped to keep their freedom by remaining on the northern plains, far from white settlements. For his part, Sully claimed that "in spite of their threats and boasts" the Sioux would never again "attempt to unite and make a stand."[27] Not for the first or the last time, military hubris had miscalculated the strength of the opposition, and a dozen years later General George Armstrong Custer would pay the price.

Sand Creek

As Sully carried the war from Minnesota into the Lakota heartland, troubles in Colorado fanned the flames of war from that direction. In 1858 prospectors discovered gold near Pikes Peak, igniting a gold rush that brought over 140,000 white miners and farmers into the region. Almost overnight the new town of Denver sprang up on the front range of the Rocky Mountains. Most Cheyenne and Arapaho Indians who lived in this area tried to avoid the newcomers. They remained wary of the army after the Cheyenne's bad experience with Colonel Summer's campaign the year before and preferred to avoid white settlements and to follow the buffalo far from the mountains. A few Cheyenne, however, felt peaceably inclined toward the Americans and were assimilating to various degrees.

In its early years Denver had frequent Indian visitors, and many major traders had at least one Indian wife. For the matrilineal Cheyenne, having a white husband represented prestige for the wife, and Cheyenne women frequently became the cultural intermediaries between the two cultures. Their mixed-blood offspring created a cultural fusion, the possibility of a blended culture. One cynical frontiersman remarked that the Indians were "fast becoming civilized. They get drunk as readily as white men and swear with great distinctiveness." An Arapaho chief, Little Raven, who promised to remain at peace with the whites, became a frequent visitor to Denver, where he impressed the whites as a "sensible and friendly" guest who "handles a knife and fork and smokes cigars like a white man."[28] But within a few years, the citizens of Denver turned toward more conventional respectability, and white society began to look down on the so-called squaw men who had married Cheyenne women. As one historian has written, polite society of the time denigrated these mixed couples by suggesting that they "carried a little whiff of blanket and boiled dog."[29] Those most equipped by language and culture to assist in the two cultures' understanding of each other were now relegated to the margins of society.

In 1861, with Denver and the mining areas of the state booming, Colorado officials forced a new treaty on the Cheyenne and Arapaho, limiting them to a small fraction of the land promised to them under the 1851 Fort Laramie Treaty. The Fort Wise Treaty, signed by leaders of the peace faction among the Cheyenne and Arapaho, limited them to a barren stretch of land south of the Arkansas River, out of the way of Denver and the Pikes Peak settlements, but also with almost no game and limited agricultural potential. (Seventy years later it would be one of the most severe areas of the Dust Bowl.) One of the leading Cheyenne chiefs to sign the Fort Wise Treaty was Black Kettle, well known for his view that the best way to preserve his people's freedom and hunting territory was to accommodate the whites. Significantly, no representatives from the Dog Soldiers, the more militant of the Cheyenne factions who stood for living the traditional nomadic life and resisting all accommodation, approved of the treaty. The Dog Soldiers remained farther north and east of Denver, where the abundant grassland still supported large herds of buffalo. They often allied with members of the Sioux who supported their more militant views.

Territorial governor John Evans wanted to subjugate all of the Indians of Colorado so that they could pose no threat to his vision of progress for the new territory. Evans had an expansive vision for Colorado and for his role in it, hoping that the territory could quickly become a state, with Denver as a station on the transcontinental railroad and with himself in the role of U.S. senator. Indians had no place in this vision. A committed antislavery and Union man, Evans feared during the Civil War years that Confederates might persuade the Plains Indians to attack settlements and isolate Denver. When some Cheyenne and Arapaho resisted his overtures to discuss the terms of the Fort Wise Treaty, he interpreted their unwillingness to negotiate away their land as preparation for war. When rumors circulated in Denver that the Cheyenne were planning to ally with other tribes and launch a major offensive in the spring of 1864, Evans believed that his suspicions of an Indian uprising, perhaps similar to the 1862 Sioux uprising in Minnesota, had been justified.

Governor Evans found support in another leading citizen of the territory, Colonel John M. Chivington, the "Fighting Parson," made famous by his victories against the Confederates in 1862 in New Mexico. At 6 feet 5 inches tall and weighing 260 pounds, Chivington was "strong as a bull elephant." He was also a born-again Methodist minister who once, when threatened with death for preaching an antislavery sermon, showed up the following Sunday wielding a revolver in each hand. Perching his revolvers openly on the pulpit, daring anyone to challenge him, he again poured down God's wrath on the evils of slavery. Chivington saw the continued presence of untamed Indians in Colorado as a barrier to progress for his state and as an impediment to his own political ambitions. As George Bent, who sympathized with the Cheyenne, said of Chivington, "the easiest way" to political office was "to attack the Indians and stir them up . . . On the frontier this was the shortest road to the people's hearts; give the Indians a whipping and the voters would give you any office you asked of them."[30]

With wide popular support, soldiers rode out in April 1864 to find and punish Indians who had been raiding the emigrant trails and came upon a large camp of Cheyenne. Starving Bear, a leading peace chief who had been to Washington, D.C., to visit with President Lincoln a year earlier, rode out to meet them. He had a peace medal from Lincoln, as well as the president's advice for assimilation: "I can only say that I can see no way in which your race is to become prosperous as the white race except by living as they do, by cultivation of the earth."[31] As Starving Bear approached the soldiers, making signs of peace, they opened fire, killing him and several others. Cheyenne warriors returned the fire and were gaining an advantage against the outnum-bered soldiers when Black Kettle rode into the middle of the fight, shouting, "Stop the fighting. Do not make war against the whites! Stop the fighting."[32] Black Kettle's courageous intervention stopped the fighting that day, but the plains were on fire throughout the summer of 1864 with raids and counter-raids. Cheyenne, especially the Dog Soldiers, raided wagon trains and in one frightful incident killed and mutilated a family only 30 miles from Denver. In retaliation, Chivington's orders that summer were to "burn villages and kill Cheyennes whenever and wherever found."[33]

Against this backdrop of violence, Evans called for "friendly" Indians to separate themselves from "hostile" Indians so that he could make war against the "hostiles." Black Kettle saw this as an invitation to initiate peace negotia-tions with the soldiers, and he traveled to Denver to meet with a surprised but not delighted Evans and Chivington, who were still hoping for the oppor-tunity for open war. Both men shared the view of Major General Samuel R. Curtis, military commander of the district, who advised Chivington, "I want no peace until the Indians suffer more . . . It is better to chastise before giv-ing anything but a little tobacco to talk over. No peace must be made without my directions."[34] At the same time, the Denver newspapers were ridiculing Chivington's ill-trained Colorado Third Regiment of Volunteer Cavalry for its inactivity, adding to the growing frenzy for fighting Indians.

Black Kettle, believing that he had negotiated peace for his people, re-turned from Denver and moved his village to winter camp on Sand Creek, where he awaited further instructions from army officials in Fort Lyon, 40 miles away. Chivington, allegedly looking for a fight against "hostile" Indi-ans, decided to attack Black Kettle's village rather than undertake a riskier campaign against the militant factions, who in any case might be harder to find. At Fort Lyon, some army officers protested that Black Kettle's people had already surrendered and were, in effect, prisoners of war. Among those who objected to Chivington's plans was Captain Silas Soule, who later was ordered to go with Chivington to Sand Creek. Colonel Chivington cut off all debate at Fort Lyon: "I have come to kill Indians, and believe it is right and honorable to use any means under God's heavens to kill Indians. Damn any man who is in sympathy with an Indian."[35]

At daybreak on November 29, 1864, the seven hundred soldiers of Chiving-ton's Third volunteers opened fire on the five hundred sleeping Cheyenne and Arapaho in Black Kettle's camp. Black Kettle, confident that the attack was a mistake, raised an American flag and a white flag over his lodge. When the fight started, Soule refused the command to order his troops to fire. As he remembered, "I refused to fire and swore that none but a coward would, for by this time hundreds of women and children were coming toward us and getting on their knees for mercy." Amid the gunfire and screams, Soule heard one officer shout, "Kill the sons of bitches," while another one proclaimed, "anyone who sympathized with the Indians ought to be killed and now was a good time to do it."[36] The warriors in the village used what arms they had to protect the escape of the women and children, but they were in no way prepared for a fight. Other Cheyenne fled, running for cover on the banks of the nearby river as the soldiers came at them from two sides, catching them in a withering crossfire. The Cheyenne dug pits in the river sand for protection, but soon Chivington ordered the howitzers focused on this area. Sand and willow leaves offered scant protection from the exploding shells.

The slaughter continued until afternoon, with Chivington's soldiers chasing down fleeing villagers and, following orders, taking no prisoners. According to John Smith, an interpreter who was present with the soldiers, "All manner of depredations were inflicted on their persons; they were scalped, their brains knocked out; the men used their knives, ripped open women, clubbed little children, knocked them in the head with their guns, beat their brains out, mutilated their bodies in every sense of the word."[37] Before nightfall, between 150 and 200 Cheyenne, two-thirds of them women and children, lay dead along the banks of Sand Creek. Somehow, Black Kettle and some of his followers managed to escape.

The next day the brutality continued. The poorly trained volunteers wandered through the village, desecrating the dead bodies and hunting for souvenirs. They carried away any valuables they could find and cut off body parts of the dead, including fingers, ears, and genitals. Then they burned what was left of the village and marched south in search of peace chief Little Raven's Arapaho village that was reported to be in the area. Failing to find this, they returned to Denver where they were greeted as heroes and welcomed by a large parade. The *Rocky Mountain News* claimed, "Colorado soldiers have again covered themselves with glory." A large audience cheered wildly at a local theater as Chivington announced his "victory" and soldiers from his Third Regiment displayed dozens of Cheyenne scalps, some of them women's pubic hair.[38]

The Sand Creek massacre was not the largest slaughter of Indians during the 1860s—the Connor massacre of a Shoshoni village on Bear Creek in Idaho in 1863 and the Baker massacre of Blackfeet Indians on the Marias River in Montana in 1869 both had higher casualty rates—but it was the most publicized massacre of Indians in the nineteenth century. Plains Indians spread the word first, as Cheyenne survivors of the massacre carried the war pipe not only to other Cheyenne but to the Arapaho and Sioux as well. As many as 1,500 warriors gathered on the central plains and for several months raided stage stations, plundered ranches, cut down telegraph wires, and even attacked the town of Julesburg, Colorado. Spotted Tail, who had been convinced of the need to make peace with the whites, was so outraged at the injustice of Sand Creek that he joined in the revenge raid on Julesburg. Chivington had said that all Indians on the plains ought to be considered hostile, and Governor Evans feared that a united Indian insurrection would isolate Denver. Because of the massacre at Sand Creek, they were very nearly correct.

Beyond the senseless loss of life, the Sand Creek massacre went a long way toward crippling the peace factions in both Indian and white societies. Many Cheyenne leaders, especially the peace chiefs, were either killed outright or had their authority severely undermined when they proved unable to protect their people. As word of the massacre spread among Plains tribes, they no longer believed that the U.S. government would deal with them justly or that the army would treat them fairly. One official later warned of the new Indian perception of troops, "An angel from Heaven could not convince them but what another 'Chivington massacre' was intended."[39]

Sand Creek also put advocates of restraint in white society on the defensive. A military investigation concluded that Chivington was guilty of a premeditated massacre and the atrocities committed by troops were a disgrace to the uniform. However, by the time of the verdict the enlistment terms of Chivington and all of his volunteers had expired, so they were beyond military discipline. During the military investigation, one witness reported that Chivington, in a public speech in Denver, had argued that the solution to Colorado's "Indian problem" was to "kill and scalp all, little and big; nits make lice." Other testimony argued that Chivington never in fact uttered this phrase, but at least one witness testified that Chivington's men made this their slogan for the Sand Creek campaign.[40] Silas Soule, who refused to fire at Sand Creek and was among those who testified against Chivington, was murdered a month later by a member of the Colorado volunteers. The man who killed him was arrested, but he later escaped and fled to California.

A congressional committee, after hearing testimony from all sides, reached a conclusion very similar to the military investigation. Led by Wisconsin Republican senator James R. Doolittle and reflecting a measure of eastern and humanitarian concerns, the committee concluded that Chivington "deliberately planned and executed a foul and dastardly massacre which would have disgraced the veriest savage among those who were victims of his cruelty."[41] The most revealing expression of the western hostility toward Indians came in 1865 when Doolittle addressed a packed audience in the same Denver theater where Chivington's men had displayed Cheyenne scalps the previous year. Doolittle pleaded for a humane approach toward Indians but was stunned when, as he later recalled, at one point in his speech a loud shout arose, "almost loud enough to raise the roof of the Opera House— 'Exterminate them! Exterminate them!' "[42]

Red Cloud's War

During the Civil War years, the Lakota shifted their focus away from the intertribal warfare that they had known for centuries and toward meeting the American invasion, which they came to see as the supreme threat to their existence. Sibley's and Sully's attacks from the east and the wars on the southern plains, especially the Sand Creek massacre, convinced many Lakota leaders that the whites, not the Crow or any other Indian people, constituted the greatest menace to their well-being. "The white men have come to take over the entire land," Lakota leaders realized, and would continue until "they will completely annihilate the Lakota people." Pushed from the east and the south, the Lakota said, "They kept crowding us until we had to fight." Or, as one Lakota remembered, "The band I was in got together and said they were not going to let the white men run over them." Another recalled the spirit of resistance that animated his generation: "At the age of ten or eleven I had a six-shooter and a quiver full of arrows to defend my nation."[43]

One of the Lakota's most prominent war leaders during these years was Red Cloud, who came of age as a warrior during this rising tide of resistance to the white invaders. White society generally treated Red Cloud as the "chief" of the "hostile" Sioux in the years after the Civil War; although he was never a chief in the sense that whites used the term, he did become a "shirt-wearer," or war leader on the basis of his fearsome exploits in intertribal warfare. Red Cloud knew the value of white traders and appreciated the importance of manufactured goods, especially guns, blankets, beads, and whiskey, but otherwise wanted to keep his distance from whites. Born in Nebraska Territory, he had come of age as a warrior along the Platte River valley and witnessed firsthand the depletion of its woodlands, the overgrazing of its grasslands, and the dispersal of the game that had once frequented the lush river bottoms. Having lost control of one ecologically rich slice of the Lakota homeland, Red Cloud was ready to make a stand in defense of another.

The Bozeman Trail, the main route to the newly discovered gold fields in western Montana, forked away from the other overland trails at Fort Laramie and headed north through what is now central Wyoming and southern Montana to the Yellowstone River. In other words, it cut directly through the Powder River country that formed one of the last best hunting lands on the continent. Bordered by the Platte River on the south and the Yellowstone on the north, with the snow-capped Bighorn Mountains on the west and the verdant Black Hills to the east, the Powder River region had elk, deer, pronghorn antelope, and buffalo in abundance. As buffalo herds elsewhere declined as a result of the increasing trade in buffalo robes, the buffalo herds here could still fill the horizon as far as the eye could see. Although the Lakota were gradually pushing westward, pushing the Crow closer to their Bighorn Mountain strongholds, the region was in the 1860s still an ecological buffer zone between warring tribes. Because of the increased risk for hunting parties of either tribe, hunters did not linger in the area and consequently wildlife gathered there in unusual abundance. When the government tried to secure passage for emigrants along the Bozeman Trail, promising to pass through without disturbing the wildlife or damaging the wood and grass resources, Red Cloud and the Lakota had reason not to believe these promises. They had heard the same words, and already watched the destruction, with regard to the Platte River valley in the 1840s and 1850s. Now they were fighting the Crow for control of the Powder River region's immense animal wealth, and they were willing to fight the U.S. government as well.

In 1865, as the Civil War came to a close, the army launched a series of offensives throughout the West with the expectation that the "Indian problem" had a military solution. General Patrick E. Connor led a massive force of 2,500 troops into the Powder River country with the instructions to subdue any Indians they could find. Connor recently had led forces in an attack against a Shoshoni village in Bear River, Idaho, that had inflicted more casualties than Sand Creek and included much of the same debauched behavior—

killing women and children heedlessly—as the more famous massacre. This time, Connor promised to "hunt them like wolves" and ordered his troops to "attack and kill every male Indian over twelve years of age."[44] But with large columns of soldiers marching through rugged landscapes dragging long supply lines behind them, the army failed to find any Indians in 1865. It almost found disaster when General Connor's large force in the Powder River country ran out of supplies and nearly starved to death after being caught in early September snowstorms.

Both the public and the government began to lose patience with making war in such a futile and expensive manner. In the aftermath of the Civil War, the public had little taste for seemingly endless engagements against the Indians, while the postwar government was anxious to reduce the size and expense of the army. Promising presents and a new peace treaty, officials succeeded in persuading many Lakota leaders to attend meetings at Fort Laramie. As the discussions were going on, Colonel Henry B. Carrington marched a battalion of infantry into the fort and announced that he had orders to go to the Powder River country and build a series of forts to protect the white emigrants. Outraged, Red Cloud abruptly called a halt to the meetings with an angry speech: "The Great Father sends us presents and wants us to sell him the road, but White Chief goes with soldiers to steal the road before Indians say yes or no."[45] Red Cloud continued with a bitter speech, accusing the whites of crowding the Lakota into an ever-smaller area, depleting invaluable grass and wood resources, and now splitting the last of the great buffalo herds. It was better to die fighting, Red Cloud said, than to die by starvation.

Ignoring Red Cloud's protests, Carrington proceeded to build three forts along the Bozeman Trail, Fort Reno, Fort Phil Kearney, and Fort C. F. Smith, although his poorly equipped soldiers could hardly defend themselves, let alone protect the emigrants. Red Cloud, after leaving the Fort Laramie meetings, organized an offensive campaign designed to close the forts and stop all traffic on the Bozeman Trail. The Lakota laid siege to all three forts, harassing the soldiers every time they strayed far from the ramparts. After months of this hit-and-run warfare, they were able to stop emigrant traffic on the Bozeman Trail and to keep the soldiers isolated in their garrisons. The decisive battle came in December 1866, the Moon of the Popping Trees (so named because in the severe cold trees actually crack as loud as a gunshot), at Fort Phil Kearney on Little Piney Creek, at the foot of the snow-capped Bighorn Mountains. On December 20 a large group of warriors sought supernatural guidance for their coming fight by consulting a *winkte*, a man who dressed as a woman and had spiritual powers. He rode from the war party to the distant hills four times, each time returning with a vision of the number of enemy soldiers who would be killed. For three times the war leaders told him that the number was not large enough, but on the sacred fourth time, the *winkte* said that he had one hundred soldiers, and the war leaders shouted as if the victory were now certain.

Following a careful plan, the Lakota sent one group of warriors to attack a party of soldiers out collecting wood for the fort. It was no accident that the fight would begin as a struggle over scarce timber resources. Fearing an attack on his men, Carrington ordered Captain William J. Fetterman to ride to the relief of the wood train. Fetterman, who like Grattan a dozen years earlier had nothing but contempt for the fighting capacity of the Sioux, had once bragged that with eighty soldiers he could ride through the entire Sioux nation. With perfect irony, he commanded eighty soldiers as he rode out of the fort that day. As Fetterman's troops approached, the warriors backed off from the wood train, while a handful of other warriors taunted the soldiers from just out of range. These were decoys, led by Crazy Horse, using one of the timeworn maneuvers of Plains warfare. This time Crazy Horse and his men played the maneuver to perfection. They rode just out of range, but never too far, sometimes making it seem as if one of their horses had a limp, other times jumping off to check a horse's foot as if it were injured. Fetterman could not resist the trap and chased the decoys for 5 miles over a ridge and out of sight of the fort, down into a draw where 1,500 warriors waited. Soldiers at the fort heard gunfire but were unable to mount a relief party until the next day. By the time they arrived, all they found were the badly mutilated bodies of Fetterman and his eighty soldiers.

Satisfied with their victory, the Lakota returned to their winter camps, celebrating what they called the "Battle of the Hundred Slain." The army, in contrast, called it the "Fetterman massacre" and demanded that it be avenged. General William Tecumseh Sherman, famous for his Civil War victories and now commander of troops in the western region, responded angrily to the news of Fetterman's debacle with one of his most bellicose statements: "Of course, this massacre should be treated as an act of war and should be punished with vindictive earnestness, until at least ten Indians are killed for each white life lost." He urged his subordinates to "not allow the troops to settle down on the defensive but carry the war to the Indian camps, where the women and children are, and inflict such punishment that even Indians would discover that they can be beaten at their own game . . . It is not necessary to find the very men who committed the acts, but destroy all of the same breed."[46]

Sherman's vengeance faltered, however, stalled by humanitarian concerns for peace and a growing recognition of the realistic limits of military power. For a public still weary from Civil War fighting and a government looking to trim the size of its military, diplomacy offered a more appealing method of dealing with the Indians than further military misadventures. A Peace Commission, headed by Commissioner of Indian Affairs Nathaniel G. Taylor, blamed white provocation for the Indian troubles. "War usually springs from a sense of injustice," Taylor believed, although he added, "civilization must not be arrested in its progress by a handful of savages." Taylor favored settlement by "an industrious, thrifty, and enlightened population," so long as civilization did not accomplish "its ends by falsehood and violence."[47] The commission recommended that the government should abandon the Bozeman Trail, persuade the Indians to live on reservations, and negotiate in a spirit of fairness. Generals Sherman, Terry, and Harney (the Lakota's "Mad Bear" from his 1855 Blue Water campaign), all appointed to the commission, could not agree with the majority. As they saw it, there was "no hope of peace until the Indians were thoroughly subdued by force of arms."[48] For the time being, however, the government pursued the plan recommended by the majority of the commission: persuade the Lakota to sign a new peace treaty. Annuities, it hoped, would be cheaper than armies.

Throughout 1867 the government continued to ask Red Cloud and other Lakota leaders to come to Fort Laramie for talks, but they refused to negotiate. Volunteer militias organized in Colorado and Montana, with more bluster than fight, and called for clearing the Indians out of the territory. Colorado citizens collected a purse of five thousand dollars for the purpose of paying twenty-five dollars each for "scalps with their ears on." The Lakota and their Cheyenne allies met for the annual Sun Dance in June, afterward conferring about which fort to attack that summer. Unable to decide, they split forces and attacked both Fort C. F. Smith on the Bighorn River and Fort Phil Kearney in the shadow of the Bighorn Mountains. In both battles the warriors were repulsed, in large measure because the soldiers had new breech-loading rifles that could shoot with greater accuracy, distance, and speed than the old muzzle-loading muskets. Whites called the battles resounding victories and initially claimed to have inflicted more than a thousand casualties on the Sioux. The body count was greatly exaggerated, however, and the Sioux retired without any sense of defeat.

Red Cloud and younger fighters like Crazy Horse did learn, just as Sitting Bull had learned in his fight against Sully in 1863 and 1864, that rifles were crucial to success in fighting against the whites. In defeating Fetterman, 90 percent of the Lakota warriors used bows and arrows. But by the time Crazy Horse surrendered eleven years later, over half of his warriors had guns. Crazy Horse also learned that new weapons would dictate new tactics. The massed charges, on foot or horseback, a familiar tactic of the Sioux for generations, were an invitation for disaster when going against coordinated rifle fire. In the face of this new technology, Crazy Horse preferred to maintain a fluid fight, using mobility and the initiative of individual Lakota warriors to isolate troops and defeat them piecemeal, the tactic that had worked so successfully against Fetterman and that would be used again even more effectively a decade later at the Battle of the Little Bighorn.

In 1868 government messengers again came to Red Cloud and other Lakota leaders, asking them to come to Fort Laramie to negotiate a new peace. Some Lakota leaders agreed, but Red Cloud only sent a message, "We are on the mountains looking down on the soldiers and the forts. When we see the soldiers moving away and the forts abandoned, then I will come down and talk."[49] In late July, the soldiers abandoned the forts, and Red Cloud and his warriors burned them down. Then later in the fall, after spending a summer hunting and storing meat, the great Red Cloud came down from his mountains and put his signature to the treaty, a triumph for his war strategy and his diplomacy. He had succeeded in his goals: emigrant traffic on the Bozeman Trail had almost ceased and the obnoxious forts were gone. To Red Cloud this looked like a success for Lakota military prowess, but there were other reasons for the government's concessions. Humanitarians were putting pressure on the government to relent because they found the ongoing Indian wars to be morally repulsive, while others pressed the government for budgetary relief from the constant financial drain of fielding armies in the West. Perhaps most of all, the anticipated completion of the Northern Pacific Railroad promised to provide a faster route to the Montana gold fields and would make the Bozeman Trail virtually obsolete.

This set of circumstances prepared the stage for the Fort Laramie Treaty of 1868, which the Lakota entered into from a position of strength and the whites entered into with the idealistic hope that it would bring peace to the plains. Like the 1851 Fort Laramie Treaty, this one proclaimed peace, established boundaries, and set up a series of annuity payments to the Sioux. Unlike the earlier treaty, this was a bilateral agreement between the government and the Lakota Sioux, not a multilateral agreement between the government and several Indian groups. From the point of view of the government, the treaty was a peaceful way to keep the Lakota on a reservation and place them squarely on the road to assimilation. For Red Cloud and the Lakota leadership, the main point of the treaty was the abandonment of the forts and the guarantee of a large land base with hunting rights for the Lakota people. In other words, the government saw the treaty as the beginning of the end of Lakota autonomy, while the Lakota viewed the treaty as an affirmation of their continued independence.

The treaty recognized a Great Sioux Reservation, including all of South Dakota west of the Missouri River, or half of the state, plus a sliver of North Dakota and Nebraska on the south. Farther west, the Powder River country in what is today eastern Montana and Wyoming remained "unceded Indian territory" that the Sioux could use "so long as the buffalo may range thereon in numbers as to justify the chase."[50] Although whites felt that they had confined the Indians to a reservation, Lakota clearly felt that they had won recognition of lasting boundaries—boundaries that included the sacred Black Hills, which they called the *Paha Sapa*, and that were very close to the boundaries identified by the Bear Butte Council in 1857. Within these limits, Lakota believed they could continue their nomadic hunting existence, now without fear of invading armies.

The seeds of future conflict, however, were sown into the language of the treaty. The buffalo in numbers sufficient to hunt would not last even for a generation, as it turned out, and so the land area was far less secure than the Lakota believed. Other provisions of the treaty, which whites did not always explain and Red Cloud later claimed never to have heard, aimed at rapid assimilation of the Lakota. The treaty required an annual census, required Lakota children to attend schools as soon as the government could build them, and encouraged agriculture and the private allotment of reservation lands. In a somewhat disingenuous move, government negotiator John B. Sanborn drew a picture of a tipi alongside a new house and farm animals as he promised the Lakota, "You can live in these houses and still live in your own way."[51]

Since most of the Lakota did not intend to settle down into houses, send their children to school, or begin farming, the government clearly had unrealistic expectations for what the treaty had accomplished. Lakota hopes of a permanent land base were even more optimistic, as whites in the coming years paid little heed to the treaty's boundaries. No wonder that Sitting Bull, Crazy Horse, and other militants rejected the treaty, distrusted diplomacy, and remained committed to fighting rather than talking as the means to preserve their homeland. As it turned out, within eight years the U.S. government would agree that soldiers' guns rather than treaty pens or ceremonial pipes would settle the boundaries of the Sioux nation.

WAR AND PEACE . . . AND WAR

I can whip the Indians if I can find them.

GEORGE ARMSTRONG CUSTER, 1868

SOMETIME BETWEEN midnight and 2 a.m. on a bitter cold night, Custer and his Osage scouts climbed carefully to the top of a hill overlooking the Washita River, lay down on the crusty snow, and peered into the valley below for signs of Indians. After traveling four days through more than a foot of snow with cold so severe that Custer and his exhausted cavalry had to walk to keep their feet from freezing, they were now breathless with excitement to locate their foe. Earlier they had found the tracks of a Cheyenne war party and were now trailing the warriors to their village, hoping to surprise the Indians who had been raiding white settlements. The Osage scouts smelled smoke and then from the top of the hill saw a herd of animals in the valley below. At first they suspected it might be buffalo, but then they heard barking dogs and a tinkling bell from what they knew must be a herd of Indian ponies. Listening carefully into the still crispness, they heard a baby's cry, positive confirmation that an Indian village was near. Moving quietly down the slope, Custer summoned his officers and began to make the plans for a dawn attack, an attack that would make him one of America's most famous Indian fighters.

Boy General

George Armstrong Custer arrived at this moment, November 27, 1868, on the banks of the Washita River in Indian Territory (later Oklahoma) by serving both his personal ambition and his national purpose. Armstrong, or "Autie" as his family and friends called him, was born on an Ohio farm one generation removed from its own Indian-fighting days. He grew up a "big-hearted, whole-souled fellow," one of his friends remembered, with a love of practical jokes and an eye for the girls. Although he was deeply ambitious, he had little aptitude for formal schooling, preferring instead hunting, horseback riding, and plenty of socializing. Like many Americans of the nineteenth century, Custer pursued social advancement through a career in the military, using family connections to obtain an appointment to West Point Military Academy in 1857. As a cadet, he earned a reputation for never allowing education to get in the way of having a good time. One friend remembered Custer as "the best-hearted and cleverest man that I ever knew" who was "always connected with all the mischief that is going on, and never studying any more than he can possibly help."[1] His attentions to women continued, and when he returned from a two-month furlough back home to Monroe, Michigan, in August 1859, he required treatment for gonorrhea, presumably the result of his active social life. On June 24, 1861, he graduated thirty-fourth in his class of thirty-four, just in time to receive a commission as a lieutenant in the United States cavalry as it headed into the Civil War.

The war started slowly for Custer, allowing him plenty of time for social activities. On one leave from staff duty, he imbibed spirits to the point of embarrassment, leading him to swear off alcohol forever, a promise that he kept for the rest of his life. On another break he met and fell in love with Elizabeth Bacon, the attractive, intelligent, and stylish daughter of Judge Daniel Bacon, a leading citizen of Custer's hometown. While courting her, he resolved to quit gambling, a promise he found difficult to keep, but refused to stop swearing, a habit he considered necessary in combat. With this as his only vice, the squeaky-clean Custer often stood out later in life among the officers on the western plains, where drinking and gambling were commonplace. Custer's clean image was important for winning over Libbie and proved useful in gaining her father's permission as well, since he initially objected to Custer's lower social status. Together the couple found the happiness and the social recognition they sought, especially after Custer's rise to fame at Gettysburg.

Early in the war the Union generals tended to use cavalry only as couriers or scouts, making it difficult for Custer or any cavalryman to achieve distinction. This changed at the battle of Gettysburg when Custer, fresh from a promotion to brevet brigadier general, a temporary, honorary promotion based on battlefield bravery, led two cavalry charges against the Confederate cavalry under the previously invincible Jeb Stuart. Shouting "Come on, you Wolverines," Custer personally led one of the most ferocious charges of the war, and one that established for the first time that the Union horsemen could fight on equal terms with the vaunted Confederate cavalry. Here, at twenty-three years old, the "Boy General" established a stellar reputation as a cavalry officer. Other officers often commended him for his personal courage, his "instant, exhaustless energy," and the "relentless power" of his attack.[2]

During the final stages of the Civil War, he served under Major General Philip Sheridan in the Shenandoah Valley campaign, embellishing his record of personal bravery and tactical acuteness while helping Sheridan clear the valley of Confederate forces. In 1864 Sheridan, described by President Lincoln as "a brown, chunky little chap, with a long body, short legs, not enough neck to hang him, and such long arms that if his ankles itch he can scratch them without stooping,"[3] was developing the strategy of total war—bringing the pain of war to the enemies' society and economy as well as its army—that would bring an end to the Civil War. Sheridan ordered the Union army to burn barns, fields, and pastures so that the Shenandoah Valley, sometimes called the breadbasket of the Confederacy, could no longer support the rebel army. Sheridan and Custer learned that an army that could not eat was an army that could not fight, a lesson that they would apply again on the western plains.

During the Civil War, Custer also established his reputation for his ability to fight under heavy fire and to charge into enemy lines without being hit. This was especially noteworthy because he dressed in a way that seemed designed to draw attention. He wore his reddish-blond hair long and curled at his shoulders, sported a brushy mustache, and had bright blue eyes and a fair complexion that burned in the sun. Taking full advantage of an officer's prerogative to wear individualized attire, Custer sported a blue sailor's shirt, black velveteen jacket, a bright red necktie, high boots with gaudy spurs, and a broad-brimmed hat. He could hardly be missed, even on a crowded battlefield. Some said he had a charmed existence and called it "Custer's luck," while others said that the secret to his apparent invulnerability was that he "never was still, he was always on the move." A few weeks after Gettysburg, Custer had written, "I believe more than ever in destiny."[4] Whatever the reason for "Custer's luck," he seems to have internalized the belief that he would

The "Boy General," George Armstrong Custer dressed in his distinctive
Civil War uniform. Portrait taken in 1865 and later reproduced by David
Frances Barry. Courtesy Denver Public Library.

always survive the next charge. Custer had gained a confidence to match his
ambition.

Custer's meteoric rise to glory during the war came to a standstill after the
war was over. As the army reorganized for peacetime duty—Reconstruction
in the South, seacoast defense in the East, and Indian fighting in the West—
officers gave up their wartime brevet ranks and found fewer opportunities

for advancement. Custer went from "Boy General" to Lieutenant Colonel Custer, actually a promotion from his prewar rank but dispiriting nonetheless. Promotions were rare in the postwar army, and for the rest of his career he remained officially lieutenant colonel, although most of those who served with him knew him by his brevet rank of major general. In October 1866 he reported for duty to Fort Riley, Kansas, where the Seventh Cavalry was organizing to fight Indians on the western frontier.

The next spring and summer may have been the most frustrating of his entire life. As the cavalry commander for General Winfield S. Hancock's 1,400-man expedition designed to intimidate the Indians of the southern plains, Custer repeatedly chased after Indian villages only to have a large trail split into so many small tracks that the entire village seemed to disappear. He learned that Indian ponies, especially when feeding on the luxuriant grasses of spring and summer, were faster than the grain-fed army horses, encumbered as they were by long supply lines and slow-moving wagons. As he later wrote, "I am of the opinion, . . . justified by experience, that no cavalry in the world, marching, even in the lightest manner possible, unencumbered with baggage or supply trains, can overtake or outmarch the Western Indian, when the latter is disposed to prevent it."[5]

Despite these frustrations with finding Indians, Custer was learning the thrill of riding horseback on the open plains. On one occasion he left the column to chase a buffalo, and then he accidentally shot his own galloping horse in the head with his revolver. It was a near disaster: a lone cavalry officer reduced to walking by himself on the rolling plains, lost in Indian country while facing an aggrieved buffalo bull. "Custer's luck" held, however, as the bull wandered away and his troops found him before the Indians did.

Nevertheless, Custer's fortunes remained troubled for the rest of the summer. His Indian opponents continued to elude him, the summer heat on the plains grew insufferable, supply problems hindered his movements, and he grew lonely for Libbie on this longest separation yet in their three-year-old marriage. In June he led his men on a 1,000-mile, month-long futile hunt for Indian warriors who had attacked stage coaches and burned mail stations. The closest he came to fighting Indians was finding the remains of Lieutenant Lyman S. Kidder and his eleven soldiers who had been trying to deliver a message to him. A large force of Cheyenne Dog Soldiers and Lakota warriors had discovered the small detachment and killed them all. "Kidder's Massacre" provided Custer with a vivid image of what it might mean to be surrounded by a superior Indian foe. He later described the scene in the terms that foreshadowed the idealized descriptions of his own demise nine years later: "A desperate struggle had ensued before the Indians were successful in over-powering their victims . . . All died nobly fighting to the last . . . No one is left to tell the tale . . . What bravery, what heroism must have inspired this devoted little band of martyrs, when, surrounded and assailed by a vastly overwhelming force of bloodthirsty barbarians they manfully struggled to the last equally devoid of hope or fear."[6]

As Custer's own hope of fighting Indians diminished, he became increasingly moody, overbearing, and petulant. Captain Albert Barnitz, initially a friend of Custer, wrote that he had become "the most complete example of a petty tyrant that I have ever seen," with numerous "instances of cruelty to the men, and discourtesy to the officers."[7] As frustration deepened in July, Custer impetuously left his command at Fort Wallace in western Kansas and rode with seventy-six troopers for fifty-seven hours over 150 miles to Fort Riley for a reunion with his wife. He later claimed that he was motivated by a concern for his wife's safety, but a more likely explanation was that he had simply grown tired and lonely. His eagerness might also have been stoked by rumors of Libbie spending many happy hours with a certain charming captain and University of Michigan graduate named Thomas Weir. Whatever the motive, Custer's commanding officer initiated a court-martial against him for abandoning his post.

To add to Custer's problems, another officer, one whom he had recently disciplined for drunkenness on duty (a commonplace event on western army posts) and who harbored a strong dislike of Custer, filed additional charges claiming that Custer had ordered deserters to be shot without trial. With morale and pay dreadfully low in the western army, desertion was a major problem. In fact, many "snow birds" signed up for pay during the winter months, merely waiting for their chance to desert to the gold fields or to western cities when summer came. The charge against Custer came after one particularly galling instance of desertion when thirty-four men slipped away from camp, some in full view of the officers. An enraged Custer ordered two officers and a group of soldiers to pursue them and "bring none in alive."[8] They brought six men back, three of them with gunshot wounds, one of which proved fatal. Although Custer defended himself vigorously, the court-martial found him guilty and suspended him from service for one year without pay. President Grant thought the verdict "lenient" but appropriate in light of Custer's previously distinguished record of military service. His first tour of duty on the plains thus ended ignominiously, a direct contrast to his Civil War accomplishments.

As Custer's luck would have it, he was to be given a second chance. Things were not going well for the army's campaign to control the Indians on the central plains. General Hancock's 1867 operation, of which Custer had been a part, proved disastrous. It had not been forceful enough to subdue the Indians but was enough of an irritant to agitate many militants and young warriors. Negotiations that summer led to a new agreement, the Medicine Lodge Treaty, but its provisions were so poorly understood on both sides that it unraveled almost as soon as it was signed. Correspondent Henry Morton Stanley, later to earn fame as an explorer in Africa, called it a "mock treaty" signed only as a "matter of form" and pointed out that no one had even read the terms of the agreement to the chiefs who signed it and that their spoken statements indicated that they had no intentions of surrendering the territory it required.[9]

The rolling tide of Manifest Destiny was against them, however, as Kansas more than tripled its white population during the 1860s. With more settlers streaming into the central and western plains, the Cheyenne faced overwhelming numbers in the competition for land, buffalo herds, and scarce timber. The inevitable small raids and counterraids occurred, and by August 1867 the Cheyenne and their allies had killed over one hundred whites and taken over one thousand cattle. The Cheyenne were hungry that summer, and their war parties went out looking to strike other tribes, to find food, and sometimes to take revenge against the whites. With memories of Sand Creek fresh in their minds while their stomachs often went empty, their mood was edgy and their actions unpredictable.

Strategy

The United States went to war on the plains with a shrinking army and no strategy for fighting Indians. The size of the Union army of the Civil War decreased rapidly in peacetime, with almost a million soldiers leaving the army within a year of Appomattox. Faced with the unpopular duties of policing Reconstruction in the South or fighting Indians and restricting white settlement in the West, the postwar army failed to generate much support from the general public. Congress appropriated funds for an army of fifty-seven thousand in 1868 and a mere twenty-seven thousand by 1876. Given the difficulty of recruitment, the actual number of soldiers may have been less than twenty thousand. With the number of troops declining, officers had little chance for promotion. Civil War officers, with ranks reduced from their brevet status to permanent levels, now competed bitterly for the few available promotions. Opportunities for battlefield success were rare, and fortune favored those bold enough to make the most of the moment when opportunity came.

Somewhat surprising given the frequency of Indian wars in the nineteenth century, the army also lacked an overall doctrine for fighting them. There was simply no strategy for what in the twentieth century would be called unconventional warfare. Most officers in the army saw Indian wars as a low-status diversion from their real job, which was preparing to fight a traditional war. The strategy for the campaign against the Sioux and Cheyenne came from the mind of General Phil Sheridan. Widely known as "Little Phil" Sheridan, he was an Irishman who became a fierce fighter for national union and believed that all obstacles, whether Confederates in the South or Indians in the West, ought to be coerced into submission by the force of arms.

His attitudes toward Indians were shaped by his pre–Civil War experience in the Pacific Northwest, where he lived with and fought against Indians and even had an Indian woman as his housekeeper and mistress. Although he denied it, he was widely attributed with saying, "The only good Indian is a dead Indian." Several people claim to have heard him say something close to this during a campaign in the Southwest. When an Indian, trying to get in Sheridan's good graces, claimed to be a good Indian, Sheridan's reply was, "The only good Indians I ever saw were dead." Whether or not Sheridan actually said this, and his biographer thinks it likely that he did, Sheridan was well known for his hostility toward Indian people. He viewed the typical Sioux as a "lazy, idle vagabond; he never labors and has no profession except that of arms, to which he is raised as a child; a scalp is constantly dangled before his eyes, and the highest honor he can aspire to is to possess one taken by himself."[10] Reformer Wendell Phillips, a critic of the Indian wars, countered, "I only know the names of three savages upon the Plains—Colonel Baker, General Custer, and at the head of all, General Sheridan."[11]

Sheridan and his commander, General William Tecumseh Sherman, believed that making war against the Indians was merely doing what their country expected of them. Duty called them to protect the white settlers who formed the steady advance of the nation, and Indians, as Confederates had been earlier, were obstacles to national development. The military was simply the fighting arm of the body politic, according to these architects of the Indian wars, and duty required that they execute the will of the people. Like the nation they represented, they often framed military action as a necessary defense against Indian aggression. By refusing to give up their nomadic ways, they believed, western Indians forced the army to retaliate as the only way of defending American lives and homes. The Indians bore the responsibility for their own destruction, as Sherman wrote in 1867 of a band of recalcitrant natives, "They must be exterminated, for they cannot and will not settle down, and our people will force us to do it."[12] Sheridan concurred with Sherman on the question of who bore the responsibility for causing the war, as he noted in a letter in 1873: "If a village is attacked and women and children killed, the responsibility is not with the soldiers but with the people who necessitated the attack."[13]

The special treachery that Indians committed to bring down the army's wrath on themselves, according to Sherman and Sheridan, was to capture and violate white women. Nothing conjured up the public's hatred toward Indians or stirred the generals' fighting spirit like the threat of Indians capturing and violating frontier women. Sheridan repeatedly spoke of the need to protect white women from being "scalped and ravished" and once refused to pay ransom for the return of a captive white woman on the grounds, more fanciful than factual, that after she had "been subjected to the fearful bestiality of perhaps the whole tribe," it would be "mock humanity to secure what is left of her." Sherman also warned that Indians "destroy houses and property" and "have seized the women and ravished them, perpetuating atrocities which could only have been planned ahead of time."[14]

The irony was that the defense of white domesticity required a military strategy that assaulted Indians in their homes. The army's frustrating experience of Indians evading the army on the open plains had convinced Sheridan that focusing on the village's women was the best way to ensure that warriors would stand and fight. The signature action of Sheridan's strategy became the dawn attack on an Indian village, if possible in the winter when Indians were less mobile. Such attacks aimed to kill or capture the fighting men and destroy food supplies, horses, lodges, and weapons. The goal was to force them into starvation and eventual submission. Regrettably, some women and children, while not targeted, would be killed. Sensitive to the criticism these civilian casualties brought, Sheridan hoped to minimize them whenever possible. He argued that the army's disciplined troops were better Indian fighters, for precisely this reason, than untrained volunteers such as those at the Sand Creek massacre.

Attacking Indian villages was hardly new in American history. Since colonial times, Americans had sometimes deliberately attacked Indian villages and destroyed crops in order to subdue the people. This strategy had already been tried on the plains during Harney's 1856 campaign against Little Turtle's village and Sully's campaign against the Santee Sioux in 1863 and 1864. But it was the "hard war" policy cultivated during the Civil War that elevated this practice into a deliberate doctrine. Sheridan's experience in the Shenandoah Valley of Virginia and Sherman's experience in the destruction of Atlanta and his march to the sea convinced both men that the "hard war" approach was the quickest way to peace. As Sheridan explained to the Prussians in 1870, while watching the siege of Paris, "The proper strategy consists in the first place in inflicting as telling blows as possible upon the enemy's army, and then causing the inhabitants so much suffering that they must long for peace and force their government to demand it. The people must be left nothing but their eyes to weep with over the war."[15] What was required on the plains, as Sherman saw it, was that the Cheyenne "be soundly whipped and the ringleaders in the present trouble hung, their ponies killed, and such destruction of their property as will make them very poor."[16]

Lacking any innovative means for how to accomplish this strategic goal, Sheridan relied on the conventional practices of the army: slow-moving columns of cavalry and infantry, burdened by heavy food requirements for horses and men, who could go no faster than their mule-driven supply wagons and stay in the field no longer than the supplies could feed them. The recurring embarrassment for the nineteenth-century army was that entire Indian villages could move faster than even the cavalry, let alone the infantry, and could be nearly impossible to track down on the vast expanses of the plains. Typical was Custer's 1867 experience pursuing an entire Cheyenne village, which left him empty-handed and "discouraged by seeing the broad, well-beaten trail suddenly separate into hundreds of indistinct routes, leading fan-shape in as many different directions."[17]

The best person to execute this hard war strategy, Sheridan believed, was his old colleague from the Shenandoah Valley, Lieutenant Colonel George Armstrong Custer. Seeking to energize what had been a lackluster summer and fall campaign, Sheridan asked for and received permission to recall the commander who, Sheridan believed, had the aggressiveness of ambition to fight the kind of war he wanted. After a month of organizing forces and arranging supplies, Custer set out on November 23, leading eight hundred men in search of Cheyenne and Arapaho Indians in southern Kansas and Indian Territory, along the Canadian and Washita rivers. His orders from General Sheridan were clear: "To proceed south in the direction of the Antelope Hills, thence towards the Washita River, the supposed winter seat of the hostile tribes; to destroy their villages and ponies; to kill or hang all warriors, and bring back all women and children." There should be "no terms with the hostile Indians except unconditional surrender." He was to "strike the Indians a hard blow and force them onto reservations," or failing this, at least to show the Indians that they "would have no security, winter or summer, except in obeying the laws of peace and humanity."[18]

The Battle of the Red Moon

There was more than a foot of snow on the ground as the Seventh Cavalry set out on November 23 from Camp Supply while the band played "The Girl I Left Behind Me." While some worried that the snow would slow their movements, Custer was elated. "We could move and the Indian villages could not," he explained. Captain Barnitz thought the morning "excessively cold" and said that it "was necessary to dismount very often, and walk in order to keep our feet from freezing," which in the deep snow was "exceedingly difficult and tiresome."[19] On November 26, after three days of hard marching, Major Joel Elliott's scouting patrol found the tracks of an Indian war party that numbered over one hundred men. They pursued them into the night, finally pausing to allow the rest of the Seventh Cavalry to catch up. Late that night Custer and his Osage scouts climbed the hill from which they saw the pony herd and heard the baby cry, letting them know that they had found their target. As Custer gave the orders to divide his command into four columns for a dawn assault, one officer asked, "General, suppose we find more Indians there than we can handle?" Custer responded, "Huh, all I am afraid of is we won't find half enough. There are not enough Indians in the country to whip the Seventh Cavalry."[20]

Although Custer did not know it, the Indians he heard in the valley below were Black Kettle and his band of Cheyenne. Despite the atrocities at Sand

Creek, Black Kettle had continued to look for a way to remain at peace with the whites. This was not a view amenable to many younger Cheyenne. For them, Sand Creek proved that whites were not to be trusted, and as a result many of them drifted toward the leadership of the Dog Soldiers or went north and allied with the Lakota. Much as he might try, Black Kettle could not control the movements of these young warriors, and now some who had participated in raids the previous summer returned to live with their relatives in his village during the cold winter months. Black Kettle, along with about six thousand Cheyenne and Kiowa allies, had chosen to spend the winter along the Washita River, a traditional river valley for wintering that offered abundant wildlife, grass for their ponies, plenty of firewood, protection from blizzards, and, they hoped, safety from the soldiers. The entire Cheyenne and Kiowa village stretched for miles along a great horseshoe bend in the river, with Black Kettle's hamlet of fifty-one tipis and perhaps 250 people set up some distance away from the rest of the camp.

Just before dawn a bright morning star illuminated the eastern sky. Custer took this as a signal of victory and called it "the star of the Washita." At the first rays of the morning sun, Custer ordered his trumpeters to sound the charge, and then the Seventh Cavalry band played "Garry Owen" as four columns of blue-coated cavalrymen converged on Black Kettle's village. "The Indians were caught napping," Custer claimed, using a phrase that he repeated to his men eight years later at the Little Bighorn.[21] Custer's head scout, Ben Clark, known to the Cheyenne as "Red Neck" for the way his fair skin burned in the intense prairie sun, reported, "The Indians were taken completely by surprise and rushed panic-stricken from their lodges, to be shot down before sleep had left their eyelids." Years later, Mrs. B. K. Young Bird, who was fourteen when the battle happened, recalled, "There was no warning; up from our sleep we jump, we did not have time to gather our clothing; just as we got up from our sleep we ran for safety . . . We all knew that Long Hair Custer was out hunting the Indians and we knew that he had found us . . . I cannot tell the horror that was experienced that awful cold morning when the soldiers started shooting and we jumped out of our sleep and ran for safety and very many of our people were shot down like rabbits."[22] When the shooting began, Black Kettle and his wife mounted his horse and rode for safety, only to be shot as they attempted to cross the Washita River. Black Kettle, hit in both the stomach and the back, fell into the icy stream and died. His wife, riding behind him, was also shot and later found nearby. His second wife was found later with a bullet in her back, near the mutilated remains of another woman and the unborn child she had been carrying.

The surprise was so complete that Custer's soldiers controlled the village in only ten minutes. Scattered fighting continued as the remnants of Black Kettle's band fled in different directions, many running barefoot downstream along the icy Washita River. Ben Clark witnessed E Company, under Captain Myers, pursuing a group of women and children, "killing them without mercy." When Clark asked Custer if women and children were to be killed, Custer responded, "No. Ride out there and give the officer commanding my compliments and ask him to stop it. Take them to the village and put them in a big tipi and station a guard over them."[23] As fighting in the village died down, troops secured the area and gathered other surviving women and children to join the prisoners in two large tipis. From the top of a small hill, Major Joel Elliott noticed a group of Cheyenne running away and, calling for volunteers to join him, galloped after them with a parting shout, "Here goes for a brevet or a coffin." Elliott and seventeen followers chased the fleeing Indians for several miles downstream, until they ran into a much larger force of mounted warriors from the villages below. Elliott and his men dismounted and made their final stand in the tall grass on top of a small knoll. In about the time it takes "to smoke a pipe four times," one Cheyenne later recalled, Elliott achieved the destiny he had so blithely sought.[24]

Meanwhile, Lieutenant Edward S. Godfrey and his platoon were rounding up a large pony herd in the hills near the village. From the top of a ridge, Godfrey later remembered, "I was amazed to find that as far as I could see down the well wooded, tortuous valley there were tepees—tepees. Not only could I see tepees, but mounted warriors were scurrying in our direction."[25] Godfrey returned the herd of ponies to camp and reported the distressing discovery to Custer. Soon mounted warriors appeared on the hills above the village, forcing Custer to adjust his plans in light of the new threat. He decided not to send a relief party after Elliott, which may have been too late anyway, and, in keeping with the concept of total war, he directed his men to destroy the Cheyenne camp and their means of transportation: the pony herd. After selecting ponies for the officers and allowing some for the prisoners to ride, the men shot the remainder of the herd, over six hundred animals. The slaughter took nearly two hours and occurred in full view of the gathering numbers of enraged warriors in the bluffs above the village. While this was going on, Custer ordered the lodges searched for evidence of participation in the summer's raids in Kansas. His troops found mail, photographs, and household goods, enough evidence for Custer to establish the village's complicity. Then Custer ordered the village and its contents burned, including, by his own account, 573 buffalo robes, 550 buffalo skins, 210 axes, 140 hatchets, 35 revolvers, 47 rifles, 535 pounds of powder, 1,050 pounds of lead, 4,000 arrows, 241 saddles, 775 lariats, 940 saddlebags, 470 blankets, 700 pounds of tobacco, and a winter supply of buffalo meat, flour, meal, supplies for cooking, and, he concluded, "everything they possessed." He also claimed that he had "now in our possession, as prisoners of war, 53 squaws and their children."[26]

By afternoon the destruction was complete, yet Custer now found his force surrounded by large numbers of warriors gathering on the hills overlooking the Washita. Having destroyed Black Kettle's village, he now faced the possibility of being wiped out by a larger force. As he wrote, "We had achieved a great and important success over the hostile tribes. The problem now was how to retain our advantage and steer safely through the difficulties which seemed to surround our position." The solution he found was to take "recourse to that maxim in war which teaches a commander to do that which his enemy neither expects nor desires him to do."[27] In other words, Custer decided on a feint attack toward the downstream Indian villages, reasoning that protection of their families was the warriors' greatest concern. Placing the prisoners in the middle of his column, he marched the regiment downstream toward the other Indian villages. Fearing their villages would be attacked next, the hilltop warriors hurried to their homes in preparation for defense. When darkness came, Custer then ordered a countermarch that took his regiment and their prisoners out of the Washita valley and back toward their base at Camp Supply.

The battle was barely over before the controversies began. Custer wrote to Sheridan of his success, "We have cleaned Black Kettle and his band out so thoroughly that they can neither fight, dress, sleep, eat, or ride without sponging on their friends."[28] He claimed to have killed 103 warriors in addition to the fifty-three women and children taken prisoner. Later, he revised this number upward, claiming to have killed or taken prisoner as many as three hundred. Cheyenne memories of killed and wounded were considerably lower, perhaps as low as one-tenth of Custer's exaggerated body count. Casualties for the Seventh Cavalry included twenty killed (eighteen of them with Elliott) and thirteen wounded. Sheridan's initial enthusiasm for Custer's "efficient and gallant services" was tempered when he learned the fate of Major Elliott and his men. Custer's explanation that they were probably lost and would show up sooner or later was, in Sheridan's words, a "very unsatisfactory view of the matter,"[29] and some officers in the Seventh Cavalry thought Sheridan understated the situation. When an anonymous letter appeared in a Saint Louis newspaper accusing Custer of abandoning Elliott and his men, Custer called a meeting of his officers, demanded to know who had authored the letter, and promised to horsewhip the villain. Captain Frederick Benteen, hand on his service revolver, stepped forward and claimed authorship. Custer stepped away rather than risk more than a verbal fight, but the dissension did not die. Fueled by the Elliott incident, and magnified by petty jealousies, personality differences, and Custer's favoritism, the factionalism in the Seventh Cavalry festered over the eight years from Washita to the Battle of the Little Bighorn, where some would hold that Benteen's bitterness played a role in the outcome.

Within weeks of what the military considered a great victory, many people were criticizing the army for committing a massacre against unarmed women and children who were in a village trying to live at peace with the whites. Samuel Tappan, a friend of the Commissioner of Indian Affairs Nathaniel Taylor, wrote that Black Kettle's village had been friendly, that Custer's attack amounted to another Sand Creek, and that only an "immediate and unconditional abandonment of the present war policy" would avoid further slaughter of innocents. Others in the Indian Bureau supported the view that Custer's attack had been a "cold-blooded butchery" of innocent women and children. Representatives of the Cherokee, Choctaw, and Creek nations, the so-called civilized tribes, saw Washita as a "brutal massacre of friendly Indians," and even retired Brigadier General William S. Harney, who the Lakota called "Mad Bear" for his brutal 1857 campaign against Little Thunder's camp at Blue Water Creek, called Black Kettle "as good a friend of the United States as I am."[30]

The *Army and Navy Journal*, however, dismissed all of this as the sentimental musings of what they mockingly dubbed the "Indian Ring"—a few philanthropists, the Indian Bureau, and "Indian agents, contractors, and peddlers" who had jobs or profited from doing business with Indians. "We are told that Black Kettle's band was friendly, and accordingly, that Custer is a second Chivington. That is not the fact," the *Journal* argued, because Black Kettle's "camp has been a rendezvous for young warriors, who start from it as a 'base' and return to it with booty." Sheridan thought that Washita was a one-sided battle, but not a massacre, because unlike Sand Creek, Black Kettle's camp was not under military protection, it harbored warriors who had recently been fighting, and the Seventh Cavalry, unlike Chivington's poorly trained volunteers, were under strict orders to spare noncombatants. Sherman dismissed criticism with the comment that "the great mass of our people cannot be humbugged into the belief that Black Kettle's camp was friendly" because it had so many stolen goods, what he called "trophies of war."[31]

From the perspective of most Cheyenne, Washita represented a devastating loss very similar to Sand Creek. Magpie, a Cheyenne chief who escaped from the village and witnessed most of the fighting, later in life visited the site "where so many of our people were killed and where the soldiers wantonly slaughtered our ponies." As he remembered, "The Indians were not to blame. They were not bad. They were not on the warpath. They had come here to be out of white man's way, so they would not have to fight the white soldiers, but Custer's soldiers hunted them out and tried to kill or to make slaves of them." A Cheyenne woman who experienced the fight gave it a different name. Mrs. Lone Wolf, in an interview years later, recalled an aspect of the battle mentioned more in Cheyenne accounts than in white versions: "The ponies, after being shot, broke away, and ran about, bleeding, until they dropped. In this way the snow on the whole bend of the river was made red with blood. This is the reason we call it [the battle of] the red moon."[32]

The most important point about Washita from the army's perspective was that it was neither a massacre nor a battle so much as merely one action in a larger campaign. If Sheridan and Sherman's principles of total war meant anything, it was this: the army would relentlessly pursue the Indians in any season, especially winter, until the Indians were forced to surrender on the army's terms. After Washita, Sheridan thought, "If we can get one or two more good blows there will be no more Indian troubles in my department." Sherman concurred, confident that "by Christmas he [Custer] will have all these Indians begging for their lives."[33] In order to make good on these promises, Sheridan went with Custer on another campaign to the Washita in December 1868 to force the Kiowa to submit to reservations and then sent Custer on a long march around the Wichita Mountains to find the Arapaho and force them to submit. Success in these campaigns came not from major battles but from the unrelenting pursuit of the Indians during a season when survival was difficult. Finally, in July 1869 the Fifth Cavalry under Major Eugene Carr defeated the largest remaining group of Cheyenne Dog Soldiers, thus effectively ending armed resistance among the Southern Cheyenne.

Despite the controversies surrounding Washita, the battle established Custer's image as the nation's premier Indian fighter. His ego fed on the publicity as his name became synonymous with fighting Indians on the western plains, even overshadowing his earlier record of success in the Civil War. To enhance this new persona, he replaced his Civil War blue uniform with a buckskin jacket and trousers, the symbol of the Plains scout and Indian fighter. In the coming years he transformed his reputation into the latest unveiling of the heroic Leatherstocking from James Fenimore Cooper's novels, the mighty hunter, master of Plains lore, and the one who possesses a keen understanding of the Indians he simultaneously identifies with and fights against. He was the self-styled avenging angel of civilization, who somewhat reluctantly cleared the plains of the Indian obstacle to ensure the inevitable progress of the civilization he served, even as he self-consciously identified with the frontier he was bringing to an end.

Custer cemented this image by writing *My Life on the Plains,* first serialized and then published in 1874. In addition to narrating his adventures in the West, Custer professed admiration for his Indian foes. "If I were an Indian," he speculated, "I often think that I would greatly prefer to cast my lot among those of my people who adhered to the free open plains, rather than submit to the confined limits of a reservation . . . " In keeping with the Leatherstocking genre, Custer affirmed the nobility of his adversaries. But if the Indian was noble, he was nonetheless a savage, according to Custer, with a "cruel and ferocious nature" that was "so deep-seated and inbred" that "he cannot be himself and be civilized." Here was the prison of the noble savage stereotype; Indians who lost their savagery also lost their nobility. "Cultivation," Custer asserted, "deprives him of his identity," while education would "weaken rather than strengthen his intellect."[34] In other words, Custer believed that Indians were most ennobled when they were in their free and "natural" state, but that there was no place for them in civilized American society. Assimilation policies were doomed to failure, Custer implied, and the noble red man appeared to be destined for extinction.

In early 1872 Custer played a leading role in a Great Plains spectacle that dramatized this romantic view of the vanishing frontier. During a celebrity tour of the United States, the Grand Duke Alexis, son of the Russian czar, made General Sheridan aware that what he most wanted was an opportunity to travel west to shoot buffalo and see wild Indians. Sheridan happily obliged the duke, treating his party of aristocratic sportsmen to a gala hunting trip in

Nebraska. In addition to his regular staff, Sheridan invited Custer and William "Buffalo Bill" Cody to the extravagant event. Sheridan completed the calculated creation of frontier authenticity by inviting Spotted Tail and his band of over five hundred Lakota to participate in the hunt. In the male-dominated world of the hunting camp, Custer chased buffalo side by side with Duke Alexis while everyone drank liberal amounts of champagne and whiskey to celebrate the hundreds of slaughtered buffalo. In the evenings the Lakota performed dances, everyone feasted on buffalo steaks, and Custer flirted brazenly with Spotted Tail's sixteen-year-old daughter, whispering in her ear and once giving her earrings and kissing her.

Sheridan welcomed these aristocratic buffalo hunters to the plains because they provided a powerful symbol for what he believed was the key to winning the war against the Plains Indians, the destruction of the vast buffalo herds that were their food source. Once numbering perhaps as many as twenty-five million, buffalo numbers had dwindled since the 1840s because of introduced diseases, drought, subsistence and commercial hunting, and habitat destruction along the overland trails. The period from 1872 to 1874, however, marked the years of the "great hunt" when the wholesale slaughter of this American icon virtually wiped out the animal on the southern plains. Aided by a new process that allowed commercial tanning of hides and by railroads that provided easy access to transporting the bulky robes, professional hunters moved onto the plains to make their fortunes. The buffalo hunter's goal was to make a "stand," that is, to establish position downwind of the herd and then shoot as many animals as possible without causing a stampede. A successful hunter might kill seventy to one hundred buffalo in one "stand," shooting so fast that only an overheated rifle barrel could slow the slaughter. The result of this industrial carnage was that over five million buffalo hides reached market between 1872 and 1874, with almost all of the meat left to rot on the plains. The naturalist William Hornaday described the southern plains in 1873 as "one vast charnel-house" where "putrefying carcasses, many of them with the hide still on, lay thickly scattered over thousands of square miles of the level prairie, poisoning the air and water and offending the sight."[35] In the second half of the 1870s, buffalo hunters turned their attention to the northern plains, where the last of the great buffalo herds lived with the last significant Indian obstacle to the nation's Manifest Destiny.

Although some Americans protested this slaughter of buffalo, many military leaders welcomed it. According to Sheridan, the buffalo hunters did more in a few years "than the entire regular Army has done in the last thirty years" to pacify the Indians. "For the sake of lasting peace let them kill, skin and sell until the buffaloes are exterminated," he concluded. Secretary of the Interior Columbus Delano supported this position, testifying in Congress that "the destruction of such game as the Indians subsist upon" would facilitate the government's policy of "destroying their hunting habitats, coercing them on reservations, and compelling them to begin to adopt the habits of civilization." The violence of Delano's language, *destroying, coercing, compelling,* indicated perhaps more than he intended about the government's assault on tribal culture. For his part, Sitting Bull understood all too well the connection between the decimation of the buffalo and the demise of his culture. "A cold wind blew across the prairie when the last buffalo fell," he lamented, "a death-wind for my people."[36]

Participation in a buffalo hunt, even a largely symbolic hunt for the Grand Duke Alexis, helped to secure Custer's role as Indian fighter and Leatherstocking of the plains. The other star in Sheridan's buffalo hunt was Buffalo Bill Cody, who competed with Custer for attention and was learning that there was more profit in staging frontier spectacles than in hunting buffalo. Wearing his hair long and attired in a "spangled buckskin suit," Cody made such an appearance that, according to one of the many journalists covering the hunt, "White men and the barbarous Indians are alike moved by his presence."[37] Although both Cody and Custer dressed and played the character of frontier scout, they had little to do with each other, as they seemed to realize that they were both vying for the same role. Only later, after Custer's death, did Cody latch onto an imagined affinity with Custer when he made Custer's last fight, along with staged buffalo hunts and Indian dances, part of the Wild West's nightly performance of the spectacle of the vanishing frontier.

For all of his self-proclaimed identity as a Leatherstocking of the Great Plains, Cheyenne culture was more complex than Custer understood. A few months after Washita, Custer and his men pursued Indians along the Wichita Mountains in the Texas Panhandle. Riding far ahead of his exhausted troops, Custer and one officer happened upon a Cheyenne village led by Chief Medicine Arrows. Showing no fear, Custer and the officer entered the village under warrior escort, hoping to negotiate the release of two white women captives. As Custer parleyed with Medicine Arrow and a holy man around a fire in the chief's lodge, the Cheyenne holy man performed a pipe ritual and other ceremonies. Custer did not realize that he was sitting under the tribe's sacred medicine arrows, nor did he understand the profound power that the Cheyenne attached to the occasion. As the holy man concluded the solemn ritual, he tapped the ashes from his pipe onto Custer's boot, telling him in Cheyenne (which Custer did not understand) that this act signified the annihilation of Custer and all of his men if Custer ever again harmed the Cheyenne.[38] For many Cheyenne, Custer's fate during his offensive seven years later at the Little Bighorn merely fulfilled this sacred prophecy.

Custer's interactions with the Cheyenne included another connection that surely meant something different to them than it did to him. According to both Cheyenne and white sources, in the months after Washita, Custer developed a long-term sexual attachment to a Cheyenne woman prisoner named Meotzi, whom he called Monahseetah. The relationship certainly began with Custer exploiting her as an object of his sexual desire. This was not unusual. According to the scout Ben Clark, "Many of the squaws captured at the Washita were used by the officers." The interpreter Raphael Romero, nicknamed Romeo for his role as the go-between, took the Cheyenne women prisoners around each evening for the sexual pleasure of the officers. As Clark recalled, "Custer picked out a fine looking one and had her in his tent every night." Custer hired Meotzi (and two other women) as an interpreter, although sources suggest that she may not have spoken much English. Custer wrote about her in intimate terms, describing her as having "bright laughing eyes, a set of pearly teeth and a rich complexion" with a "luxuriant growth" of "beautiful" hair, "rivaling in color the blackness of the raven and extending when allowed to fall loosely about her shoulders to below her waist."[39] He wrote to Libby that "one of the squaws that I have here as a prisoner had a little papoose."[40] After birthing this child, Meotzi remained the object of Custer's sexual attentions for at least another three months, and Cheyenne tradition claims that later in the year Meotzi gave birth to a light-haired son whose father was Custer.

Although such exploitation of Indian women prisoners was a common practice among army officers on the Indian frontier, a "gentlemen's agreement" kept them from talking openly about these arrangements. The Cheyenne saw it differently. From their perspective, the sexual union of a white leader and a native woman might represent the coming together of the two peoples in a kinship relationship. Cheyenne sources suggest that Meotzi came to think of her connection to Custer in this way. After all, she was the daughter of Chief Little Rock, and the great white chief Long Hair Custer had chosen her as his bedmate for several months. Bearing a son with a chief of the enemy might enhance her status within her people and become the basis for peace between the warring peoples. If so, it would not be the first time in American history that an Indian woman served as the cultural intermediary between white and native societies. That this possibility never developed in this case, that Monahseetah did not become the Pocahontas of the prairie, was because Custer never realized the larger social meaning of his sexual appetites. Nevertheless, for the rest of his life, even when he attacked a Cheyenne camp at the Little Bighorn that fateful summer seven years later, at least some Cheyenne thought of Custer as a member of their extended family.

A Chance for Peace

On January 25, 1869, a delegation of Quakers visited President-elect Ulysses S. Grant at his Washington, D.C., home to urge him to adopt a new approach to Indian policy. Fresh from a national meeting on Indian matters that had condemned the violence of Indian wars and advocated assimilation through peaceful means, the Friends urged Grant to pursue an Indian policy based on Christian compassion and to appoint, as much as possible, Indian agents who would stand as examples of Christian kindness. The Friends told the grizzled Civil War general and future president that the example of justice and Christian morality would do more than force of arms to elevate the Indians into mainstream society. To their great surprise, Grant responded: "Gentleman, your advice is good. I accept it. Now give me the names of some Friends for Indian agents and I will appoint them. If you can make Quakers out of the Indians it will take the fight out of them. Let us have peace."[41]

Grant's peace policy, however, represented not a conversion to kindness so much as a pragmatic consideration of the failures of existing practice. The great constant of nineteenth-century American Indian policy was that assimilation represented the only alternative to extinction. For the first half of the century, Indian removal to a line west of settlement, a "permanent" Indian frontier, had been a way of allowing Indians to postpone eventual assimilation, but the claims of Manifest Destiny in the 1840s left the remaining Indians entirely surrounded by white settlement and necessitated a means of hastening the assimilation process. The idea of reservations developed during the 1850s and 1860s as a kind of internal removal, a way to concentrate

Indian populations in small areas, in the words of Nathaniel Taylor's Peace Commission, "such as will most likely insure civilization for the Indians and peace and safety for the whites." Reservations, it was assumed, would protect Indians from the contaminating influences of the frontier, especially whiskey and guns, while simultaneously opening up land for white homesteaders. Moreover, some advocates of reservations argued that forcing Indians onto increasingly smaller parcels of land would actually *benefit* Indians because they would find it necessary to abandon their nomadic hunting ways and take up agriculture, a crucial step on the road to civilization. Reservations would be only temporary, however, as once Indians became farmers then reservation lands could be divided in severalty as Indians became private landowners and achieved full citizenship, albeit no longer as Indians. In an age of national consolidation, when immigrants and freed slaves were expected to learn the values of free labor and become absorbed into the American mainstream, scarcely anyone could imagine a future for Indian reservations as a locus of cultural continuity. Reservations, it was widely agreed, were the humane alternative to extermination.

The difference between the military leadership and civilian reformers was not about the ultimate goal of assimilation but about the means of achieving it. Reformers assumed that Indians would want to "improve" themselves through education and assimilation if given a fair chance, that is, if they were presented with the honest, peaceful side of Christian civilization instead of deceit, corruption, and alcohol. Lydia Maria Child, for instance, was a noted abolitionist and peace advocate who rejected "our haughty Anglo-Saxon ideas of force" in favor of recognizing Indians "simply as younger members of the same great human family, who need to be protected, instructed and encouraged, till they are capable of appreciating and sharing all our advantages."[42] Military leaders shared this paternalism but thought that the Indian "children" needed more discipline in the form of a sound whipping from the army. The difference was whether coercion or kindness would be the best means of achieving assimilation, whether Indians would join mainstream American society by compulsion or choice.

Grant had given careful thought to the Plains Indian wars and decided to give the reformers a chance because he believed that the corruption and inefficiency of Indian agents was a major part of the problem. Instead of dispensing government annuities and providing opportunities for education and uplift, Indian agents in Grant's view skimmed profits, made jobs for political cronies, and served Indians a steady diet of whiskey and degeneration. In his first message to Congress, Grant complained that Indian policy "has been a subject of embarrassment and expense and has been attended with continuous robberies, murders, and wars." In place of this, he favored "any course toward them which tends to their civilization and ultimate citizenship."[43] In one sense, his "peace policy" simply recognized that churches might be more successful at this than the government had been. Grant's ideas on this were influenced by his friendship with Brevet Major General Ely S. Parker, a Seneca chief who also had been General Grant's aide-de-camp and military secretary during the Civil War. At Appomattox, while Grant spoke, Parker recorded the terms of surrender for Lee's army. With a foot firmly in both worlds, Parker represented the ideal of the acculturated Indian. In appointing Parker as Commissioner of Indian Affairs, Grant scored a political home run: Parker was the first native to hold this position, and the reformers respected Parker as the ideal of an assimilated Indian, yet he also had long experience as an army officer and remained a loyal friend of the president.

As it turned out, Grant was considerably more interested in the Quakers' reputation for "strict integrity and fair dealings" than he was in their pacifism, their belief that Indians as well as whites possessed an "Inner Light," or their history of just dealings in colonial Pennsylvania. As the *New York Times* editorialized, the union of "Broad-Brim and Breech-Clout" might lead to a "peaceful and cheap administration of Indian Affairs." Even the *Rocky Mountain News* of Denver, hardly sympathetic to Indians, could appreciate the potential economic savings to the government by using the Friends: "There are no shrewder business men than the broad brimmed sect furnishes." Grant had not turned pacifist; he made it clear that his peace policy was merely a tactic to be used whenever possible, not a commitment to avoid war. As he said, "All Indians disposed to peace will find the new policy a peace-policy. Those who do not accept this policy will find the new administration ready for a sharp and severe war policy." Grant affirmed his support for General Sherman's approach to Plains Indians as a "double process of *peace* within their reservation and war *without*."[44] Ironically, during the eight years of the Grant administration's peace policy, the government engaged in over two hundred military actions against Indians, including the most famous of all at the Little Bighorn.

In the spring of 1870, Red Cloud launched a peace policy of his own by announcing that he wanted to visit Washington, D.C., in order to discuss with officials the terms of the 1868 treaty. The overture met a mixed response from white society. Some saw it as a way to open more Indian land for white settlement; others hoped that diplomacy could avoid another war. The *New York Times* announced high hopes for the negotiations, based largely on its assessment of Red Cloud's importance and character: "The visit of Red Cloud to Washington cannot but do good . . . Red Cloud is undoubtedly the most celebrated warrior now living on the American Continent . . . The friendship of Red Cloud is of more importance to the whites than that of any other ten chiefs on the plains . . . He is a savage, but a powerful and wise man." General Sherman held the opposite view; he advised that the government should dictate terms to the Sioux, not negotiate with them, which he believed would do "more harm than good" by unfairly raising their expectations. Major General Christopher Augur cautioned against high expectations for Red Cloud's visit on the basis that Red Cloud was not as important a leader as the *Times* and many others had come to believe. Nor, Augur asserted, could Red Cloud control the Sioux. To the contrary, he argued, to the extent a chief became "friendly to the whites [he] will cease to exert any influence over the hostiles."[45] President Grant, hoping to avoid another war with the Sioux and demonstrate the effectiveness of the peace policy, approved the visit of Red Cloud and his twenty associates to Washington, D.C., with the proviso that Brulé chief Spotted Tail, known for his more accommodating stance toward the whites, also be invited.

Spotted Tail and his delegation of Brulé leaders, ostensibly invited to provide a moderating influence on Red Cloud's more bellicose position, arrived first in Washington, D.C., and made the most of their initial negotiations. When he met with the secretary of the interior, Spotted Tail immediately listed his people's grievances: their hunting rights were being denied to them, they wanted to choose where to live on their reservation, they should not be forced to live near the Missouri River where the whiskey traders were corrupting them, and their annuities must be delivered on time and in full. The secretary responded sternly "that a man must expect some trouble in his life and should face it in a manly way, not by complaining." Spotted Tail laughed as he replied that if the secretary had experienced as much trouble as he had, "he would have cut his throat long ago."[46] Spotted Tail also visited the Great Father, President Grant, at the White House. After a pleasant time smoking on Grant's meerschaum pipe, Spotted Tail began again to explain his grievances. Grant responded with the suggestion that Spotted Tail and his people ought to take up farming and, in gesture of goodwill, offered to pay for one of Spotted Tail's sons to attend school. Spotted Tail, whom whites thought of as a peace chief, politely declined, stating that his sons were to be warriors and that his sixteen-year-old had already taken a Pawnee scalp.

Aside from diplomacy, a major reason for the government to bring the Sioux leaders east was to dazzle them with the superiority of American technological and cultural might. The Sioux delegation was shown around the city, with views of the Capitol and from the Senate gallery with legislation in process. More interesting for the Lakota leaders was a trip the next day to the Arsenal and the Navy Yard, an excursion designed to impress upon the Sioux the military might of the United States. The 15-inch canon that sent a large shell 4 or 5 miles down the Potomac River did not have quite the intended effect, however. The Lakota women covered their ears in advance of the firing, suggesting that they already knew what a loud noise the gun would make, and the men agreed that this was indeed a mighty weapon, but any warrior on a horse could easily ride to the side of the fearsome gun. After all, what man would be foolish enough to stand still in front of such a gun while it was being loaded?

The campaign to dazzle the primitives next turned from military to cultural sophistication, with similar results. In the East Room of the White House, President Grant hosted the Lakota leaders to a formal dinner with the members of the Cabinet, a few congressmen, and officials from the diplomatic corps and the Indian Bureau. After servants lit the chandeliers, each dignitary was formally introduced, and then the entire party moved to the State Dining Room for a formal dinner. The Lakota drank little of the wine but relished the rest of the food, most especially the strawberries and ice cream. Spotted Tail pointed out that the whites were holding out on the Indians by not sending them their best foods in their annual rations. The response was that this was because the whites had given up a life of following war and the hunt for the more prosperous life of agriculture. Spotted Tail replied that he too would switch to farming "if you will always treat me like this and let me live in as big a house."[47]

When formal negotiations began, Red Cloud demonstrated again that however impressed the Lakota were by white military power and cultural sophistication, they were not in the least bit intimidated. After speeches from several government officials, Red Cloud stood up, shook everyone's hand, and launched into a lengthy speech:

Look at me. I was a warrior on this land where the sun rises, now I come
from where the sun sets. Whose voice was first sounded on this land—the
red people with bows and arrows. The Great Father says he is good and kind
to us. I can't see it. I am good to his white people. From the word sent me
I have come all the way to this house. My face is red, yours is white. The
Great Spirit taught you to read and write but not me . . . The white children
have surrounded me and have left me nothing but an island. When we first
had this land we were strong, now we are melting like snow on the hillside
while you are growing like spring grass.[48]

The speech continued with a precise statement of Lakota demands: no roads
or settlements in Sioux lands from the Black Hills to the Bighorn Mountains,
the agency should be near Fort Laramie rather than on the Missouri River,
annual provisions of supplies should be larger and include guns and ammunition for hunting, and no more corrupt Indian agents. The *New York Times*
called it a remarkable speech, noting that "the clear conception which this
unlettered savage possesses" of his rights and grievances showed that "the attempt to cajole and bamboozle them, as if they were deficient in intelligence,
ought to be abandoned, no less than the policy of hunting them down like
wild beasts."[49]

   In further negotiations the Sioux leaders revealed a keen sense of their audience. They complained that whiskey traders along the Missouri River cor-
rupted Indian society and pointed out that most army officers on the plains
drank too much whiskey, an objectionable habit that interfered with their
ability to understand clearly the complaints of the Indians. There is no record
of what the notoriously hard-drinking president thought of these complaints,
but they certainly appealed to the Christian reformers who were sympathetic
to the Lakota. Later, during a tense moment in the negotiations, Commissioner Parker asked Little Swan if he would maintain peace. Little Swan replied that he had just been to Congress, where the white leaders could not
even agree among themselves. Parker then asked if Little Swan had become
a great chief by killing people. "Yes," Little Swan answered, "the same as the
Great White Father in the White House."[50]

   After days of speechmaking and misunderstanding, the negotiations ended
inconclusively and Red Cloud reluctantly accepted an invitation to visit New
York City. In his farewell to Washington, D.C., Red Cloud said, "Tell your
children to keep the peace . . . I want to raise my children on my land, and

therefore I want my Great Father to keep his children away from me."[51] In New York, Red Cloud saw some of the sights and gave one more oration, by this time demonstrating the direct simplicity of speech for which he was becoming known. He was learning to tailor his message to a white audience, specifically to one that was prepared to see him in the role of a dignified, noble savage. With studied simplicity that demonstrated a sophisticated understanding of the liberal sensitivities of his audience, he laid out his views to a sympathetic New York audience:

> My Friends. The Great Spirit placed me and my people on this land poor and naked. When the white men came we gave them our lands, and did not wish to hurt them. But the white men drove us back and took our lands. Then the Great Father made us many promises, but they are not kept . . . The Great Spirit placed me here poor and naked. I appear so before you, and I do not feel sorry for that. I am not mad—I am in good humor—but I have received no satisfaction . . . My people understand what I come here for, and I should lose my power if I did not stick to one course. You are my friends. You always talk straight to me and I am not blaming you.[52]

Later that day Red Cloud and his delegation, objects of curiosity for thousands of city dwellers, went to Central Park and then spent the evening at the Grand Opera House, where, according to the *New York Times*, "they, sad to say, appeared to take especial delight in the fantastic gambols of the semi-nude coryphées and the gorgeous display of parti-colored fustian, glittering tinsel and red fire." Apparently, the newspaper was sad that the same Indians who could be so noble in the morning could in the evening enjoy the same semi-naked dancers and cheap costumes that delighted the rest of the sophisticated New York audience.

What it all meant was difficult to say. Neither side got what it hoped for, although Red Cloud did win helpful concessions. White officials, however, viewed him as a blustering, deceitful negotiator, full of tricks and bluff. They learned, most of all, that his peace policy was not an accommodation policy, but rather resistance by diplomacy instead of by arms. Despite the effort to dazzle the Indians into submission, the negotiations revealed the Lakota to be clever, witty, and often skilled at making demands and changing the terms of discussion to their ends. Red Cloud kept his word and never again made war against the United States, but much to the frustration of Indian agents in Washington, D.C., and for the next several decades, his peace policy was anything but passive. For their part, the Lakota hoped that Red Cloud's trip to Washington, D.C., had bought them the chance to continue living as nomadic hunters. Despite Red Cloud's remarks, however, the government could not, or at least did not, keep whites away from Sioux lands. General Augur's warning about the trip turned out to be prophetic: the chief who befriended the whites would begin to lose his authority. As Red Cloud tried to find that narrow line between loyalty to his people's needs and peace with the whites, more and more Lakota moved north, away from the overland trails and the railroads and toward the leadership of the last bastion of armed Lakota resistance, Sitting Bull.

Making War

The nearly constant warfare imposed strains on the Lakota people. On the one hand, the pressures of white advances heightened factionalism among the Sioux. On the southern and eastern borders of Sioux country, where contact with whites along the overland trails had been greatest, many Lakota were learning to live alongside the whites at their government-sponsored agencies. Given that white population in the Dakota Territory increased nearly ten times during the 1870s, from 14,000 to 135,000, many Lakota felt that they had no choice but to adapt. In the northern and western ranges of Sioux country, where there had been comparatively little contact with whites, the Lakota and some Northern Cheyenne allies were determined to maintain their nomadic hunting ways. Yet paradoxically, the same pressure from white intrusions also led to an increased centralization of authority as Lakota attempted to meet the military threat that surrounded them. For a people always at war, leadership fell to war chiefs at the expense of peace chiefs as military concerns took priority over the normal affairs of domestic life. Hunkpapa and their allies attempted to elevate Sitting Bull to the unprecedented position of chief for the Sioux nation in matters of war and peace, while separately, but in a parallel fashion, the Oglala declared Crazy Horse to hold the unprecedented position of supreme war chief of all of the Oglala. In the highly individualistic Lakota society, these claims of personal authority were unprecedented, but they certainly did not indicate the sort of centralized command that existed in white society, especially in white military society. Not even Sitting Bull or Crazy Horse could give orders as a general or a president could do, and they would continue to lead through example more than compulsion. Sitting Bull also led through his powerful oratory, seeking to reach consensus through the art of persuasion. Wooden Leg, a Northern Cheyenne, commented that when the bands came together, "the chiefs of the different tribes met together as equals," but Sitting Bull was recognized as "being above all the others . . . the one old man chief of all the camps combined."[53]

During the early 1870s, Sitting Bull led the northern Lakota toward an isolationist position, hoping to avoid contact with whites and to continue the hunting life in the vast northern plains. This meant that Sitting Bull abandoned his attacks against Fort Buford, which for years had been the hated symbol of U.S. authority on the upper Missouri. Sitting Bull's more defensive posture of the 1870s left the fort alone and made it clear to whites that he had no fight with them, that he wanted most of all simply to be left alone. As Sitting Bull's uncle Four Horns advised, "Be a little against fighting, but when anyone shoots be ready to fight." Another time Sitting Bull challenged agency Indians, "Look at me. See if I am poor, or my people either. The whites may get me at last, as you say, but I will have good times till then. You are fools to make yourselves slaves to a piece of fat bacon, some hard-tack, and a little sugar and coffee."[54]

As much as Sitting Bull wanted to avoid the whites, the coming of the railroad to the northern plains made war inevitable. The railroad represented both the symbol of national progress—the engine of history—and the reality of a transcontinental rail link connecting the Great Lakes with the Pacific Northwest. General Sherman called it a "national enterprise" because of its potential to integrate the cattle ranges and mines of the northern plains and mountains into the national market. Since the 1840s westerners had viewed railroads as the linchpin for western development and lobbied the federal government to support railroads as the crucial link that would connect western people and resources to distant cities and markets. Preliminary surveys suggested that the best route for a northern transcontinental railroad would be along the Yellowstone River. Sherman recognized that building the railroad would mean the end of Lakota autonomy and that they would be "hostile in the extreme degree." The demands of economic progress justified the inevitable war, Sherman believed, which would "help to bring the Indian problem to a final solution." Custer agreed with his commander: "No one measure so quickly and effectually frees a country from the horrors and devastations of Indian wars" as a successful railroad.[55] If there had to be a war, they expected it to be the last.

For the northern Lakota and their Cheyenne and Arapaho allies, the railroad was an intolerable intrusion into their last best hunting grounds. The Elk River, as they knew the Yellowstone, contained the concentrations of elk and buffalo that were the key to their economic independence. The Lakota believed that the Elk River was included in the unceded lands of the 1868 treaty, and certainly within their usual hunting territory, and therefore was protected by the treaty. After watching the central transcontinental railroad spell the end of the buffalo and independence for their Oglala and Brulé relatives along the Platte River, the northern Indians felt that they must stop this one even if it meant a fight to the death. Spotted Eagle spoke for many when he warned that he would "fight the railroad people as long as he lived, would tear up the road, and kill its builders."[56] They too realized that this war might be their last.

In the summer of 1872 the government authorized two military expeditions to protect railroad survey crews as they planned a route along the Yellowstone. Colonel David S. Stanley, with six hundred soldiers, left Fort Rice on the upper Missouri River heading west, while Major Eugene M. Baker, leading five hundred soldiers, left from Bozeman heading east. Near Arrow Creek, a small tributary of the Yellowstone near present-day Billings, Montana, the Lakota warriors attacked Baker's infantry, who immediately assumed a strong defensive position on the riverbank. Unable to penetrate Baker's defense, the warriors kept up a steady fire throughout the night and encircled the soldiers, looking for an opening. In the morning, Sitting Bull arrived on the bluffs overlooking the river, watched the battle below for a while, and then invited anyone inclined to smoke to go with him. Followed by four others, he walked slowly down the hill to within range of the soldiers' guns. As bullets whizzed in the air around them and struck the dirt nearby, Sitting Bull calmly sat down, carefully loaded tobacco into his pipe, took a meditative puff, and then passed the pipe to his friends, who drew quick, deep breaths on the pipe, the fastest he had ever smoked a pipe, one later confessed. With the tobacco gone, Sitting Bull carefully cleaned the pipe, then slowly got up and walked uphill out of rifle range.

After this remarkable feat of courage, the "bravest deed possible" according to one observer, Sitting Bull announced, "That's enough, we must quit,"[57] and the warriors broke off the engagement. Having solidified his position as war leader and bravest of all the northern Indians, Sitting Bull turned his attention east along the Yellowstone River where his warriors met Colonel Stanley's command. After several days of inconclusive skirmishes, Stanley's soldiers and surveyors turned back for Fort Rice. Although they had inflicted only a handful of casualties, the fact that both survey parties retreated to their forts encouraged the Lakota to think that they had stopped the progress of the railroad.

The following year, however, brought only a renewed determination from General Sherman to provide the necessary military assistance to protect the "national enterprise" against the "most warlike nation of Indians on this continent."[58] Sherman assured Congress that he would provide the military muscle that would allow the captains of industry to lay the tracks for economic development in the region. Realizing that infantry lacked the mobility to defeat mounted warriors, this time the army called on Lieutenant Colonel George Armstrong Custer and his Seventh Cavalry. With ten companies of the cavalry, Custer accompanied nineteen companies of infantry under Stanley's command to ensure the safety of the Northern Pacific's surveyors. Including both white and Indian scouts, the 1873 Yellowstone Expedition numbered over 1,500.

Even with such a strong force, the campaign brought mixed results. As usual, Custer seized the opportunity to ride ahead of the main party, scouting and hunting for the expedition. He killed great quantities of elk, buffalo, and deer to feed the soldiers, bragging to Libbie, "I have done some of the most remarkable shooting I ever saw, and it is admitted to be such by all."[59] One day when he was in his typical place ahead of the main party, some Lakota used the lame horse decoy tactic in hopes of ambushing Custer. He at first gave chase but then astutely avoided the trap and raced back to his infantry skirmish line, where he organized a successful defense. When Stanley ordered a counterattack, Sitting Bull's warriors provided cover while the accompanying village filled bull boats and crossed the Yellowstone River, leaving the army in the familiar position of being unable to follow an entire village of Indians across the open plains. Because the battle over the Yellowstone coincided with the financial panic of 1873, which bankrupted the Northern Pacific and forced a halt to railroad construction, the Lakota had reason to believe that an armed campaign could force the government to abandon, or at least delay, its railroad through Sioux lands. Not without reason, they could hope that the success of closing the forts on the Bozeman Trail might be repeated along the Yellowstone.

The panic of 1873 may have temporarily stalled the construction of the Northern Pacific, but it also brought increased demand to exploit another part of Sioux land, the Black Hills. For years there had been rumors of gold in the Black Hills, but the government discouraged development in the region for two reasons: the idealistic hope of abiding by the Fort Laramie Treaty, which clearly placed the Black Hills entirely within the Great Sioux Reservation, and a pragmatic reluctance to strain army resources with more Indian wars than it could handle. The financial panic, however, created an increased urgency to develop the region in the hope that an infusion of gold into the nation's economy would boost the monetary supply and stimulate the economy, while the migration of miners would serve as a safety valve to drain off the nation's unemployed workers. For a band of fifteen thousand or so hunters to occupy an area larger than half the state of South Dakota made no sense to a white society anxious for economic development in every last corner of the continent. National development demanded that all available resources be exploited to their fullest potential.

In 1874 General Sheridan received permission to send a military expedition into the Black Hills for the purpose of locating a fort closer to the nomadic bands of Indians who had fought against the railroad. The unstated but generally understood purpose of the trip was to investigate the truth behind the persistent rumors of gold in the hills. Newspapers in the Dakota Territory responded that the treaty was an "abominable compact with the murdering bands" of Indians and asserted an almost sacred duty to break the treaty and explore the hills: "As the Christian looks forward with hope and faith to that land of pure delight, so the miner looks forward to the Black Hills, a region of fabulous wealth."[60] For the Sioux the Black Hills were especially sacred, the *Paha Sapa*, a place possessed with *wankan*, or mysterious spirituality, and a source of life for all animals of the plains. The Black Hills also had an economic purpose for the Sioux, according to Sitting Bull, who argued that they were "the food pack of the people,"[61] a central place to which the nomadic people could always return. Because of their ecological variety, the Black Hills were a special place of unique abundance, a green oasis in a landscape of browns and grays. In Sitting Bull's "food pack" metaphor, the Black Hills constituted a reserve food supply and an alternative to dependence on government rations.

"Custer and Indian Scouts." Attired in the buckskins of a western scout, Custer consults with Bloody Knife (kneeling on Custer's right) and other Arikara scouts (Goose standing and Little Sioux kneeling) during the 1874 Black Hills expedition. Standing behind Custer is Private John Burkman, whose job it was to care for Custer's horses and beloved staghounds. Courtesy Little Bighorn Battlefield National Monument.

Brushing aside these arguments, Custer organized a large expedition in the summer of 1874 that included over one thousand men, including cavalry, infantry, geologists, and sixty-five Arikara scouts; among them was Bloody Knife, Custer's favorite. Lest there was any doubt about the implied purpose of the trip, they also took with them two miners and a number of reporters. The large party met no resistance and enjoyed a picnic atmosphere for most of the trip. Custer used the opportunity to augment his self-proclaimed fame as a hunter with a photograph and letter to Libby, "I have reached the highest rung of the hunters ladder of fame. I have killed my grizzly after a most exciting hunt and combat." The photograph included Bloody Knife and another officer in the frame, but what Custer did not tell Libby was that the grizzly bear carcass had not only two of his own bullets but three from Ludlow and Bloody Knife. "We have discovered," Custer wrote to his wife, "a rich and beautiful country."[62]

The only Sioux Custer's expedition encountered was a small camp that they quickly surrounded and entered under a flag of truce, even smoking a pipe of peace with the camp's chief, One Stab. Face to face with their enemies, Custer's Arikara scouts dressed for war and threatened to kill all of the Sioux, who responded with a swift mass exodus. Custer managed to retain One Stab in custody, noting wryly that he had "effected arrangements by which Chief One Stab remains with us as a guide." The expedition returned with the fabulous news that there was gold in the Black Hills "from the grass roots down." The journalists did their job, and the headlines proclaimed rich veins of gold for the taking. One Bismarck newspaper suggested that the Black Hills might become the "El Dorado of America." For the Sioux, the new El Dorado was still *Paha Sapa*, and they named Custer's route through the hills "Thieves' Road."[63]

Attempts at peaceful resolution of the Black Hills conflict ended in failure. Red Cloud led a delegation to Washington, D.C., to protest against Custer's expedition, but the secretary of the interior politely suggested that the Sioux should consider allowing themselves to be removed to Indian Territory. The delegation left Washington, D.C., in exasperated disbelief. Meanwhile, President Grant sent a commission headed by Edward Allison to negotiate a purchase of the hills from the Sioux. The commission first traveled north in hopes of persuading the nonagency Indians to participate in negotiations. Crazy Horse agreed with Sitting Bull, who stated the Lakota position in a few simple declarative sentences: "I will not go to the reservation. I have no land to sell. There is plenty of game for us. We have enough ammunition. We don't want any white men here."[64]

After failing to persuade the northern leaders to come to the negotiations, Allison opened up negotiations with the southern Indians at the Red Cloud Agency. Some Lakota considered a proposal to lease mining privileges in the Black Hills in exchange for subsistence provisions for seven generations of Sioux. Yet this Seven Generations Plan never had a consensus even among the agency Sioux, and certainly no plan could find agreement among all of the various factions. When the government mentioned a purchase price, it turned out to be a small fraction of what Indian agents had already told the Sioux was a reasonable price. The government's stinginess doomed any chance that negotiations might have had, but any remaining hope was dashed when Little Big Man, an Oglala shirt-wearer from Crazy Horse's camp, led a mock charge, guns blazing, into the middle of the negotiations and threatened death to anyone who signed away the Black Hills.

With negotiations having failed, the government turned to war as a means of dispossessing the Lakota from gold country. Meeting in the White House in November, President Grant and several of his top civilian and military advisors decided on a plan that would create an excuse for forcing the Sioux to surrender the Black Hills. The army would withdraw the troops who were currently preventing miners from entering the hills, thereby allowing the trickle of migration to become a flood. If Indians attacked miners, the government could legitimately begin a military campaign that would bring all of the Sioux into submission and force them to sell the Black Hills. With flagrant disregard for the terms of the 1868 treaty, President Grant also decided that the hunting bands should be compelled to abandon the unceded lands promised to them and be required, under military force, to live on the reservation. On December 3, the secretary of the interior issued an ultimatum that all Sioux living outside of their reservation must report to the agency by January 31, 1876. Since, under the terms of the 1868 treaty, the Sioux had a right to live and hunt in the unceded lands of eastern Montana and Wyoming, this amounted to a unilateral redefinition of the treaty, if not an outright violation. By the end of 1875 there were already fifteen thousand miners in the Black Hills, and even though their presence was a violation of the treaty, they exerted considerable political pressure to "extinguish the Indian title" from any land they found desirable. Given a choice between honoring the government's treaty obligation to protect Indian lands and yielding to popular opinion, Grant chose the latter.

Not for the first time in American history, a president manipulated conditions in order to manufacture a war and then blamed the opponent for starting it. Having chosen war, the government adopted rhetoric designed to make it seem to be the inevitable result of Indian behavior. Government officials cloaked their breaking of the law by complaining about the "untamable and hostile" Indians under Sitting Bull who defy "all law and authority, and boast that the United States authorities are not strong enough to conquer them . . . They laugh at the futile efforts that have thus far been made to subjugate them, and scorn the idea of white civilization." Faced with Indians who refused to bend to the will of the dominant society, one official recommended simply sending "troops against them in the winter, the sooner the better, and *whip* them into subjection."[65]

Meanwhile, far off in the deep snows of a northern plains winter, messengers braved the severe cold to deliver word of the government's ultimatum. Those Lakota who heard it received the news politely, interpreting the ultimatum as an invitation for yet another parley, and promised to come for a visit to the agency when it was convenient, after the snows had melted and the weather allowed for travel. Most hoped to remain at peace with the United States. What they could not possibly hear were the drums of war that were beating ever louder all across the country, and especially in Washington, D.C., where the decisions made would bring war once again to the land of the Lakota.

3 { # CUSTER'S LUCK AND SITTING BULL'S MEDICINE

The simple truth is that Custer met the combined forces of the hostiles, which were greater than his own, and that he had not so much underestimated their numbers as their ability.

OHIYESA, ALSO KNOWN AS DR. CHARLES EASTMAN, SANTEE SIOUX

Surely in the Grand Strategy we ought not to allow the savages to beat us, but in this instance they did.

GENERAL WILLIAM TECUMSEH SHERMAN

ON A soggy morning in mid-May 1876, the Seventh Cavalry prepared to leave Fort Abraham Lincoln, the largest garrison in the Dakota Territory, heading for what they expected would be the last great battle of the Indian Wars. The twelve companies of the Seventh had spent several rain-soaked days gathering supplies and making ready for travel. They formed the major part of the Dakota column, which marched under the command of General Alfred Terry and totaled nearly one thousand men. The Seventh Cavalry comprised about three-quarters of the Dakota column and expected to be the mobile strike force for the expedition. In addition to the Seventh, the column included 140 soldiers of the Sixth Infantry and a detachment of over forty scouts, mostly Arikara but including four Dakota Sioux and "Lonesome" Charley Reynolds, widely considered to be the best white scout in the territory. With the scouts came two interpreters, Frederic Gerard, married to an Arikara woman, and Isaiah Dorman, an African-American who was married to a Dakota Sioux woman. Accompanying the expedition were the 150 mule-led wagons of the supply train, loaded with food, ammunition, and two

Gatling guns. To convey news of the expedition to a waiting public, journalist Mark Kellogg traveled along and sent dispatches to newspapers in Bismarck and New York.

Although commanded by General Alfred Terry, the energizing personality in this thousand-man march, according to Kellogg, was "General George A. Custer, dressed in a dashing suit of buckskin . . . The General is full of perfect readiness for a fray with the hostile red devils, and woe to the body of scalp-lifters that comes within reach of himself and his brave companions in arms."[1] Custer's commanding presence gave confidence to the expedition, and despite the dreary rain, spirits were high as they prepared for departure. As Private Charles Windolph wrote, "You felt like you were somebody when you were on a good horse, with a carbine dangling from its small leather ring socket on your McClelland saddle, and a Colt army revolver strapped from your hip; and a hundred rounds of ammunition in your web belt and in your saddle pockets. You were a cavalryman of the Seventh Regiment. You were part of a proud outfit that had a fighting reputation, and you were ready for a fight or a frolic."[2]

To build morale among the departing soldiers and to reassure family members left behind, Terry and Custer arranged for the entire expedition to march by the garrison's living quarters in an impressive display of strength and precision. Fort Abraham Lincoln, like most western forts, was a collection of buildings without a stockade, designed more for launching an attack than defending against enemies. The expedition wrapped itself around the buildings and proceeded through the parade grounds while the Seventh Cavalry Band played "Garry Owen," an old Irish tune used frequently during the Civil War that had become the signature melody of Custer and the Seventh. The soldiers stopped for family farewells, including a teary embrace between Armstrong and Elizabeth Custer, and then rode away as the band played "The Girl I Left Behind Me," another Civil War favorite. As the 2-mile column crawled out of the river valley into the morning mists, the sun broke through the clouds, and as Elizabeth Custer later recalled, a "mirage appeared which took up about half the line of cavalry, and thenceforth for a little distance it marched, equally plain to the sight on the earth and in the sky."[3] Here was a mythmaking moment, at least in Libbie's later memory, shaped by her desire to memorialize her husband's reputation. Even if the memory was enhanced, the image is nevertheless irresistible: Custer and the Seventh Cavalry riding from the Dakota prairie and into the timeless mists of the heavens.

Three hundred miles to the west and two months earlier, the Centennial Campaign, the last of the Sioux wars, had already begun with tragedy rather than mythology. Sheridan had wanted a winter campaign in order to strike when the grass was frozen and the Indian ponies were weakest. General George Crook did his best to meet Sheridan's timetable, leading his forces into northeastern Wyoming on March 1 in a blinding snowstorm and bitter cold. Crook, undeterred by the northern plains winter, claimed, "The worse it gets, the better; always hunt Indians in bad weather."[4] Crook's hunt for Indians might not have been successful except for the work of the scout Frank Grouard. Born in the South Sea Islands to a Polynesian mother and a Mormon missionary father, Grouard had lived eight years with the Lakota and had once been adopted by Sitting Bull. Known to the Lakota as "The Grabber," Grouard led Crook's column through the Wyoming winter to find a camp of sixty-five lodges of Northern Cheyenne on the Powder River on March 17.

Four hundred soldiers attacked at dawn while temperatures hovered near 25 degrees below zero, forcing 150 frozen warriors into a rushed defense while families ran, some nearly naked, to hide in the nearby bluffs. Although casualties were light on both sides, the soldiers burned the village, including all of the tipis, winter food supplies, clothes, and weapons. Miraculously, most of the villagers survived while the warriors regrouped to follow the soldiers and recover many of the village's horses. Crook returned to Fort Fetterman to resupply his troops, not fully aware that his attack had failed to discourage the nontreaty Indians. Rather, the effect of Crook's winter assault was to bring them together for a summer of unity based on a growing realization that this was not to be another fight over limited grievances. This fight would be a battle for their existence as a free, nomadic people, a stand against the encroaching confinement of reservation life.

As the refugees faced a bitterly cold spring with no food, clothing, or shelter, they went first to Crazy Horse's Oglala camp several days away where they were met with great generosity. "Cheyennes, come and eat here," Oglala women said as they welcomed the refugees into the warmth of their lodges. But the village was too small to feed the refugees for long, so Crazy Horse took the Cheyenne to Sitting Bull's Hunkpapa, who had over one hundred lodges and constituted the largest single village of northern Indians. Here, the Sioux extended their generosity to the Cheyenne, welcoming them with food, shelter, and gifts. Wooden Leg, a Northern Cheyenne who was among the refugees, recalled the hospitality of Sitting Bull's people: "When we arrived there they set up at once two big special lodges in the center of their camp circle . . . Women had set their pots to boiling when first we had been seen. Now they came with meat. They kept coming, coming with more and more meat. We were filled up, and we had plenty extra to keep for another day . . . Crowds of women and girls came with gifts . . . Whoever needed any kind of clothing got it immediately. They flooded us with gifts of everything needful . . . Oh, what good hearts they had! I never can forget the generosity of Sitting Bull's Hunkpapa Sioux on that day."[5]

Over the next several days as the refugees gained food, clothes, robes, and even horses and sacred pipes from their generous hosts, the chiefs met in council to decide on a course of action. As they listened to the story of the dawn attack on the Cheyenne village, even moderates realized that the fight had come to them whether they wanted it or not. Their best hope, they concluded, would be for the Lakota and Cheyenne alike to stay together in a single large encampment for the summer. Until now, the Cheyenne had little experience with the Hunkpapa, but for this summer at least their destinies were linked. Threatened by invading soldiers, the leadership of Sitting Bull and the generosity of the Hunkpapa provided the glue to hold this otherwise unlikely camp together long enough for them to win the single greatest victory in the Plains Indian wars. Crazy Horse, who rarely spoke in council, declared, "This is it." Although he had "never made war on the white man's ground," he is reported to have said that "he would now strike a blow that would be remembered by those who invaded his country." Sitting Bull's camp sent messengers south to the agency Sioux, inviting them to a great Sun Dance on the Rosebud River in early June. With the invitation came a simple message: "It is war."[6]

The Gathering of the Army

The army that went to war in the late nineteenth century was hardly of one mind as to the nature of their Indian opponent. Generals Sherman and Sheridan, with some of their bellicose statements, sometimes created the impression that they favored extermination of Indians, and many westerners saw Sheridan as their Indian avenger. As one Texan wrote, "Give us Phil Sheridan and send Philanthropy to the devil."[7] Although westerners associated Sheridan with the saying, "The only good Indian is a dead Indian," his views were actually more complicated. He agreed with his nation's goal that

Indians should be assimilated, but he disagreed with some on the means for achieving this lofty purpose. Whereas the Indian Bureau and humanitarian reformers held out the promise that Indians could be assimilated peacefully, Sheridan thought that Indians would assimilate only after they were subdued militarily. At times, he even seemed to sympathize with their plight, "We took away their country and their means of support, broke up their mode of living, their habits of life, introduced disease and decay among them, and it was for this and against this they made war. Could anyone expect less?"[8] However sympathetic he could sound at times, Sheridan firmly believed that Indians constituted an inferior race and a barrier to national progress. In making war against them and conquering their lands, he saw himself as the military instrument of a national consensus that required the subjugation of native peoples.

Not all officers shared Sheridan's harsh views. General Crook, who struck the first blow in 1876, blamed the war not so much on Indian atrocities as on unscrupulous Indian agents and greedy white settlers, the very people with whom Sheridan identified. Tall, eccentric, and thoughtful, Crook on campaign looked as unconventional as Custer, often riding a mule and wearing civilian clothes with either a pith helmet or a high-crowned black hat. He believed that Indians were fully human, "gifted with the same god-like apprehension as the white man, and inspired by the same noble impulses." They were victims of "unjust treatment" and had been "pushed beyond endurance," so that when war came he declared, "our sympathies were with the Indians." He once went on the lecture circuit with the theme "The Indian is a Human Being," a speech in which he explained how nomadic hunters could become "happy Indian farmers" who, once given the right to vote, would make better citizens than many frontier settlers. His reputation for success in the Indian wars depended on his ability to "think like an Indian,"[9] which led him to use mules instead of wagon trains to carry supplies and thereby travel over difficult terrain where wagons could not go. Perhaps his most important innovation was his use of Indians, even those within the same tribe, to fight against other Indians. Most officers, including Sheridan, distrusted the loyalty of these scouts and thought Crook to be naively wrongheaded in trusting them as much as he did.

General Alfred H. Terry, another leading player in the Sioux War, also differed from Sheridan in important ways. Terry, a tall, soft-spoken man, did not attend West Point and became a general by leading a volunteer regiment from Connecticut during the Civil War. When the war ended, President Grant rewarded his services with the command of the Department of the Dakota, which the general supervised from his office in Saint Paul. General Terry, who had studied at Yale Law School, viewed the miners' invasion of the Black Hills as a blatant violation of the 1868 treaty. He saw the whites as the ones who had "audaciously and flagrantly violated the law," while the Sioux, he maintained, had obeyed it.[10] He was initially reluctant to prosecute the war, but he relented when Sheridan emphasized to him the military duty to follow a presidential order. He preferred administrative duties to field command and would rather have remained in his office in Saint Paul than embark on the strenuous journey into Indian country. Terry had little motivation or inclination for the aggressive offensive that Sheridan required, so he was happy to have Custer as his attacking arm.

Custer's thoughts on western Indians fit within the range of other army officers of his day. On the one hand, he was fascinated by the "rude interchange of civilities, their barterings, races, dances, legends, strange customs, and fantastic ceremonies." At times Custer romanticized the freedom of the natives he fought; he also argued that however noble the Indians might be, they were still savages. "Stripped of the beautiful romance," he wrote, "the Indian forfeits his claim to the appellation of *noble* red man. We see him as he is . . . a savage in every sense of the word . . . one whose cruel and ferocious nature far exceeds that of any wild beast of the desert." Even with this view of Indians as savage animals, Custer did not think that "a Christian or civilized nation" or anyone who understands "the necessities of the Indian question" could advocate extermination. The solution, Custer and most of his associates believed, was to "civilize" the Indians with the "stern arbitrary power" of the army.[11]

The problem for the army in the years after the Civil War was not so much *fighting* Indians as *finding* them. On the wide-open prairie spaces, entire villages could rapidly disperse in the face of imminent attack by the slower-moving soldiers. The recurring problem for the army was that villages would disappear into the trackless plains, only for the warriors to appear later ready to harass supply lines or small groups of soldiers. General Philip Sheridan's solution was to send out several columns originating from different places and converging where the Indians were likely to be found. The goal was not necessarily for the columns to meet in simultaneous attack, as this would have been nearly impossible given the limited communications and immense distances involved. Rather, the different attack forces would press the Indians from different directions, keeping them off balance and always on the move, denying them any chance to rest, restore food supplies, or resume normal living. Sheridan preferred that these campaigns come during the winter, when there was little grass for the Indians' horses and when villages were more likely to stay hunkered down out of the fierce plains weather. Specifically, Sheridan planned a three-pronged attack in early 1876 that would see Crook lead a force north from Fort Fetterman in Wyoming, Colonel John Gibbon direct the Montana column from Fort Ellis near Bozeman east along the Yellowstone River, and General Terry, with Custer leading the Seventh Cavalry, head up the Dakota column west from Fort Abraham Lincoln near Bismarck.

Although Custer was the most famous of the officers who were gathering for the last great Indian campaign, he almost missed what turned out to be his final and most famous hour. Armstrong and Libbie Custer had spent the winter of 1875–76 among society friends in New York. They attended the theater, dined with the famous Shakespearean actor Lawrence Barretts, and visited the artist Albert Bierstadt in his studio. Custer pursued his dream of wealth by investing heavily in the stock market, only to lose over eight thousand dollars, an amount equal to twice his annual salary. He was far more successful with his writing, where he was regarded as an expert on the western plains, hunting, and "the Indian question." His reputation in these matters led to an offer to go on the lecture circuit, starting after the summer campaign, for fees of up to one thousand dollars per week, enough to offset his business losses.

After his winter in New York, Custer reported for duty in Saint Paul on February 15, 1876. The Northern Pacific, aware of its special relationship with the army, arranged for a special train to carry him through the winter snows to Bismarck. On March 7, three locomotives, two snow plows, Custer's private car, and four coaches carrying the Twentieth Infantry and their three Gatling guns ground to a halt in the face of a blinding blizzard. A week later the relief party, a mule-drawn sleigh, carried Armstrong, Libbie, and their hounds into Fort Abraham Lincoln near Bismarck, only for Custer to receive a telegram calling him back to Washington, D.C. Democrats in Congress were spearheading an investigation of corruption in Indian affairs, what some called "the frontier swindling business,"[12] a path of corruption that already led directly to the Grant administration. Most officers kept silent about what they knew, or supported Grant out of loyalty, but Custer could not resist giving public testimony to what he believed, that Indian agents and army post traders diverted rations intended for Indians and sold them again, leaving Indians hungry and traders rich. Custer's highly visible testimony implicated administration officials and enraged the president, who promptly ordered Custer to be relieved of his command. Only after Custer appealed personally to Grant did the president yield and reinstate him to his role as field commander in the coming campaign.

The 750 soldiers and officers of the Seventh Cavalry appeared a formidable sight as they paraded through the grounds of Fort Abraham Lincoln on that foggy day in mid-May of 1876, but under the impressive veneer there were weaknesses that would inhibit their effectiveness in the coming campaign. Custer was a popular but divisive leader, and the Seventh had its share of admirers and detractors. Heading the list of admirers was what one officer called the "royal family" of the Seventh, Custer's own brothers Tom and Boston and his brother-in-law James "Jimmi" Calhoun. For Custer's indigenous opponents, the kinship-based societies of the Plains Indians, favoring one's relatives was normal. In Custer's society, this sort of favoritism went by the name of nepotism. Although this was common practice in the army, the inner circle of the Custer family stood out above the rest. Tom Custer, appointed to serve as his older brother's assistant during the Civil War, had recently been promoted to captain. Younger brother Boston, new to the region, had signed on as "guide" during the Black Hills expedition. He loved the action and hoped that the western air would be good for his health. Calhoun had married Armstrong's sister Margaret in 1872 and joined in with the brothers on family practical jokes. Other notable officers friendly with the Custer "royal family" were Captain Myles Keogh, the brave and charming Irishman who had joined the Union army during the Civil War, and Captain Thomas Weir, the University of Michigan graduate known for his engaging conversation and ability to charm the officers' wives, including First Wife Libbie.

Leading the anti-Custer faction was Captain Frederick Benteen, still angry for what he considered Custer's desertion of Major Elliott at Washita, and like Custer, a courageous, competent leader under fire. The two men respected each other's military capabilities, but the closest they could get to liking each other was grudging respect, and Benteen usually did not get that far. In neither camp was Major Marcus Reno, who had joined the Seventh in 1869 but not yet served with Custer. Reno commanded little respect from the men and had the reputation of being a social misfit and a drunk, this in an army and a command known for its love of whiskey. With fourteen of its officers on detached service or leave, the regiment was stretched thin, and many of the thirty-two officers were asked to perform the duties of a higher rank. The coming campaign would expose all of these weaknesses in the leadership of the Seventh.

The 718 enlisted soldiers who served in the Seventh comprised a snapshot of the rag-tag army of late nineteenth-century America. Gone were the enthusiastic volunteers who believed in "the cause" during the Civil War, and in their place stood what one general called "the dregs from the Union and Confederate Armies and of recent immigrants from Europe." Others were less kind, describing the ordinary soldiers as "vile and wicked,"[13] criminals, thieves, gamblers, and murderers. Nearly half of the soldiers that fought in Sheridan's last great campaign for national unity were immigrants, one-third from Ireland, many from Germany, with a sprinkling of Italians and other nationalities. Custer remarked that conversation in the Seventh was "a parody of Babel,"[14] and most of the regiment's band spoke German. Many Germans, ironically, moved to the United States in order to escape conscription in the Prussian Army. Typical was young Charles Windolph, who left his home in Bergen, Germany, in 1870, one step ahead of the Prussian draft board, to become "the greenest thing that ever hit New York." He spoke only a few words of English and could not find a job, so he took the advice of an older immigrant to "join the army and learn English" so that he "could amount to something."[15]

Windolph found that difficult on wages of thirteen dollars per month, a wage that when combined with the stale food, rampant disease, and overwhelming boredom of the frontier soldier's life led many of Windolph's comrades to desert. Desertion rates reached one-third for the army during the decades after the Civil War, and many easterners during these years enlisted so that the army would provide a free ride west to the gold fields. The Seventh was a mostly veteran unit, with an average age of twenty-seven, three-quarters of whom had served for more than one year, and one-quarter of whom had served for more than five years. Only 10 percent of the Seventh's enlisted men were new recruits in 1876. Even so, the army offered little training beyond drilling for show on the parade ground, and many soldiers in the Seventh Cavalry had little experience riding horses or firing weapons, and almost no experience doing both simultaneously. Man for man, the average

Plains Indian warrior could outride, outfight, and probably outshoot the average army soldier. The soldiers' strength lay in superior weapons, coordinated movements, and concentrated firepower, all of which would come into play during this upcoming Centennial Campaign.

Vital to the chances of success in this war with the Sioux were the services of the scouts who accompanied the Seventh. Accurate intelligence about the location and numbers of the "hostile" Indians depended on forty Arikara Indians recruited to serve in this fight against their long-time enemies, the Lakota. Some, like Custer's favorite Bloody Knife, held personal grievances against members of Sitting Bull's encampment. Raised by an Arikara mother and a Hunkpapa father, Bloody Knife spent 16 years among the Hunkpapa, much of it being tormented by other boys for his mixed parentage. He developed a special hatred for a young Lakota named Gall. As Bloody Knife entered adulthood, his mother moved the family to be with her people at an Arikara village along the Missouri River, where he saw Sioux raiders scalp and kill two of his brothers. In 1865 he led a detachment of soldiers to arrest Gall, who by then was wanted for attacks against whites along the upper Missouri River. When Gall resisted, the soldiers bayoneted him and left him for dead. When Bloody Knife raised his rifle to shoot the apparently lifeless man, a soldier knocked aside his rifle as he fired, saying there was no reason to shoot a corpse. Somehow, Gall survived his injuries and grew to become a war leader in Sitting Bull's camp, a fact that Bloody Knife knew very well.

Also fighting with the army during the Centennial Campaign were contingents of Shoshoni and Crow Indians, recruited because of their long-time antagonisms with the Sioux. Serving with the U.S. military offered the Crow and Shoshoni a way to continue their warrior culture, to count coups and have scalp dances, to put off the decision to become farmers, and all the while get paid for it. Ironically, the same government that wanted them to assimilate was now employing them to act, at least for a season, in the traditional warrior ways of their culture. Most of all, welcoming the whites as allies against the Sioux represented a survival strategy in a shrinking world. The great Crow chief Plenty Coups explained, "Our decision was reached, not because we loved the white man who was already crowding other tribes into our country, or because we hated the Sioux, Cheyenne, and Arapahoe, but because we plainly saw that this course was the only one which might save our beautiful country for us. When I think back my heart sings because we acted as we did. It was the only way open to us."[16]

Overall, the army that Sheridan sent to overcome the last military resistance to national unity in the continental United States was surprisingly indigenous, as its intelligence was entrusted to Native Americans, and astonishingly foreign, as its fighting capacity was one-half immigrant. Custer's army was indeed, as one historian has written, a "foreign legion" in service of national unity.[17]

The Gathering of the Tribes

As spring and then summer came to the northern plains, the large camp of hunting bands under the leadership of Sitting Bull swelled in numbers and confidence. After Crook's attack on the Powder River in March, they all knew that protection required unity. As Wooden Leg, an eighteen-year-old Cheyenne warrior, recalled of the Cheyenne decision to attach themselves to the Hunkpapa, "They had not invited us. They simply welcomed us. We supposed that the combined camps would frighten off the soldiers."[18] The same harsh weather that had slowed Sheridan's plans for a winter campaign had made it difficult for the government to deliver its annual rations to the Red Cloud and Spotted Tail agencies, leaving many of the agency Indians poor and hungry. This presented a stark contrast with the word from Sitting Bull's camp that the buffalo were plentiful. By May the prairie grass greened up and the ponies were feisty, giving confidence to the warriors and mobility to the villagers. As Sheridan feared, the change in seasons had shifted the environmental advantage from the army to the nomads. Agency Indians began a steady exodus toward the Powder River country, the vast unceded territory of eastern Montana and Wyoming that contained the best remaining hunting grounds in the United States. Oglala, Miniconjou, Sans Arc, and Blackfeet Sioux joined the Cheyenne and Hunkpapa to form what Wooden Leg called "the swarming of angered Indians." Even some Santee Sioux, refugees on the plains since being driven from Minnesota a dozen years earlier, joined the camp. Their leader, Inkpaduta, now nearly blind but still mentally sharp, found in Sitting Bull a natural ally who shared his hostility toward the whites. By early June nearly 350 lodges of other tribes had joined the approximately 150 lodges of the Hunkpapa to form a northern alliance of almost 500 lodges with at least one thousand fighting men. And more agency Indians were arriving daily.

This great alliance of Lakota and Cheyenne wanted peace, but they were prepared for war. Scouts scoured the countryside, looking for buffalo herds or soldiers on the move. The threat of attack put the camp under increasing military discipline, with war leaders, or *blotaunkas*, given greater voice in the counsels and the camp police, or *akicitas*, active in enforcing decisions. Previous skirmishes with the army had demonstrated the advantages of improved weaponry, and perhaps as many as one-quarter of those with Sitting Bull had acquired breech-loading or repeating rifles. Ammunition was still scarce, as it often was in the army, so neither soldiers nor warriors had much practice in marksmanship. Even so, these rifles still marked a significant improvement in firepower for the Indians since the Fetterman fight, when most of the Sioux fought with bows. Sitting Bull's favorite rifle was a Model '73 Winchester that he had acquired by trading buffalo robes. Other weapons came into the camp with the steady arrival of agency Indians, who brought with them rifles and ammunition. An especially notable weapon came with Red Cloud's son Jack, who carried with him the engraved Winchester that had been presented to his father on a visit to Washington, D.C., the previous year. Even as the camp prepared for a battle, the elders counseled that they should fight only if attacked. As Wooden Leg noted, "Many young men were anxious to go for fighting the soldiers. But the chiefs and old men all urged us to keep away from the white men . . . Our combination of camps was simply for defense. We were within our treaty rights as hunters. We must keep ourselves so."[19]

For a camp this large to stay together this long was unprecedented in Sioux history. Both the divided political structure and the logistics of finding food, water, grass, and firewood for so many people and horses made this kind of unified display of power extremely difficult. What made it possible, other than the threat of imminent attack, was the growing reputation of Sitting Bull. The Sioux knew him as a war leader and a holy man, brave under fire and possessing an uncanny ability to discern the insights of the spiritual world. Sitting Bull demonstrated this power again in mid-May when the village was near the mouth of the Rosebud River. He walked to a nearby hilltop to pray to *Wakan Tanka*, the Great Spirit or Great Mystery, and received a dream of a great dust storm that came from the east, with soldiers, horses, and weapons visible in the swirling sand. From the other direction came a cloud with the conical peaks of Indian tipis. The storm hit the cloud with a violent crash of thunder and lightning, and then the dust storm dissolved into air. That evening at the village counsel he described the dream, and the elders agreed that it signified a great victory over soldiers from the east. Scouts were instructed to look carefully toward the east for approaching soldiers. Custer's forces had left Fort Lincoln but were still hundreds of miles away; Sitting Bull's dust storm was still well out of sight.

A few weeks later, in early June, Sitting Bull again went to a hilltop to pray, this time taking with him three friends and his ceremonial pipe wrapped in sage. He prayed, "*Wakantanka*, save me and give me all my wild game animals and have them close enough so my people will have enough food this winter, and also the good men on earth will have more power so their tribes get along better and be of good nature so all the Sioux nations get along well. If you do this for me I will sun dance two days and two nights and will give you a whole buffalo." As he promised in his prayer for prosperity and unity, Sitting Bull then organized a Sun Dance. After fasting and purifying himself in a sweat lodge, Sitting Bull entered the dance circle and performed the ritual pipe ceremony with the elders. Then he sat with his back against the dance pole while his adopted brother White Bull carefully cut 50 small pieces of flesh from each arm. With the blood flowing, Sitting Bull began the slow dance shuffle around the pole, always staring at the sun. After several hours he stopped, nearly fainted as if in a trance, and then collapsed into the arms of his assistants. When water had revived him, he explained what he had seen in a soft voice to Black Moon, who repeated Sitting Bull's vision for all to hear: soldiers and some Indians, upside down with hats off and looking like grasshoppers, were falling from the sky into an Indian camp. "These soldiers do not possess ears. They are to die, but you are not supposed to take their spoils."[20]

While Sitting Bull rested and recovered from the temporary blindness created by staring at the sun, the camp stirred with the news that soldiers would come right into the camp, but they would all be destroyed in a great victory. The cautionary note to avoid taking any plunder from the bodies was largely forgotten, while the overwhelming image of soldiers falling into camp generated great confidence and righteousness, even a sense of invincibility, among the warriors. Sitting Bull had discerned the will of heaven, and victory was inevitable. Sitting Bull's medicine was on a collision course with Custer's luck.

While Sitting Bull dreamed and the Sioux celebrated, Sheridan's three-pronged campaign began to take shape. Gibbon's Montana column had met with Terry's Dakota column, and the two were busy seeking information and making plans. Meanwhile, the largest of the three forces, Crook's Wyoming column, left Fort Fetterman on May 29 only to encounter a snowstorm on June 1. Undeterred, Crook continued north with his army of 1,000 cavalrymen and infantry, 51 officers, a pack train with 81 men and 250 mules, a wagon train with 116 wagons and 106 men, and 5 reporters. Such a large force proceeded with great confidence but also required significant planning simply to feed the men and mules. Crook had tried to recruit agency Oglala for this campaign, but they refused the offer to do battle against their kinsmen. Red Cloud pointedly stated that he had promised that his fighting days were over. Crook successfully recruited among other tribes, and on June 15 a force of 86 Shoshoni and 175 Crow warriors rode into camp. Now with a fighting force of over 1,300 men, Crook set out toward the Rosebud River where he expected to find the "hostile" camp.

On June 16 Cheyenne scouts, known as wolves, watched Crook's force enter the valley of the Rosebud, some 25 miles from their own camp. The chiefs counseled immediately and, agreeing with Sitting Bull, decided not to attack the slow-moving soldiers. Most chiefs urged a defensive posture, and some even thought that the soldiers might negotiate before attacking. But as darkness came, many young warriors slipped away and traveled in small bands south toward the soldiers' camp on the Rosebud. Realizing that most of the camp's warriors were on the move, Crazy Horse (and perhaps Sitting Bull; accounts differ on this point) left camp and joined the warriors traveling through the night to fend off Crook's force. The next morning, June 17, Crook had stopped for coffee and reconnoitering before advancing through a narrow canyon toward the village he mistakenly believed was only 8 miles away. As the Crow scouted several miles ahead, the Lakota and Cheyenne warriors charged them, forcing them back. They entered Crook's camp shouting the warning, "Lakota! Lakota!"

Crook's Crow and Shoshoni warrior allies thwarted the initial charge and bought time for Crook to organize his troops into battle formation. The battle raged until mid-afternoon before the Lakota and Cheyenne broke off the engagement. By most accounts it was a standoff, with furious fighting on all sides. The Cheyenne warrior Wooden Leg summarized the battle as a series of "charges back and forth. Our Indians fought and ran away, fought and ran away. The soldiers and their Indian scouts did the same. Sometimes we chased them, sometimes they chased us."[21] Many Cheyenne remembered the fight for one particular instance of great daring. Chief Comes in Sight had his pony shot out from under him, and while he lay on the battlefield with bullets zinging everywhere, his sister, Buffalo Calf Road Woman, rode in front of the soldiers' guns, stopped her pony to allow her brother to hop on, and rode off unharmed. The Cheyenne named this battle "Where the Girl Saved Her Brother." A Crow woman named Other Magpie also fought at this battle, counting coups and avenging the death of her brother at the hands of the Sioux. The fighting among the different tribes of Indians was so intense, and so crucial to the outcome of the battle, that many Sioux named this "The Battle with Our Indian Enemies."[22]

Although Crook claimed a victory because the enemy left the field of battle, in truth the Battle of the Rosebud effectively removed him from action until after the Little Bighorn. Captain Anson Mills later remarked, "We were lucky not to have been entirely vanquished."[23] In order to resupply and care for his wounded, he retreated back to Fort Fetterman. Crook's Crow and Shoshoni allies, disgusted at his refusal to follow up against the Sioux, returned to their homes. Some military observers suspected that he had been intimidated by the ferocity of the Sioux and Cheyenne warriors. Mills compared the Sioux warriors favorably to any cavalry he had ever seen. "In charging towards us," Mills wrote, "they exposed little of their person, hanging on with one arm around the neck and one leg over the horse, firing and lancing from underneath the horses neck."[24] Lieutenant John Bourke described the Cheyenne and Lakota fighters as "extremely bold and fierce," fighting not only for individual honors but displaying "excellent style" in coordinated maneuvers.[25] They retreated in the face of massed charges, only to re-form their positions into flanking maneuvers and then charge again at any weakened spot in the soldiers' line. Showing no fear, the Lakota and Cheyenne force of roughly seven hundred fighting men and one woman had attacked a force of nearly twice its size and kept it on the run for most of the day. This unprecedented boldness and unusual cohesion directly challenged army officers' perception that Plains Indian warriors fought only for individual honors and would flee in the face of a disciplined army. Unfortunately for Terry and especially for Custer, news of the Rosebud fight, either of Crook's retreat or of the new-found confidence among the Sioux and Cheyenne, did not reach them until after it was too late.

As Crook awaited reinforcements at Fort Fetterman, agency Indians arrived at Sitting Bull's camp in large numbers, more than doubling its size in less than a week. Even a detractor of Sitting Bull, agent James McLaughlin, recognized the great appeal that he had for agency Indians: "He had a great reputation on account of his medicine, and people at the agencies had come to believe that his medicine was invincible."[26] The number of lodges went from about 450 to 1,000, increasing the total population to approximately seven or eight thousand people. Of those, perhaps as many as two thousand were fighting men. This enormous group moved their six circles to the west, into the valley that they called the Greasy Grass. There the cottonwood trees provided summer shade and firewood, the game was plentiful, and the new grass supplied abundant forage for their immense pony herd. The villagers felt supremely confident in the power of their numbers, the righteousness of their situation, the natural abundance of the season, and the power of Sitting Bull's vision. Sitting Bull knew that the Rosebud was not the "soldiers falling into camp" of his vision and nervously expected another big fight. Every evening he left the camp for the surrounding hills to pray to *Wakan Tanka* for guidance and protection. On the evening of June 24, White Bull accompanied him across the river and to a high hill east of the village. There, with the Greasy Grass snaking peacefully through the valley and the snow-capped Big Horn Mountains in the distance, Sitting Bull prayed, "*Wakantanka*, pity me. In the name of the tribe I offer you this peace pipe. Wherever the sun, the moon, the earth, the four points of wind, there you are always. Father, save the tribe . . . We want to live. Guard us against all misinformation or calamities. Pity me."[27]

The next afternoon on that same hill, overlooking the Greasy Grass River, which the whites called the Little Bighorn, General Custer would fight his last battle. Later, the United States would place a monument on that hill to General Custer and the men who died with him at what they called "Last Stand Hill." Before the monument, however, was Sitting Bull's prayer to save his people in their very different kind of last stand.

Hunting Indians

As General Terry and Lieutenant Colonel Custer left Fort Abraham Lincoln on May 17, 1876, Private Windolph summarized their situation:

We were Indian hunting in rolling, mountainous country, far removed from all civilization. We knew that . . . west of us there was a considerable force of hostiles, but we had little accurate knowledge of how many warriors we would meet, or whether they would run or fight . . . Custer and most of our officers thought they'd have to whip somewhere between a thousand and fifteen hundred. And they expected most of these to be poorly armed and poorly led. From experience they figured the Indians would fight only a rear-guard action, while the women, children, old men, and pony herds got away.[28]

The officers had some information about the location, size, and disposition of their opponent, information that was fairly accurate for the first two categories. They hoped to find Sitting Bull's camp along the Little Missouri River (within the boundaries of the Great Sioux Reservation) or farther west along the Powder, Tongue, or Bighorn rivers (within the boundaries of the unceded territory). As it turned out, finding the Indians did not prove difficult. The officers also had a reasonably accurate estimate of the numbers of Indians they would face. Army intelligence reports predicted at least three thousand Indians with eight hundred fighting men and perhaps nearly double that, an estimate that turned out to be only slightly less than the actual numbers: seven or eight thousand Indians in the camp and 1,800 to 2,000 fighting men. The most serious miscalculation, made by Sheridan, Terry, and Custer alike, was not so much the numbers of Indians as the disposition of the warriors he would face. Terry confidently told Sheridan that he had "no doubt of the ability of my column to whip all the Sioux we can find." With equal confidence, Sheridan responded that Terry's column would be "fully equal to all the Sioux which can be brought against it." Citing the "impossibility of any large number of Indians keeping together as a hostile body for even one week," Sheridan could "only hope that they will hold fast" to meet the attack.[29]

Far from operating blindly, Custer had available some of the best intelligence the military could gather. Leading his scouts was Charles Varnum, who the Arikara called "Peak Face" for his high forehead and large nose, a recent West Point graduate who had impressed Custer on the earlier Yellowstone expedition. In addition to Arikara and Crow scouts, Varnum had at his disposal the highly regarded "Lonesome" Charley Reynolds, who had earned Custer's confidence serving in the Yellowstone and Black Hills expeditions. He had recently returned from a solitary trip through Lakota country that had convinced him that the Lakota were in greater numbers and better armed than expected. Interpreting for the Arikara was Frederick Gerard, the army's interpreter since 1872, who had traded with the Arikara for years and had gained a reputation as a Sioux fighter by helping the Arikara repel several attacks. Gerard had also traded with Sitting Bull, who once nearly killed him but now professed a respect for the trader. Interpreting the Sioux language for the army was Isaiah Dorman, a well-respected former slave from New Orleans now married to a Dakota Sioux woman.

If Custer's scouts and interpreters knew their enemy well, even intimately, the same was not true for Custer and the officer corps of the Seventh Cavalry. One-half of them had previous experience fighting Indians, and ten had been at the Washita, but most of this experience had been in small skirmishes. This experience had led them to believe that a trained army with better weapons, training, and discipline could overwhelm a much larger force of Plains warriors. By coordinating troop movements and directing firepower, Custer and his officers thought that they could outfight a force two or three times their size. After spending a winter at Fort Lincoln listening to the old-time soldiers, one recruit concluded, "About all there was to it was to surprise an Indian village, charge through it, shooting Indians as they ran, and then divide the tanned buffalo robes and beaded moccasins before burning the lodges and destroying the supplies."[30]

Two weeks of marching from Fort Lincoln brought the Dakota column to the Little Missouri River, where a reconnaissance found no evidence of Sitting Bull's camp, so Terry continued west toward the Powder River, afraid that "they have scattered and I shall not be able to find them at all."[31] In early June when he reached the confluence of the Powder and Yellowstone rivers, near today's Miles City, Montana, Terry received new intelligence from Colonel John Gibbon's Montana column. They had departed on April 3 from Fort Ellis, near Bozeman, and marched slowly eastward along the Yellowstone River. With over four hundred men, both infantry and cavalry, and twenty-five Crow scouts, the column constituted the third of Sheridan's converging columns. Gibbon's force also included Mitch Boyer, the Sioux-French mixed-blood scout who was fluent in Crow, Sioux, and English and knew the eastern Montana country better than any of the white scouts. Boyer brought with him six Crow, carefully selected from the much larger contingent of scouts accompanying the Montana column, who had lived, played, and hunted in the territory that they believed still belonged to them. Gibbon reported that his scouts had located a large Lakota camp on the Rosebud River, so Terry now knew that his elusive quarry was camped on one of the nearby rivers that flow north from the Wyoming mountains and into the Yellowstone River.

A reconnaissance force under Major Reno scouted along the Powder, Tongue, and Rosebud rivers, finding recent evidence of a large number of Indians along the Rosebud. On June 21 Terry met with his officers to pore over maps and lay out his new plan, which was a variation on a traditional pincer movement. Since the location of the enemy was not known precisely, Custer would lead a fast-moving attack force in a long-range sweeping movement south along the Rosebud River, then west to the Little Bighorn, and back north toward the Yellowstone. Gibbon and Terry would proceed with the slower-moving infantry along the Yellowstone to the mouth of the Bighorn to serve as a blocking force that would prevent any Indians from escaping north. Sitting Bull's camp would be trapped between the hammer and the anvil. Terry estimated that Gibbon's force would be in place by June 26, but this did not mean that the attack would be coordinated for that day. Terry's instructions to Custer made it clear that the commanding officer had "too much confidence in your zeal, energy, and ability to wish to impose upon you precise orders, which might hamper your action when nearly in contact with the enemy."[32]

Custer's orders included a wide discretionary authority because the officers' overriding concern was to locate the Indian camp rather than to coordinate a precise plan of attack. For similar reasons, Custer refused Terry's offer of four additional companies of cavalry and the two Gatling guns. The Gatling guns, as the only wheeled vehicles in his party, would only slow him down. Custer wanted "to live and travel like Indians, to go wherever the Indians can."[33] Custer even refused the extra cavalry on his often-stated grounds that the Seventh could defeat any Indians in the country, a confidence that many army officers did not consider exaggerated. Because finding the Indians was their first priority, Custer accepted the services of Mitch Boyer and six Crow scouts. "The idea pervading the minds of all of us," according to Gibbon, was "to prevent the escape of the Indians."[34]

At noon on June 22 the Seventh Cavalry rode out in search of the last and largest encampment of "hostile" Indians in the country. Custer's Seventh included approximately 650 men, including about 570 enlisted men, 31 officers, over 40 scouts, several packers, and 1 journalist, Mark Kellogg. Five weeks and 350 miles from the nearest fort, official uniforms had given way to faded blue pants, sweat-stained shirts, and a mixture of Government Issue black wool hats and light straw hats recently purchased from an intrepid trader who had visited their camp. A few soldiers had also purchased shirts from the trader, while Custer and a half-dozen or so other officers wore buckskin outfits. Shaggy hair and beards were the norm, although Custer had cut his long curly hair short for this campaign. Each soldier carried a single-shot, breech-loading 1873 Springfield carbine with one hundred rounds of ammunition and a Colt .45 with at least twenty-four rounds. As Custer said good-bye to General Terry, Gibbon called after him, "Now Custer, don't be greedy, but wait for us." Custer laughed and replied, "No, I will not," leaving it eternally ambiguous as to whether he would not be greedy or would not wait.[35]

After a leisurely 10 miles the first day, the Seventh camped for the night. That evening Custer called the officers to his tent for an unusual briefing. He first addressed procedures for their trip, especially reducing their noise, limiting their dust cloud, and remaining on alert for surprise attack. Then he told the officers that they could expect to meet a warrior force of 800 to 1,000, and perhaps as many as 1,500 if reports of the migration of agency Indians were reliable, although he did not put much stock in them. Then Custer did a most un-Custer-like thing: he asked for suggestions. Accustomed to his curt style of giving orders, this surprised some of the officers present at the meeting, so much so that one later recalled it as a premonition that Custer would be killed in the coming fight. There were other unusual conversations that evening. Lieutenant Godfrey remembered a conversation later that evening with Bloody Knife and some other scouts. Bloody Knife asked Godfrey how many Sioux he expected to find, to which Godfrey answered, "between one thousand and fifteen hundred." Bloody Knife then asked, "Well, do you think we can whip that many?" "Oh, yes, I guess so," Godfrey responded. Bloody Knife had the last word, "Well, I can tell you we are going to have a damned big fight."[36]

On the second day Custer's men found several old campsites, and on the third day they found the remains of an old Sun Dance, including a white scalp and several drawings left behind in the dirt. Arikara scouts examined the remains carefully, especially the picture of upside-down soldiers falling toward camp, and pronounced that the Lakota were confident of victory. The fresh trail led west, over the divide between the Rosebud and the valley of the Little Bighorn. Custer decided to approach this high ridge under cover of night, then rest hidden while his scouts performed a reconnaissance to learn more about the size and location of the village and its surrounding landscape. That evening Mark Kellogg wrote his final dispatch: "We leave the Rosebud tomorrow and by the time this reaches you we will have met the red devils, with what results remain to be seen. I go with Custer and will be in at the death."[37]

At 2 a.m. the weary soldiers stopped for the night, just short of the divide, while scouts approached a vantage point known as the Crow's Nest. The Crow, from years of experience fighting with the Lakota over this land, knew this place for its panoramic view of the Little Bighorn valley. At dawn they saw smoke from the Lakota and Cheyenne village 15 miles away. Although the village itself was concealed behind hills, they also saw the large Lakota pony herd grazing on the benchland west of the village. Chief of scouts Varnum, still new to the vast distances on the plains, could not see any evidence of the large village until the scouts showed him to "look for worms" on the distant hillside that were in fact a large horse herd.[38] When the scouts sent word back to Custer of their find, they discovered him in conversation with some of the Arikara scouts, including Bloody Knife. Custer asked the interpreter what Bloody Knife had said. "He says we'll find enough Sioux to keep us fighting two or three days." With a smile, Custer responded, "I guess we'll get through them in one day."[39] Then Custer rode off to the Crow's Nest to look for himself.

As the morning of June 25 wore on, more information came into camp that decisively altered Custer's plans. From the Crow's Nest, he and the scouts sighted what appeared to be a small camp about halfway between their position and the main camp. Custer next learned that several small parties of Lakota had already spotted his soldiers. Custer interpreted these signs as indications that the large camp was aware of his presence and that the Indians were beginning to scatter in different directions. Custer decided to scratch his plan for further reconnaissance and attack the village as soon as possible. Scout Charley Reynolds protested that this was the largest encampment of Indians he had ever seen. Mitch Boyer also informed Custer that this was the largest village he had ever seen in thirty years of living on the plains. Custer, preoccupied with the overwhelming concern that the village would disperse before he could attack it, told Boyer that he and the other scouts did not have to fight, that finding the village, not fighting it, was their job. Boyer responded that he would go anywhere with Custer, but if they crossed the divide into the valley of the Little Bighorn, "they would both wake up in hell the next morning."[40]

About noon Custer led the Seventh Cavalry across the divide into the valley of the Little Bighorn and toward his destiny. Proceeding down a broad coulee later named Reno Creek, Custer aimed toward the small village he had seen from the Crow's Nest. Perhaps with the goal of repeating the tactics that had worked so well at the Washita, Custer divided his men, sending Benteen and three troops (118 men) to his south to scout for any villages in that direction while he and Reno continued down Reno Creek. Custer would take the right bank, and Reno with his three troops (about 140 soldiers plus 35 Arikara scouts) would go ahead on the left. The pack train, moving slowly as always, would follow with an escort in the rear. As Custer gave these orders, the Crow scout Half Yellow Face spoke up, "Do not divide your men. There are too many of the enemy for us, even if we stay together. If you must fight, keep us all together." Custer replied, "You do the scouting, and I will attend to the fighting." As Half Yellow Face stripped his clothes and painted his face, he explained to Custer what this meant: "You and I are going home today, and by a trail that is strange to us both."[41]

When Reno and Custer converged on the first target, they found that the small outlying village had already disbanded. There was now only a single tipi standing, containing the body of a warrior who died a week earlier at the Rosebud, although the cook fires were still smoldering. Custer ordered the tipi burned, while from a nearby hill interpreter Fred Gerard waved his hat and yelled, "Here are your Indians, General, running like devils." Down the valley and moving away was a rear guard of forty warriors, covering the retreat of the small village. Custer ordered Reno and his Arikara scouts to pursue them "as fast as you think prudent and charge the village afterwards, and you will be supported by the whole outfit."[42] Reno followed the fleeing Lakota to the river, where he stopped long enough to water his horses, and then moved out into the valley floor in the direction of the Hunkpapa circle at the south end of the village. While at the river, the scout Gerard had realized his error: the Indians were no longer running away, they were now coming from the large village toward the soldiers and preparing to fight. "Hell, Custer ought to know this right away, for he thinks the Indians are running," Gerard muttered. "I'll go back and inform him." He started back to get the message to Custer, but the word did not arrive in time to make a difference.[43]

Custer, for reasons that can only be speculated upon, did not follow Reno into the valley but veered north into the high bluffs overlooking it. Most likely, Custer intended to attack the camp from a different approach, as he had done at the Washita, and support Reno by forcing the Indians to defend themselves from two different directions. As Custer's troops crossed a high hill, they could see the immense village for the first time even as they saw Reno's men advancing toward the camp from the south. At this point Custer must have realized that the size of the village would mean a bigger fight than he had expected. He sent a message with Sergeant Daniel Kanipe back to the pack train telling them "to bring the pack train straight across the high ground—if the packs get loose don't stop to fix them, cut them off." Also, Kanipe was to tell Benteen that there was a big Indian camp and he should hurry to join Custer. As Kanipe was leaving, the troops yelled with excitement, and some of the soldiers' horses bolted past General Custer. "Boys, hold your horses," Custer shouted, "there are plenty of them down there for us all."[44]

Custer led the advance north along the ridge through a series of small hills and ravines until a broad coulee, now known as Medicine Tail Coulee, opened in the direction of a river. Starting down this coulee toward what appeared to be a likely ford in the river and a second spot to attack the village, Custer decided to send another courier to bring up all of his forces. He called for Giovanni Martini (later anglicized to John Martin), the trumpeter who before coming to the United States had served with Garibaldi in Italy. Not trusting Martini's command of English, he ordered Adjutant William Cooke to write the message: "Benteen. Come on. Big Village. Be Quick. Bring packs. W. W. Cooke. PS bring pacs." With this hastily scrawled, misspelled message in hand, Martini hurried his horse back along the direction they had just come, stopping briefly to glance over his shoulder toward Custer. "The last I saw of the command they were going down into the ravine."[45] Back at Fort Lincoln six weeks earlier, Libbie Custer claimed to have seen a vision of her husband ascending into the clouds; now here on the Little Bighorn, the last surviving soldier to see Custer alive presented a vision of him riding not up toward the heavens but down into the earth.

Homeland Defense

It was a hot, dusty day along the river the Lakota named the Greasy Grass and the Cheyenne called Goat River, the kind of day that encourages napping in the shade and swimming in the river. Inkpaduta, the Santee leader who had spent the last fifteen years on the plains with the Lakota, was fishing in the river with his two young grandsons. A few boys and some of the men were tending to the horses on the bench west of the camp. Black Elk, thirteen at the time but destined for fame as an Oglala holy man, was just getting ready to join some other boys swimming in the river. As he remembered, "We were in our own country all the time and we only wanted to be let alone. The soldiers came there to kill us, and many got rubbed out. It was our country and we did not want to have trouble."[46] Low Dog, an Oglala warrior, said, "I did not think it possible that any white man would attack us, so strong as we were." The camp was peaceful enough that many young men had spent the night dancing and were now sleeping late into the day. Red Feather, in the Oglala camp, recalled, "We did not know the soldiers were so near, and the morning they attacked I was asleep in my tent. The sun was quite high, but I was sleepy and I came near sleeping too long to get into the fight."[47] Farther north in the Cheyenne circle, Wooden Leg had also spent the night dancing, then had a midday swim and was now napping in the shade along the river. Although a Cheyenne shaman had a dream of soldiers attacking and warned the men to keep their horses near their lodges, most of those in the camp believed that they were safe and, at least temporarily, at peace.

The women were the first to sound the alarm, according to Moving Robe Woman, one of the Hunkpapa women in the hills east of camp digging turnips. "I saw a cloud of dust rise beyond a ridge in the east. The morning was hot and sultry. Several of us Indian girls were digging wild turnips . . . We girls saw a warrior ride swiftly, shouting that the soldiers were only a few miles away, and that the women and children, including old men, should run for the hills in the opposite direction." Moving Robe Woman and the others hurried back to camp, which was now in pandemonium. As bullets rattled the tipi poles, mothers began searching for children, young men ran for their horses, warriors began preparing for battle, and old men shouted encouragement. Moving Robe Woman remembered, "I heard a terrific volley of carbines. Two bullets shattered the tipi poles. Women and children were running away from the gunfire. In the tumult I heard old men and women singing death songs for their warriors who were now ready to attack the soldiers . . . The soldiers kept on firing. Some women were also killed. Horses and dogs too! The camp was in great commotion." She learned that her brother had been killed, and as she watched her father prepare for battle, she sang a death song for her brother. As she later recalled, "My heart was bad. Revenge! Revenge! I ran to a nearby thicket and got my black horse. I painted my face with crimson and unbraided my black hair. I was mourning. I was a woman, but I was not afraid."[48]

As Reno's soldiers began firing, the nearest warriors rode out to meet the charge, riding back and forth in front of the village to create a screen of dust to protect the people. While young men retrieved their horses and reinforced the south end of the village, the old men helped the women and children move to the north, away from the firing. As the noncombatants fled to safety, war leaders encouraged the young men to battle. Sitting Bull, too old to be expected to participate actively in the combat, shouted to his warrior followers, "Brave up, boys, it will be a hard time. Brave up." A few miles to the north in the Cheyenne camp, Wooden Leg awoke to hear the cry of an old man, "Soldiers are here! Young men go out and fight them." The Cheyenne war leader Two Moons called from the center of his tribal circle, "I am Two Moons, your chief. Don't run away. Stay here and fight. You must stay and fight the white soldiers. I shall stay even if I am to be killed."[49]

The Hunkpapa, who bore the brunt of the initial attack, made a stand that halted the troopers about 600 yards from the edge of the village. There Reno ordered his 135 men to dismount and form a skirmish line. According to standard cavalry practice, one out of every four soldiers would hold the horses, leaving the other three free to fire. While ninety-five soldiers spread across 400 yards of the valley floor and continued firing at the village, more warriors rushed forward and quickly began to move around the skirmish line to the west, effectively flanking it within fifteen minutes. Facing fire from warriors beside and behind them, the soldiers in the skirmish line retreated back to the trees along the river, forming another temporary defensive position. At this point casualties were light, reflecting the lack of firearms training on both sides. Most of the soldiers' bullets went high, hitting the tops of the tipis. This first phase of the battle produced the only noncombatant deaths, six women and four children, perhaps killed by the Arikara scouts. Custer had told these scouts that they did not have to fight, but they could take as many horses as possible in order to reduce the mobility of the village. According to Arikara memories, several of them got close enough to the Hunkpapa circle to renew intertribal hostilities by shooting at women in the camp. Included in these first casualties were two of Gall's wives and three of his children.

Crazy Horse took his time getting into the fight, waiting twenty minutes or more to perform his ritual preparations and to have his horse brought to him. He may have simply wanted to be sure his medicine was strong, or he may have hoped to delay his charge until the decisive moment when his reinforcements could prove the tipping point in the battle. If the latter, it worked better than he could have known. After his preparations, he exhorted the warrior followers who had gathered outside of his tipi, "Here are some of the soldiers after us again. Do your best, and let us kill them all off today, that they may not trouble us anymore. All ready! Charge!" He rode south from the Oglala circle toward the fighting south of the village as a call of excitement spread among the warriors, "Crazy Horse is coming! Crazy Horse is coming!" The Oglala war leader and his followers, according to Black Elk, came yelling "Hokahey!" and made a sound "like a big wind roaring, and making the tremolo; and you could hear eagle bone whistles screaming."[50]

They joined the attack on the troops in the timber just at the critical moment when Reno's defense was collapsing. Confusion reined among Reno's men as they formed in small groups in the timber while Lakota and Cheyenne maintained a steady fire from nearly all sides. As Crazy Horse arrived and Reno's command lost all formation or discipline, a bullet struck Bloody Knife in the head, splattering his blood and brains onto Reno's face. After rapidly ordering his soldiers to dismount and then mount again, Reno shouted, "Any of you men wish to make your escape, draw your revolvers and follow me." As he raced his horse out of the woods and toward the river, one of his men shouted, "Every man for himself!"[51]

Crazy Horse and hundreds of other warriors galloped after Reno's fleeing troops in a phase of the battle that was often said to be "like chasing buffalo." In his chase Crazy Horse caught a trooper struggling to stay on his horse, flung himself onto the horse, brained the soldier with his coup stick, and galloped on, shouting, "Come on! Come die with me! It's a good day to die! Cowards to the rear!" As Two Moons recalled this action, "The Indians covered the flat. They began to drive the soldiers all mixed up—Sioux, then soldiers, then more Sioux, and all shooting. The air was full of smoke and dust. I saw the soldiers fall back and drop into the river bed like buffalo fleeing."[52]

The soldiers crossed the river and continued up the bluffs on the other side, but many did not make it. Warriors used their war clubs to knock the soldiers from their horses or shot them with bow and arrows as they galloped full speed into the chase. Wooden Leg used his "captured rifle as a club" and "knocked two of them into the flood waters." He also heard the Lakota taunting the soldiers during the chase, "You are only boys. You ought not to be fighting. We whipped you on the Rosebud. You should have brought more Crows or Shoshones with you to do your fighting."[53] All told, the Lakota and Cheyenne killed about forty of Reno's fleeing soldiers, while the rest found refuge on top of the bluffs on the east side of the river.

With the soldiers gone, warriors and some women and children who had not retreated began to spread over the valley floor, killing the wounded, mutilating the dead, and searching for plunder. Men claimed guns and ammunition and then hurried on to the rest of the fight. Women looked for useable clothes or other merchandise. Black Elk returned to the flat along the river to see "people stripping dead soldiers and putting the clothes on themselves." A warrior encouraged him to take the scalp of a soldier who was "still kicking." Black Elk dismounted and started to lift the scalp, but his knife was dull and the soldier struggled, so Black Elk shot him in the forehead and then took the scalp. On his way to show his mother his new trophy, Black Elk noticed a "very pretty young woman among a band of warriors" motivating them for the fight by singing this song, "Brothers, now your friends have come! Be brave! Be brave! Would you see me taken captive?" When he found his mother and showed her the scalp, his mother "gave a big tremolo just for me."[54]

Sitting Bull rode onto the field and saw a badly wounded Isaiah Dorman, "Custer's Black White Man," the interpreter who was married to a Hunkpapa woman. Sitting Bull dismounted from his horse to give the dying man a drink of water, as Dorman said, "My friends, you have already killed me, don't count coup on me." Sitting Bull responded with the instructions, "Don't kill that man, he is a friend of mine."[55] After Sitting Bull rode away toward the soldiers on the bluffs, a Hunkpapa woman named Eagle Robe, mourning for her ten-year-old brother who had been shot earlier that day, shot Dorman in the head. Other women, outraged at a man they considered a traitor to his wife's people, mutilated his body to make certain he would not fare well in the spirit world.

As Reno's demoralized men began to regroup on the hillside, warriors crossed the river in pursuit. Sitting Bull, having seen to the protection of his people, urged the warriors to let the soldiers escape so long as they were not a threat to the village. But not even the greatest chief of the Lakota could call off the warriors in the middle of a fight. Many scrambled up the steep hillside and began to surround Reno's position on the hilltop. Only when warriors sighted a new group of soldiers approaching the village from the north did they relent from attacking Reno. These new soldiers threatened the northern end of the village, where the noncombatants had taken refuge and were currently only lightly defended. According to Red Horse, "On a hill the soldiers stopped and the Sioux surrounded them. A Sioux man came and said that a different party of soldiers had [taken] all the women and children [as] prisoners. Like a whirlwind the word went around, and the Sioux all heard it and left the soldiers on the hill and went quickly to save the women and children."[56]

As warriors streamed toward this new group of soldiers, Sitting Bull rode back through the village, then west to a small creek on the far side of the valley where many of the noncombatants had gathered. There, Sitting Bull, his friend Inkpaduta, and some other men stood guard to protect them. With the collective memories of Killdeer Mountain, Sand Creek, Washita, and other smaller village assaults in mind, the huddled old men, women, and children hoped that this time the warriors could keep the soldiers from the village.

Although the warriors rushing to defend the river crossing did not know it, the soldiers approaching the river were part of Custer's Seventh Cavalry. After sending Martini back with the message to Benteen to hurry forward, Custer advanced along some high bluffs and toward Medicine Tail Coulee, a broad dip in the land affording a possible avenue of attack against the village. Before continuing down the coulee, he heard news from his scouts, Mitch Boyer and Curley, who had waited on the bluffs long enough to witness Reno's retreat. Knowing that the first prong of his planned attack had failed might have caused some commanders to adopt a cautious strategy, perhaps to backtrack toward Reno and Benteen in order to unite the command. But Custer had made a career of going on the offensive, and he continued to do so at this critical juncture. Instead of uniting his forces, he split them again, sending his old friend Captain George Yates and two companies, nearly eighty men, down Medicine Tail Coulee to its ford on the Little Bighorn River. While Yates charged toward the village, Custer and three companies (134 men) were holding to the high ridges about a mile east of the river.

Many students of the battle suggest that Custer intended these two companies to be a show of force that would draw the warriors away from Reno's beleaguered men. Custer's intentions cannot be known with certainty, but his personality and a few hints from the testimony of those who saw him last suggest that he continued in an offensive mind-set. Curley's story was that Mitch Boyer, after giving the news of Reno's retreat to Custer, told Curley to escape if possible. "That man," Boyer said pointing at Custer, "will stop at nothing. He is going to take us right into the village, where there are more warriors than we are. We have no chance." Years later Martini testified that Custer, before dispatching his final message to Benteen, looked at the village for a while and saw children, dogs, and ponies, but no warriors (presumably because they were fighting Reno). Custer said to his men, "We will now go down and make a crossing and capture the village." Martini continued, "The consensus of opinion seemed to be among the officers that if this could be done the Indians would have to surrender when they would return, in order not to fire upon their women and children."[57]

Certainly many of the villagers understood the soldiers' presence at Medicine Tail Coulee as a threat not to the warriors but to their families. Yates's charge started a new round of flight to the north and west, an exodus that probably was visible to Custer and may have influenced his next movements. At Medicine Tail Ford the warriors met the soldiers' assault and halted the advance. As Yates and his two companies fell back from the river, hundreds of warriors crossed in pursuit. Yates led his men back up the shallow coulee in a fighting retreat to rejoin Custer on the high ridge. There, at the southern end of the ridge now known as Calhoun Hill, Custer stationed Captain Myles Keogh, the Irish soldier of fortune who had combat experience in Europe and the Civil War, and three companies of men to hold this high ground. From Calhoun Hill the soldiers held a field of vision that could slow the flow of Lakota and Cheyenne coming from that direction, as well as serve as a lookout for Benteen's troops, who Custer must have been hoping would follow his orders to come quickly with the pack train.

Although Custer's plans at this point cannot be known for certain, army officers immediately after the battle and some historians later have speculated that Custer was attempting to recreate his success at the Washita by capturing the families of the warriors. At that battle, holding fifty-three women as hostages had kept hundreds of warriors at a distance. In *My Life on the Plains*, he had written, "Indians contemplating a battle, either offensive or defensive, are always anxious to have their women and children removed from all danger." In earlier encounters, Custer realized that placing soldiers in "close proximity of their women and children" would "operate as a powerful argument in favor of peace."[58] Now, from his vantage point at Battle Ridge, he could see the exodus of women, children, and old men from the village toward the north. If he could find a convenient ford of the Little Bighorn and capture some of them, perhaps he could still hold off the warriors and control the village. The archaeological evidence and testimony from Indian survivors suggest that, with the remaining two companies, just under eighty men, Custer rode north across the high ground now known as Battle Ridge, past the hill now known as Last Stand Hill, and northwest from there for perhaps a mile or more toward the river. At this attempted river crossing, northeast of the current battlefield site, warriors met the soldiers with a fierce resistance, forcing Custer back toward Battle Ridge. The Oglala warrior Flying Hawk said that the place where Custer approached the river "was right above the women who had collected down the river."[59] Journalist Mark Kellogg, along to capture the glory of the last great Indian battle, died near the river, perhaps as Custer began shifting his priorities from offense to defense.

While Custer was exploring his attack options in the north, and perhaps waiting for Benteen's reinforcements, the Lakota and Cheyenne were infiltrating the area around Battle Ridge from every direction. Although the high ground commanded a good field of vision, the wrinkled landscape provided many small furrows for warriors to hide. For perhaps an hour or so, even as hundreds of warriors infiltrated closer to the troops, the fight was at a standstill, with warriors applying pressure but still held back by the disciplined fire of the soldiers.

Among those who were gradually surrounding Custer's forces on the mile-long ridge was Moving Robe Woman, still seeking vengeance for her brother's death. With her father and some young warriors, she crossed the Greasy Grass River downstream from Medicine Tail Ford and infiltrated her way toward the ridge. Dust from the horses and powder smoke from the carbine fire "made everything dark and black." In the midst of all the "whooping and hollering," Moving Robe Woman heard Red Horse shout, "There was never a better day to die!" She also heard "cries from troopers" but could not understand their English. Rain in the Face, later made famous (falsely) as the alleged killer of Custer in Longfellow's poem "Hiawatha," saw Moving Robe Woman and shouted, "Behold, there is among us a young woman! Let no young man hide behind her garment!"[60] He used his words to inspire bravery, knowing that the men would be more likely to compete for war honors when a pretty young woman was among them.

After a time of what some battle veterans characterized as an even fight, a series of warrior actions that combined individual bravery with acute tactical awareness initiated a sudden collapse among the soldiers. The sheer weight of numbers began to take its toll, as warriors by the hundreds continued to stream from the village to the battlefield, approaching the high ground from ravines and creases in the furrowed landscape. But it was more than the weight of numbers that overwhelmed Custer's soldiers; tactical awareness learned from previous battles with the whites also helped the Lakota and

Cheyenne prevail. Gall fought on the south side of Calhoun Hill, and he described his tactic to chase the horses away from the cavalry: "They fought on foot. One man held the horses while the others shot the guns. We tried to kill the holders, and then by waving blankets and shooting we scared the horses down that coulee, where the Cheyenne women caught them."[61] The tactic of taking the horses away from the soldiers left them without any mobility and hastened their sense of panic.

Other warriors made "bravery runs," riding near the soldiers while clinging to the far side of the horse so as not to expose themselves, and some warriors led charges directly to the soldiers' lines. Bravery runs could attest to one's individual bravery, but they had the tactical advantage of testing the enemy's firing strength and could turn into a charge if warriors perceived a weakness. The Cheyenne chief Lame White Man led one crucial charge against the bluecoats. In the middle of a sweat bath when the fighting started, Lame White Man had rushed quickly into battle, taking time only to put on his moccasins, wrap a blanket around his waist, and grab his gun. Sensing a weak spot from the soldiers on the hill, he gathered other Cheyenne and Lakota warriors around him and shouted, "Come, we can kill all of them!" With that, according to Wooden Leg, "the Indians began jumping up, running forward, dodging down, jumping up again, down again, all the time going toward the soldiers."[62] At the cost of his own life, Lame White Man's charge overwhelmed the soldiers at that spot on the hill. Another crucial charge happened when Sitting Bull's nephew White Bull made a bravery run and then, along with Crazy Horse, dashed directly through the line of soldiers. "Hokahey, brother! This life will not last forever," White Bull called to Crazy Horse as they split the soldiers' defenses. Crazy Horse's courage inspired others to follow the charge, as Red Feather remembered, "The soldiers all fired at once, but didn't hit him. The Indians got the idea the soldiers' guns were empty and charged immediately on the soldiers." The rout was on, as Crazy Horse's charge "broke through and split up the soldiers into two bunches," according to He Dog.[63]

This combination of bravery and tactics caused the soldiers to lose their cohesion and sense of discipline. In short, some of them panicked. As warriors charged over Calhoun Hill, soldiers fled north toward Custer's position on the other end of the ridge. Then, according to one Oglala woman, "The Indians acted just like they were driving buffalo to a good place where they could be easily slaughtered."[64] The remnants of Custer's forces gathered on the hilltop at the north end of Battle Ridge, known as Last Stand Hill, killed their horses for breastworks, and fought for their lives. One warrior noted that in the close combat, soldiers and warriors were "near enough to look each other in the eyes."[65] With the smell of blood all around them, a group of soldiers, perhaps as many as forty and including Mitch Boyer and Boston Custer, desperately broke toward the river and took cover in Deep Ravine, where they perished in close fighting.

Then, according to Wooden Leg, "The shots quit coming from the soldiers. All of the Indians then jumped and rushed forward. All of the boys and old men on their horses came tearing into the crowd. The air was full of dust and smoke. Everybody was greatly excited. It looked like thousands of dogs might look if all of them were mixed together in a fight."[66] When the firing stopped, warriors continued to ride over the battlefield, finishing off any wounded soldiers and taking clothes or ammunition. According to Kate Bighead, boys rushed onto the field to count coup on the dead soldiers, "as that was considered a brave deed for a boy. There was such a rush and mix up that it seemed the whole world had gone wild." According to Bighead, one badly wounded soldier was sitting up and rubbing his head "as if he did not know where he was nor what was going on in the world."[67] Three Lakota men ran to the man, knocked him flat, and cut off his head. In their anger, other Lakota and Cheyenne women mutilated some of the bodies, partly out of the belief that the bodies would go into the next world disfigured that way. Cheyenne historian John Stands in Timber provides another reason, noting that most of the mutilation was done by those who had lost relatives at Sand Creek or Washita.

Although most of the villagers did not know the identity of the soldiers they had been fighting, a few recognized Custer among the corpses. Kate Bighead said the warriors did not know it was Custer they had fought until later. She added, however, that two Southern Cheyenne women who knew Custer from his earlier campaigns in Kansas saw his body on the field and prevented anyone from mutilating it. "He is a relative of ours," they said, thinking of Meotzi. The women then pushed a sewing awl into each of his ears to "improve his hearing, as it seemed he had not heard what our chiefs in the South said when he smoked the pipe with them."[68]

With the village defended and Custer defeated, the warriors turned their attention again to Reno's soldiers on the hilltop 5 miles to the south. During the interim between chasing Reno's soldiers up the bluff and returning to

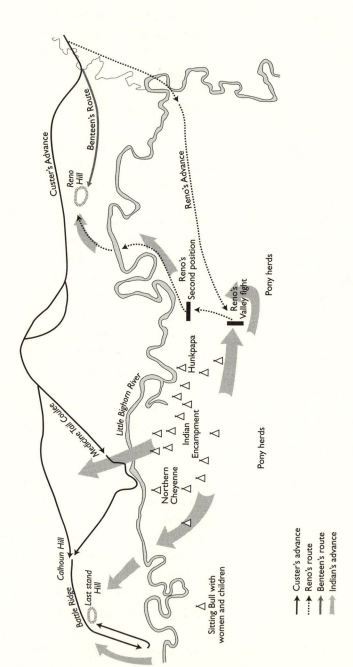

The Little Bighorn River snakes along a broad valley floor where the large encampment of Lakota and Northern Cheyenne moved in the last week of June 1876. Approaching from the southeast, Custer sent Reno to cross the river and attack the south end of the village, while he led his troopers along the high bluffs on the east side of the river. Indians rushed from the village to repulse Reno's advance and forced him to retreat to high bluffs on the other side of the river. Part of Custer's force approached the village at Medicine Tail Coulee, later rejoining the main force along Battle Ridge. Custer apparently searched for another site to ford the river, across from where Sitting Bull was with the women and children, but then retreated toward Battle Ridge for the last desperate fighting.

the same bluffs after defeating Custer, Benteen had arrived at the scene. "For God's sake, Benteen, halt your command and help me. I've lost half my men. We are whipped," Reno said despondently.[69] Either to help Reno, or because Reno was his commanding officer, or because of his hatred of Custer, Benteen stopped his command and helped Reno establish a defensive perimeter around a saucer-shaped hilltop. When the pack train caught up with them, they had about 350 soldiers and plenty of ammunition. Captain Thomas Weir, a better friend of Custer than either Reno or Benteen, led a contingent of soldiers to a high point about a mile away, from which he saw horses running, guns firing, and much dust. With a large number of warriors approaching, Weir retreated back to the Reno hilltop, not understanding what was happening in the confused battle scene 4 miles away.

The soldiers on the hilltop with Reno, with warriors gathering in force around them, spent a frightened night wondering if they would make it through the next day. No one knew what had happened to Custer and his men. Some speculated that Custer had abandoned them, an idea that Benteen fueled by reminding them that Custer had deserted Major Elliott at Washita. Not everyone sided with Benteen in this eight-year-old argument, but still they asked on this lonely night, "Where is Custer?" While considering answers to this perplexing question, Charles Windolph heard loud drumming from the village and imagined that the Indians were having "wild victory dances." "We were terribly alone on that dangerous hilltop. We were a million miles from nowhere. And death was all around us."[70]

The villagers that evening also felt the presence of death, for they had suffered some thirty to forty deaths and many more injured in the day's fighting. The drumming and singing that Windolph heard were not victory dances but mourning songs. As Moving Robe Woman remembered, "The Indians did not stage a victory dance that night. They were mourning for their own dead." According to Wooden Leg, "There was no dancing nor celebrating of any kind in any of the camps that night. Too many people were in mourning, among all of the Sioux as well as among the Cheyenne. Too many Cheyenne and Sioux women had gashed their arms and legs, in token of their grief. The people generally were praying, not cheering."[71]

The next day warriors returned to the fight on the hilltop where Reno's desperate men were surrounded. Although there was some fierce fighting, these soldiers were more numerous, better organized, and had a better field of fire than the soldiers on Battle Ridge. Most of all, the warriors had al-

"Custer's War" by the Lakota artist One Bull. A battle participant, One Bull later (probably about 1900) painted this pictographic view of the full sweep of the battle. Bareback riders rush from the camp circles to meet Reno's attack and chase troopers across the river. On the hills at the other end of the camp, warriors surround Custer's forces in close fighting. In the center, One Bull rushes into battle carrying a war club and Sitting Bull's shield. Courtesy Minneapolis Institute of Arts.

ready defended themselves from the attack on their families and now had less desire to risk their lives in order to finish off the bluecoats. "Let them go now," Sitting Bull advised, "so that some can go home and spread the news."[72] About midday word arrived that more soldiers were approaching from the north. This was Gibbon's Montana column, which included infantry, which many Lakota avoided fighting whenever possible because of their superior marksmanship.

Weary of fighting, the camp decided to move south and let the soldiers on the hilltop live. Women struck the tipis and packed their belongings while three hundred young men went north to slow Gibbon's advance. In the evening, the village started its southern migration, stretching out for 2 miles as it walked past the valley floor where Reno had started the fight and under the bluffs where he now huddled. From their vantage point, some of Reno's men watched as the village of approximately seven thousand people, with all of their belongings and about twenty thousand horses, took several hours to pass from their sight. Never again would this many natives gather together to defend themselves from the military authority of the United States. As Moving Robe Woman knew all too well, "The brave men who came to punish us that morning were defeated; but in the end, the Indians lost."[73]

In a sense, Moving Robe Woman was correct. The army quickly retaliated, and soon the victors at the Little Bighorn were defeated. But the memory of that one day, the day Long Hair was rubbed out, remained with the people. It was a memory of a successful finish to a battle they had not sought. Sitting Bull said simply, "When Indians must fight, they must." Lakota warrior Flying Hawk elaborated:

> It was hard to hear the women singing the death song for the men killed, and for the wailing, because their children were shot while they played in the camp. It was a big fight; the soldiers got just what they deserved this time. No good soldiers would shoot into the Indian's tepee where there were women and children. These soldiers did, and we fought for our women and children. White men would do the same if they were men.[74]

This memory of triumph in defending the people would provide a spark of hope in the onslaught that was to come.

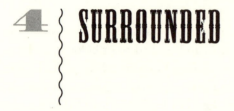

SURROUNDED

Wherever we went, the soldiers came to kill us, and it was all our
own country.

BLACK ELK

ON THE day that Custer rode to his last fight, Colonel Anson Mills
hooked one hundred trout in the cool mountain waters of Goose Creek, Wyoming, less than 60 miles to the south. Mills was part of General Crook's expedition that had been stymied at the Rosebud battle. Tending to their wounded
and awaiting reinforcements, the officers and enlisted men of Crook's army
basked in the luxuriant beauty of the rolling foothills and clear waters at the
base of the Big Horn Mountains. The most popular activity was fishing in
the trout-laden waters of Goose Creek. Captain Bourke estimated that in the
month that Crook's army was encamped near Goose Creek, they caught and
ate at least fifteen thousand trout.

Despite the spectacular scenery and Edenic abundance, some officers in
the camp worried about the month-long wait. The absence of any kind of
news about Terry's column along the Yellowstone created anxiety among the
officers and fed questions about Crook's strategy. In addition to fishing, the
officers and men read old newspapers and any books that could be found;
Bourke and another officer even "made an arrangement to peruse each day
either one of Shakespeare's plays or an essay by Macaulay, and to discuss
them together." The camp's packers organized a mule race that immediately
became the occasion for much betting. The cavalry officers played "a game
of base-ball" against the infantry officers in which, Bourke reports wryly,
"quite a number managed to hit the ball, and one or two catches were made."[1]

General Crook led a four-day "informal reconnaissance" to the peaks of the Bighorn Mountains, officially to scout but mostly to hunt and fish the high mountain lakes. Journalist John Finerty, with the expedition reporting for the *Chicago Times*, relieved the monotony by shooting his first buffalo.

In the midst of this fishing, hunting, gambling, and storytelling idyll, Crook and his officers sought news of the war around them. In addition to his angling exploits on June 25, Colonel Mills hiked up some hills near camp that gave him a view of the distant horizon. To the north at a great distance, he noticed a "dense smoke," which most officers concluded was a "prairie fire or something of that kind."[2] The few Indian scouts left in Crook's camp thought otherwise; they saw the smoke as a sign of a great defeat for the soldiers. Five days later some mixed-blood Indians rode into Crook's camp with news of a big fight in which a large band of Sioux had wiped out some "pony soldiers." Most officers refused to believe the story, thinking that it was a typically exaggerated rumor of their own fight on the Rosebud. Nevertheless, General Crook sent two scouts to find the Crow and encourage them to return to his camp. The scouts traveled no more than 20 miles before returning because of the large number of hostile Indians in the area. On July 7, Crook next ordered Lieutenant Frederick Sibley and a twenty-four-man escort to reconnoiter the Little Bighorn. Two days later the bedraggled soldiers returned with a story that they had been surprised and trapped by four hundred Cheyenne warriors. They escaped only by leaving their horses behind during the night and walking 50 miles through deep forest, rocks, mountains, and canyons to safety.

On July 10 General Crook learned that his Indian scouts had been right all along. Two messengers from General Sheridan arrived in camp with details of Custer's stunning defeat. "The shock was so great," Bourke wrote, "that men and officers could hardly speak when the tale circulated from lip to lip."[3] That night some Sioux and Cheyenne set fire to the prairie around Crook's camp, attempting to harass them and deprive them of forage. Three days later Crook's camp received another shock from three riders from General Terry's camp on the Yellowstone River. Traveling through the war zone at the risk of their lives, Terry's men carried dispatches describing the Custer fight sewn into their clothes. The news meant that the month of restless waiting was over, and Crook became impatient to set out after the hostile Sioux and Cheyenne. Yet his desire to enhance his reputation as an Indian fighter was balanced by his newfound respect for the size and power of the Sitting Bull alliance. Custer's defeat at the Little Bighorn had weakened the confidence of the army. Commanders were now reluctant to move unless they possessed overwhelming force. Before setting out after the hostiles, Crook decided to wait for the arrival of the reinforcements that Sheridan had promised.

While Crook waited, the village that had defeated Custer moved leisurely along the upper regions of the Rosebud and Tongue rivers, stopping whenever possible to hunt buffalo and prepare the meat and hides. The herds were harder to find this summer, in part because hide hunters were moving onto the northern plains, decimating the herds for hides and tongues. Consequently, the nomadic hunters divided into smaller groups that had a better chance of finding buffalo or other game. They regrouped in early August on the Powder River and then split again, with Sitting Bull heading east toward Killdeer Mountain, the site of his battle with General Sully in 1864, while Crazy Horse led another group toward the Black Hills. The necessity of defense urged them to stay together, but the logic of subsistence dictated that the northern nomads must split in order to feed themselves and put in stores for the coming winter. More than either Crook or the Indians realized, the rest of the Great Sioux War would depend largely on the ability to find food.

Avenging Custer

Custer did more in death than he had done in life to advance the Indian wars. News of the Little Bighorn shocked the nation out of complacency and moved Congress to open the floodgates of financial support for the army's solution to the "Indian problem." No longer did Congress, the public, or the generals debate the causes of the war or the legitimacy of the nation's claim to the disputed Black Hills. The pendulum of public opinion swung toward retribution in the wake of what was increasingly being called the Custer "massacre." Schoolboys in Custer's Ohio hometown made a solemn vow to kill Sitting Bull on sight. Newspapers across the country demanded revenge. The *Bismarck Tribune* argued that the Indians who killed Custer should be "exterminated root and branch, old and young, male and female," while the more lenient *New York Times* suggested, "We must beat the Sioux, but we need not exterminate them."[4]

With Congress in a mood to support his every request, Sheridan could now implement his long-standing plan for victory over the Sioux: more soldiers, two new forts, and military control of Indian affairs. His immediate aim was to flood the war zone with reinforcements. On July 7 Sheridan ordered Colonel Nelson Miles and the Fifth Infantry to transfer from Fort Leavenworth, Kansas, to join General Terry along the Yellowstone. Also reinforcing Terry were six companies of the Twenty-second Infantry, coming from the Great Lakes and even as far away as New York. Sheridan also ordered the Fifth Cavalry under Colonel Wesley Merritt to hurry north to reinforce Crook's command at Goose Creek. Congress authorized funds for 2,500 new recruits to replenish the depleted Seventh Cavalry, and by August the first of the "Custer avengers" began to move west. Within the year almost 40 percent of the entire U.S. Army would be ready to fight against the Sioux and Cheyenne in the largest military action since the end of the Civil War.

Congress also agreed to Sheridan's request to build two new forts near the war zone. Sheridan had long argued for these forts as the best way to impose military control over the nomadic Lakota and Cheyenne, but only in the wake of Custer's defeat did Congress see the wisdom of appropriating two hundred thousand dollars for this proposal. Congress also acceded to Sheridan's request to give the military control over the Indian agencies in order to enforce a separation between "agency" Indians and "hostile" Indians. Sheridan had long wanted to deprive the nomadic bands of the support, trade, and comfort that came from the free movement of agency Indians and nontreaty Indians. Now, in the wake of the Little Bighorn, Sheridan would have the military authority to divide the two populations more completely than ever.

The first test of Sheridan's strategy came on July 17 in northwestern Nebraska. Colonel Wesley Merritt, while en route to join General Crook at Goose Creek, received word that several hundred Cheyenne planned to leave the agency and join their kinsmen in the north. Merritt ordered his Fifth Cavalry on a grueling ride, 85 miles in thirty-one hours, in order to prevent this migration. Reaching War Bonnet Creek first, Merritt's forces skirmished briefly with the Cheyenne and forced them back to the agency. The fighting was minimal, but it did enforce Sheridan's strategy of separating the agency and nonagency Indians. Moreover, War Bonnet Creek was the first good news for the army since the campaign began the previous winter. The immediate effect was a strategic victory for Sheridan—the agency Indians were forced to stay away from the war zone—and a morale boost for soldiers still reeling from the psychological pain of Custer's demise. As Danish immigrant Chris Nelson, who rode with the Fifth Cavalry at War Bonnet Creek, said, "It was the first scalp for Custer, the first victim of the vengeance which more than anything had been the goal of my regiment."[5]

Fresh from his victory at War Bonnet Creek, Merritt proceeded to join Crook's command in Wyoming on August 3. Two days later the two-thousand-member Big Horn and Yellowstone expedition began its eastward march, hoping to locate the Sioux who had already moved hundreds of miles east in their summer migrations. Because they were so far behind the Indians, Crook ordered all heavy equipment left behind with the wagons. The necessary rations and ammunition would travel with the expedition on mules, the tactic that had worked so well in increasing Crook's mobility in his fight against the Apaches in the Southwest. But with his confidence still shaken by the Rosebud and Little Bighorn defeats, Crook undermined his mobility by joining Terry's reinforced Dakota column on the Rosebud River and creating a daunting but cumbersome force of nearly four thousand men. Unable to provision such a large army for more than week, the commanders appeared tethered to their Yellowstone River supply lines. Worse, the cavalry's grain-fed horses, left to subsist on only prairie grasses, began to weaken and die. Cavalrymen walked and left behind a line of dead horses to mark their path. By late August the Crow and Shoshoni scouts, demoralized because this expedition would never catch the Sioux, returned to their homes. Buffalo Bill Cody and most of the journalists, also disgusted with the mismanagement of the expedition, left for their occupations in the East.

Disheartened, Crook and Terry separated their commands; Terry turned north to prevent the Sioux from escaping into Canada, while Crook followed a trail leading east toward the Black Hills. Fearing that white settlements in the Black Hills might be under attack, Crook cut loose from his supply base on the Yellowstone River and set out across 200 miles of country completely unknown to him. For nearly three weeks Crook's men struggled through rain and mud with scarcely any provisions in what became known as the "Starvation March." Slogging 20 to 40 miles a day, the men survived by eating the mules and horses that died along the way. Private Thomas Lloyd of the Third Cavalry remembered how one would "shoot an old sore back mule, take your butcher knife, cut as nice a slice as you could get and eat it raw." The soldiers weakened, sometimes falling behind or collapsing along the way. Lieutenant Walter Schuyler saw "men become so exhausted that they were actually insane" and other "men who were very plucky" and would "sit down and cry like children because they could not hold out."[6]

In desperation, Crook sent Captain Anson Mills with an escort of 150 cavalrymen ahead to the Black Hills settlements to procure food for his starving expedition. Traveling at night, Mills's detachment nearly stumbled into a village of thirty-seven Lakota lodges. Mills and his officers spent the rest of the foggy night hiding in a ravine and debating their next move. Fearing that this village might be part of a much larger encampment, most of the officers argued that their relatively small contingent should avoid a fight. Against this advice, Mills ordered a dawn assault, still hanging onto the widely shared belief that the size of the warrior force would be irrelevant if the soldiers had surprise and discipline on their side. Some of the men must have had the Custer fight in mind as they spent the night fearful that dawn would bring a disaster for the troops. If Mills thought of the Little Bighorn, he didn't pay it any mind as he ordered a three-pronged dawn assault that had become the standard tactic for the army, Custer's experience notwithstanding.

As it turned out, Mills was right about the dawn assault, and his officers were also correct in thinking that other Sioux in the area might jeopardize their small force. Catching the village by surprise, the mounted soldiers rode "pistols in hand, yelling and firing into tepees" while the Miniconjou warriors struggled to return fire. "Dismounted men followed . . . with a deadly fusillade into the village." According to Miniconjou warrior Red Horse, who was in the village, "It was early in the morning, still dark and misting. We were all asleep. The first we knew we were fired upon, we caught up what arms we could find in the dark, the women taking the children and hiding among the rocks." Some of the warriors who escaped into the rocky bluffs gathered their ponies and rode several hours to Crazy Horse's camp for help. Adding to the horror of the attack was the fact that, as Red Horse explained later, "We were coming in here to stay, to give ourselves up, when we were attacked."[7] Not only was this village traveling to the agency to surrender, but they were at this point on their own Great Sioux Reservation.

As Mills had hoped, the warriors had scattered and his soldiers controlled the village in a matter of minutes. They found saddles, cooking utensils, ammunition, and sacks of flour, corn, and beans, as well as two thousand animal skins and 5,000 pounds of dried meat. Any lingering doubts about attacking the village vanished when they discovered a Seventh Cavalry guidon, a few army saddles, and some clothing from Custer's old regiment. Avenging Custer, in their minds, more than justified any regrets about killing villagers. For Charger, a young Lakota man in the village, this loss of property was devastating. As he remembered, villagers caught what ponies they could and fled, some riding double. "All their tents, food, and other articles such as beadwork were destroyed by the fire, leaving some of the fleeing Indians almost helpless, and in a destitute condition."[8]

The soldiers discovered a horrified three- or four-year-old Lakota girl in the camp screaming in fear. Struck by her "beauty and grace," Captain Mills calmed her "by petting her and giving her food," and she began to follow him around. Later that day, as Mills was inspecting the dead and dying in a ravine, the girl suddenly shrieked in grief as she "ran and embraced" one of the "bloody and mangled" corpses lying on the ground. "The sight," Mills remembered, "was enough to touch the heart of the strongest man." He resolved "to adopt this little girl, as I had slain her mother."[9] In the end, however, he never did. His wife, he realized on further reflection, would never accept the social disapproval of bringing an Indian child into their home.

Crook's column caught up with Mills, and by afternoon the only sounds were "the barking of stray puppies, the whining of children, the confused hum of the conversation going on among two thousand soldiers, officers, and packers" in the small village. Suddenly, the "sharp crack of rifles and the whizzing of bullets" announced the arrival of Crazy Horse with a force of Lakota warriors strong enough to contest the soldiers. After several hours of inconclusive fighting from a distance, the warriors realized that it was no use to fight further against such a large, entrenched force and pulled back. Crook distributed the dried meat to his famished men, although some of them preferred to feast on the two hundred Indian ponies that had been captured. The soldiers burned the rest of the contents of the village, and the next morning Crook prepared to move on south toward Deadwood in the Black Hills. Before departure, Crook spoke to the women and children captives, telling them that they were free to leave because "we were not making war upon such as they." One young warrior prisoner, Charging Bear, declined the offer to leave and remained with the soldiers as a scout, "rendering most efficient service in the campaign during the following winter," Captain Bourke recalled.[10]

Crook claimed this battle, known as Slim Buttes for the nearby rock formations, as a victory, but having finally encountered Crazy Horse and the Lakota who fought Custer, he proved unable to follow them. The cavalry horses, some without their accustomed grain for the entire summer, had no energy for the chase, and the riders were more concerned with filling their bellies than avenging Custer's killers. Torrential rain and fierce hunger tormented the men as they struggled toward Deadwood, where finally the sun broke through the clouds and a herd of beef cattle awaited them. They had survived the Starvation March, but Slim Buttes was not much of a victory to celebrate. "The general impression in this command," one reporter noted, "is that we have not much to boast of in the way of killing Indians." Many soldiers blamed Crook, as one discouraged member of the Fifth Cavalry summarized, "So far the result of this expedition has been nothing but disaster, and a depletion of the public purse. Custer and his 300 brave soldiers still remain unavenged, and the Indian Question is further from solution than ever." The *Chicago Times* added caustically, "At Last Crook Can Make a Showing for His Summer's Work. The Net Results Being Several Indians, Two Squaws, and a 'Nit' Killed."[11] As Lieutenant Bourke described matters, the local bloodlust was not yet satiated: "When the whites succeeded in killing an Indian, which happened at extremely rare intervals, Deadwood would go crazy with delight; the skull and scalp were paraded and sold at public auction to the highest bidder."[12]

What the newspapers and the military missed was the simple fact that Indians were also hungry. Kept on the move for most of the summer, with buffalo herds beginning to dwindle, Lakota and Cheyenne hunters struggled to put away enough meat for the coming winter. While Crook was pursuing them, the Cheyenne and Lakota had burned the prairie in order to deny the cavalry horses grazing, an action that now compounded their own problems as they retraced this blackened landscape. As summer rains became autumn and winter snows, their ponies began to starve. Like the soldiers, the hungry nomads ate the lean horseflesh. In small family groups, some of them drifted toward the agencies. There, at least, they would have food.

Closing the Circle

While the press and much of the public continued to demand vengeance, General Sheridan kept his focus on victory, and he knew the difference. He realized that his army did not need to defeat the Lakota alliance in battle if it could compel them into submission through fear and starvation. This tactic may not provide the public with the catharsis it longed for after Custer's defeat, but it would achieve the national goal of subjugation nevertheless. In some ways Sheridan's strategy in the fall of 1876 anticipated the counterinsurgency strategies of the twentieth century. He realized that the army might not be able to engineer a decisive battle that would win the war. Instead, victory over the Sioux would come through control over the flow of Indians at the agencies and the occupation of the Powder River region, the area that still had enough wildlife to supply them with sustenance. Forts in the middle of the nomads' hunting lands and military control over the agencies would prove more decisive than battles. The strategy would be to separate the militants from the agency Indians, concentrate the loyal Indians near the agencies where rations could be controlled, and starve the hunters into submission.

During the late summer and fall of 1876, Sheridan began to implement this strategy of concentration, isolation, and control. In August, while Crook was on his Starvation March, Congress had passed a bill that made future appropriations for food rations for the Sioux (required by treaty) contingent upon their agreeing to relinquish the Black Hills and all of the unceded hunting lands of the 1868 Fort Laramie Treaty. In September a commission chaired by humanitarian George W. Manypenny traveled to the Lakota agencies to secure a fig leaf of legal title for the government's seizure of the Black Hills. The commission proceeded more by dictation than negotiation, making it clear to Lakota leaders that their future food rations depended on providing signatures and that even if no one signed the government would simply take the Black Hills and the unceded lands of eastern Montana and Wyoming anyway. Disregarding previous treaty commitments, Congress now required the Sioux to submit or starve.

Even in this coercive situation, most Sioux refused to give in to the commission's demands. In the end, fewer than 10 percent touched the pen, far less than the three-quarters of all adult males required by the 1868 Fort Laramie Treaty for any changes in its terms. As far as Manypenny and the army were concerned, the seven million acres of the Black Hills and the forty million acres of the unceded territory from the 1868 Fort Laramie Treaty now legally belonged to the United States. The army's next step was to ensure that those Sioux who were concentrated near the agencies would remain isolated from the wandering militants. In a carefully orchestrated maneuver, the army surrounded two separate villages of Lakota camped near the agencies, disarmed 150 warriors, and confiscated 750 ponies.

With the agency Indians contained, Sheridan then sent his generals on a winter campaign to harass the remaining bands of still-roaming Indians. With winter coming on, the seasonal advantage again shifted toward the army. Grass-fed Indian ponies would provide limited mobility for the warriors and make villages vulnerable, while the army's grain-fed horses could still travel over long distances. General Crook held down a post in northern Wyoming between the Black Hills and the Bighorn Mountains, while the ambitious Colonel Nelson A. Miles established a post at the confluence of the Tongue and Yellowstone rivers. Sheridan hoped that constant military patrols in these areas would deny a safe haven or good hunting to the militants and gradually force the Lakota alliance to disintegrate into smaller family units who would come to the agencies for food and safety. Colonel Miles had chafed under the cautious restraint of General Terry during the summer campaign and welcomed the opportunity to lead the army's cause in the northern war zone. Miles was nearly the same age as Custer and shared many of the slain general's characteristics: both were Civil War heroes, veterans of Indian wars, aggressive, energetic, confident to the point of vanity, distinctive in dress and appearance, and obsessive in pursuing the scarce promotions available in the post–Civil War army. In addition to maintaining a military garrison at the mouth of the Tongue River (near present-day Miles City, Montana), Miles was determined to use his eight-hundred-man Yellowstone command to keep the northern Lakota on the run for the entire winter. To Miles's way of thinking, "the only way to make the country tenable for us was to render it untenable for the Indians."[13] Because Miles wore an overcoat trimmed with bear fur and a fur cap on his winter campaigns, the Sioux came to know him as Bear Coat.

The first fighting of the fall broke out in October over Miles's attempts to resupply his garrison at the Tongue River. Sitting Bull's scouts noticed the supply wagons and began firing at them from protected positions along the route. On the second day of this running skirmish, the supply wagons came upon a note left in their path. Dictated by Sitting Bull, the note said in part, "I want to know what you are doing traveling on this road. You scare all the buffalo away. I want to hunt in this place. I want you to turn back from here. If you don't, I will fight you again."[14] Under a truce flag, a few Lakota chiefs asked the soldiers to leave the country but also said they were hungry, in need of food and ammunition, and desired peace. As they moved away, Colonel Miles saw a chance to negotiate with Sitting Bull and rode after the Lakota. On October 20, a day drenched in sunshine but frigid with a bitter cold wind, they met on a buffalo robe laid out on the prairie between their opposing armed forces. Miles wore the fur-trimmed coat that gave him his name, while Sitting Bull came dressed in leggings, moccasins, a breechcloth, and a buffalo robe, but no feathers or ornamentation. The intense cold added to the tension that seemed to many present as if it could break into open violence at any moment. Bear Coat was still relatively new to the northern plains, but Sitting Bull commanded respect from all as the man who, at least by reputation, had engineered the defeat of Custer.

In the first meeting during the Great Sioux War between a government representative and a leader of the northern Lakota alliance, the two men shook hands and then shared the sacred pipe. According to another chief who was with them, Sitting Bull "filled a pipe and, presenting it to the Great Spirit, called upon Him to have mercy upon his people; to allow nothing to be said on either side but the truth; to look down upon them and influence the hearts of the Indians and the whites so that they might do what is right." In the tumultuous hours of discussion that followed, Sitting Bull expressed a desire to hunt buffalo in peace and agreed that Indians would not fight with soldiers if only they were left alone. Miles insisted that the only path to peace was for the Lakota to submit to the authority of the federal government and live on the reservation. Sitting Bull replied, "God Almighty made him an Indian and did not make him an agency Indian."[15] As it became clear that, sacred pipe ceremony notwithstanding, there would be no agreement, talks broke off with the only accession being to meet again the next day.

The tensions continued during the fretful night as both sides considered initiating an early morning attack against the other. In the morning Miles ordered the infantry to approach the Indian camp in preparation for battle, while in the distance they could see Lakota women and children packing camp and leaving "like a vast herd of buffalo." As the meeting commenced, there was little trust on either side. From time to time warriors casually rode around the talks, sometimes giving Miles the feeling that he was being surrounded. Once he told Sitting Bull to order the warriors to retreat or the talks would be over. Although there was supposed to be a ban on firearms at the council, Miles concealed a handgun under his coat and at one point briefly entertained the thought of killing Sitting Bull. "But that would have been violating a flag of truce," he wrote to his wife, "and the whole civilized world would have denounced it."[16] Other accounts suggest that some Sioux unsuccessfully attempted to deliver a carbine to Sitting Bull, concealed under a large buffalo robe. With talks restating the previous day's irreconcilable positions, Miles offered an ultimatum: surrender at once or the attack would begin.

The skirmish that followed, which whites called the Battle of Cedar Creek, proved more consequential in its aftermath than in the fighting itself. Outnumbered two to one, the soldiers might have briefly felt alarmed; at least one observed that "many a strong heart grew weak as our thoughts flew back to the Custer massacre."[17] But disciplined infantry maneuvers backed by artillery soon chased the warriors from the field of battle, although neither side suffered heavy casualties. Even though the Lakota slipped away and eluded Miles's pursuit, in the next weeks and months Lakota began to surrender as individual families and small groups began to peel off to find food and shelter at the agencies.

While Miles was busy with Sitting Bull in eastern Montana, Crook was preparing a winter campaign designed to crush the Indian resistance in Wyoming. Not wanting a repeat of his Starvation March, Crook made the Powder River expedition his best-equipped expedition yet. With prairie grass scant during the winter months, the expedition's horses needed 30,000 pounds of grain each day to maintain their strength. Crook arranged to have 500,000 pounds of grain available for the horses, in addition to enough winter clothing, rations, and supplies to last the soldiers for five months. Transportation costs alone for the Powder River expedition totaled sixty thousand dollars per month. Tapping the immense resources of the nation in a way his adversaries could not, Crook had this vast amount of grain, food, and equipment transported by Union Pacific Railroad to Fort Laramie and then freighted by wagons northward. While his Indian opponents had to rely on subsistence to find their fighting strength, Crook's operation used the nation's surplus wealth channeled to the plains of Wyoming on the new transcontinental railroad.

The most noticeable addition to Crook's Powder River expedition was the more than 350 Indian scouts that Crook had recruited especially for this mission. Crook was well known for his use of Apache scouts in his southwestern campaigns, and he believed that the lack of scouts and their intimate knowledge of the countryside had contributed to his difficult summer campaign. Yet having this many Indian scouts, constituting roughly 20 percent of his entire command, was unprecedented. In addition to Sioux recruited from the agencies, Crook hired Cheyenne, Arapaho, Shoshoni, Pawnee, Crow, Bannock, and one Nez Perce. Crook's policy was a tacit admission that without the help of Indians, the army could not find and defeat Indians. For their part, the various tribes who scouted for the army saw their participation as a way to accommodate white demands while still enjoying familiar pursuits. In the spring of 1876 Crook had been unsuccessful in recruiting Sioux and Cheyenne scouts, but by autumn of that year he recruited successfully from both tribes largely because he allowed scouts to keep their mounts and weapons. Some younger Lakota allied themselves with Crook for this campaign because they thought it would bring better treatment for their people and especially would allow them to keep their agencies on the western plains rather than being removed to Indian Territory or forced to move to agencies along the Missouri River. These mostly younger Lakota rejected the militancy of Red Cloud, Crazy Horse, and Sitting Bull because they judged cooperation rather than resistance to be the best strategy for holding on to a portion of their homeland.

Recruiting other tribes to fight against the Sioux was comparatively easy for Crook. For most of the nineteenth century, the expansionist Sioux had fought against the Pawnee, the Shoshoni, and the Crow. Our contemporary focus on Indian resistance to white invasion obscures the fact that during the nineteenth century more Indians died in intertribal warfare than in fighting against the whites. Many nineteenth-century Indian war memories recalled more about intertribal wars than they did about the "Indian wars" against the whites. Whereas whites tended to think of "Indians" as a monolithic "people," their own identities on the plains in the nineteenth century were much more local, more tied to extended family and band. From the perspective of the Crow, Shoshoni, or Pawnee, they did not assist the army so much as welcome the army as an ally in their fight against the Sioux in what they considered a mutually advantageous relationship of equals. At that time Indians who fought against the government were stereotyped as "bad," the "sullen" Sitting Bull for instance, while the "good" Indians were those like the "noble" Spotted Tail who negotiated for the best terms they could get. In recent years the categories are sometimes reversed, with Sitting Bull as a "patriot" and Spotted Tail as a collaborator, maybe even a traitor, and scouts sometimes portrayed as "mercenaries." None of these categories would have made any sense to the native peoples of the nineteenth century, who negotiated to the best of their abilities to protect their interests and serve the cause of their relatives. For some this meant resistance, for others accommodation, but for many the strategies blended, never more than in the fall of 1876 when some warriors who had fought against Custer now considered that the best way to protect their "people" was to join Crook's army.

Through the harsh November cold this unlikely assemblage proceeded north from Fort Fetterman to Cantonment Reno, the well-supplied garrison near present-day Buffalo, Wyoming. The temperature stayed below zero most days, but the expedition was well prepared for the Wyoming winter. Despite the fact that Crook had told his Indian allies, "We don't want to kill the Indians, we only want to make them behave," the expedition was determined to have a fight. As Lieutenant Bourke wrote, "We begin to fear that Crazy Horse may surrender without a blow; a fight is desirable to atone and compensate for all our trials, hardships and dangers for more than eight months."[18] Although Crook had started out in search of Crazy Horse, he changed plans when he learned from scouts that a Cheyenne village was camped in the Big Horn Mountains on the Red Fork of the Powder River. With such a convenient target available and Crazy Horse still not found, Crook ordered Mackenzie to take his cavalry and the Indian allies for what had become the trademark of the Great Sioux War: a dawn assault on an Indian village. As fate would have it, the attack commenced on the morning of November 25, exactly five months after Custer's fatal attack on many of these same Cheyenne.

The Cheyenne village, led by Dull Knife (sometimes called Morning Star), rested in a walled canyon about 1 mile wide and 5 miles long. The site had fresh water, abundant timber, and plenty of grazing land for horses. A favorite wintering spot for the Cheyenne, the canyon offered a refuge from the cold northern winds while being situated to catch the warm westerly chinook breezes. In the village were 173 lodges, home to about 1,200 people and perhaps 300 warriors. Numbers had grown in recent weeks as several family groups, alarmed by the army's seizure of guns and horses from agency Indians, left the agencies to spend the winter in this traditional place. Many Cheyenne leaders were present, including holy men, political leaders, and war chiefs, representing perhaps the most complete assemblage of Northern Cheyenne people in the same place in the several decades of intermittent warfare. Scouts for the village had been watching Crook's movements, and the day before the attack a blind holy man named Box Elder saw a vision of soldiers assaulting the camp. This news made some in the camp anxious to move, but Last Bull, chief of the warrior society known as the Kit Fox soldiers, insisted that they remain where they were and dance through the night to celebrate their recent victory against a Shoshoni hunting party.

While the Cheyenne danced, Mackenzie moved his cavalry and Indian allies into position as they listened to drumming and singing from the village, a noise that only stopped shortly before dawn. Then, as Cheyenne battle veteran Beaver Heart recalled, "Gray light was seeping into the canyon when the charge came. The thunder of hoofs and the war chants of enemy scouts awoke the village. Rifles and pistols took up their song of death."[19] Mackenzie's Indian allies charged first, followed closely by the cavalry. Bullets rattled the tipis as villagers scrambled in the chaos to retreat into the hills on the far side of the charge. Pawnee advanced through the village sounding their war whistles made from eagle bones. Dogs barked and gunfire cracked as warriors attempted to protect their families and the village pony herd. The Cheyenne woman Iron Teeth fled to the hills while her husband and two sons defended the village. Interviewed in 1929 at the age of 95, Iron Teeth still had vivid recollections of that day. "My husband was walking, leading his horse, and stopping at times to shoot," she remembered. "Suddenly, I saw him fall. I started to go back to him, but my sons made me go on, with my three daughters." The last she saw of her husband, "he was lying there dead in the snow."[20]

In an hour of chaotic fighting, Mackenzie's men took complete control of the village and chased the Cheyenne into the rocky ridges on the western end of the canyon. The cavalry performed their tasks efficiently, with the only exception coming from some of the new recruits—the Custer avengers—who faltered for lack of training and discipline. Later in the morning firing slowed down as it became apparent that the Cheyenne could not be forced from their strongholds in the rocky heights. At one point they sent out a white flag of truce, asking for talks. Dull Knife said he had lost two sons and was ready to surrender, but other chiefs vowed to hold out. In a comment that emphasized the critical role of the expedition's Indian allies, one Cheyenne leader shouted from the rocky heights to the Indians in the village below, "We can whip the white soldiers alone, but we can't fight you too."[21] By afternoon the Cheyenne had lost their horse herd and almost all of their valuables in the village. Mackenzie ordered the village and its contents burned, a sight that sent the Cheyenne in the hills into mourning. During the night they slipped away into the mountains.

On Mackenzie's orders, soldiers inspected each lodge before they burned it, and the resulting inventory represents a vivid portrait of Northern Cheyenne material culture. There were weapons of all sorts, including plenty of ammunition and even a keg of gunpowder. The camp was rich in dried meat and buffalo hides, enough that the Indian allies loaded fifty mules with robes before burning the rest. There was also a long list of manufactured goods: shovels, axes, knives, saddles, hammers, scissors, canteens, kettles, pots, china saucers, coffee pots, frying pans, and forks and spoons. There were even beaver traps and bottles of strychnine used to poison wolves. In addition, the camp held many priceless artifacts representing Cheyenne artwork, including eagle feather war bonnets, buckskin shirts trimmed with human hair, dresses trimmed with beadwork and elk's teeth, and porcupine quill pipe bags. One gruesome item saved was a necklace made of beads mixed with eight human fingers. The soldiers' most grisly discoveries, however, were two scalps of young girls, a human hand and forearm, and a buckskin bag filled with the right hands of twelve Shoshoni babies, apparently victims of a recent Cheyenne attack on a Shoshoni village. This discovery sent the Shoshoni into "the most abject grief, and letting hair hang down over face and shoulders," they "danced and wailed" until the next morning.[22] The soldiers took great interest in the remnants from the Seventh Cavalry—various books, saddles, articles of clothing, canteens, and a guidon (made into a pillowcase)—proof enough for Mackenzie's soldiers that these Cheyenne had participated in killing Custer.

Mackenzie's assault on Dull Knife's village was the closest thing to a decisive battle in the months after the Little Bighorn. Crook praised Mackenzie's "brilliant achievements and the gallantry of the troops under his command." "This will be a terrible blow to the hostiles," Crook added, "as those Cheyennes were not only their bravest warriors but have been the head and front of most all the raids and deviltry committed in this country."[23] The army suffered seven casualties, while the Cheyenne fatalities totaled approximately forty, with perhaps twice that number wounded. That number does not count those who died from exposure to the severe cold, including fourteen babies that froze to death during the first two nights after the fight. In keeping with Sheridan's notions of total war, Mackenzie had denied the Cheyenne people the means to feed, clothe, or transport themselves and therefore weakened both their will and ability to resist. As Iron Teeth remembered the battle's aftermath, "We wallowed through mountain snows for several days. Most of us were afoot. We had no lodges, only a few blankets, and there was only a little dry meat food among us. Men died of wounds, women and children froze to death."[24]

Chased without food or shelter into the frigid Wyoming winter, Dull Knife's Cheyenne traveled for eleven days in search of Crazy Horse's Lakota, the same refuge as they had found in March after Crook and Reynolds had attacked their village to launch the Great Sioux War. Crazy Horse's village helped the Cheyenne as best they could, but this time the Oglala were themselves closer to the bone and had little to share. Generosity based on abundant food supplies had held the northern coalition together during the summer months, but now food shortages added to the factionalism inherent in Lakota and Cheyenne societies. In the months to come, both Crook and Miles exploited the growing factionalism among the Lakota confederation to peel away strength from the militants. As Sheridan and his generals had expected, the Great Sioux War ended not with the storm of a great battle but with the steady drizzle of harassment and starvation.

During the cold months the Lakota and Cheyenne alliance met frequently in council to debate their options for war and peace in this time of stress. With the Cheyenne refugees present as evidence of the high costs of war, militants led by the Oglala Crazy Horse and supported by Cheyenne leaders Two Moons and Ice (the holy man who had promised a bulletproof fight nineteen years earlier) maintained that vigilance and solidarity were the best way to protect their homeland. The peace faction was distressed by the continuing costs of war, amply illustrated by the attack on Dull Knife's camp. Many in this group were animated by the prospect of negotiating with the government to establish an agency somewhere in the territory of the Yellowstone and Powder rivers, the land that many increasingly favored as their home. Complicating the internal dynamics of this debate was the fact that both Miles and Crook had enlisted informants from the agency Indians who acted sometimes to encourage the peace faction and sometimes as spies who slipped back to Crook or Miles with information on the location and temperament of the militants.

In mid-December the divided camp of Crazy Horse agreed to send peace delegates to Miles's garrison on the Tongue River to explore what concessions Miles might be willing to make if they would surrender. As they approached the post, a group of Crow scouts greeted them with handshakes but, while grasping hands, dragged them from their horses and shot, beat, clubbed, and hacked the Lakota to death. The Crow justified their action as retaliation for a Lakota raid earlier that fall; one of the peace delegates was riding a horse that had belonged to a Crow woman who had been killed during that raid. Furious at the loss of a chance for negotiations, Miles ordered his Crow scouts to leave and sent gifts to the Lakota, but the damage had been done. For the time being at least, the peace faction among the Lakota lost ground as it appeared that Miles could not be trusted.

For the militant faction to prevail, however, it would have to prevent defections, and to do this required a degree of coercion that was unprecedented in Lakota society. The *akicitas*, or camp police, typically enforced group decisions such as where to hunt or when to send a war party. During this winter of discontent the *akicitas* imposed a kind of martial law and Crazy Horse assumed power well beyond any typical chief. In one instance, as a council in a neighboring village of Miniconjou discussed their desperate situation and weighed the possibilities of negotiated surrender, Crazy Horse and a gang of bodyguards threw open the tent flap, entered the lodge, and announced that no one would be allowed to leave the camp. When several families attempted to slip away during the night, Crazy Horse and his *akicitas* followed and stopped them. In a cruel echo of the government's surrender terms, they then took their weapons, shot their horses, and forced them to return to camp.

Such an unprecedented intervention was a sign of the increasing militarization of Lakota life. After nearly a quarter century of constant warfare, the *akicitas* now played a much larger role in camp life. War chiefs had eclipsed the hereditary chiefs who normally came to the fore during times of peace. Just as mainstream American society often turned to generals in times of war and mainstream history usually remembers war leaders more than peace advocates, so Lakota society trusted its war chiefs during this time of crisis and Indian history remembers the names of Sitting Bull and Crazy Horse rather than any leaders who emerged during earlier times of peace. The Great Sioux War is sometimes portrayed as the last chance for "traditional" Plains Indian society, but the growing militarization and the increasing reliance on trade goods, especially guns and ammunition, made this a society already in the throes of rapid change. Standing still in time, remaining "traditional" Indians, was one choice the Lakota and Cheyenne did not have in the winter of 1876.

The Lakota's and Cheyenne's choices were made in the midst of a series of small battles that emphasized that there could be no respite for the usual enjoyments of winter camp. On December 18 a portion of Miles's troops led by Lieutenant Frank Baldwin struck Sitting Bull's camp at Ash Creek, not far south of the trading post at Fort Peck. The skirmish left only one Lakota killed but forced Sitting Bull's village to abandon their food and possessions. In January Miles led a winter expedition that ran into a Lakota offensive organized by Crazy Horse, who was still anxious to prove that the militant strategy could produce results. In the Battle of Wolf Mountains, Crazy Horse's decoys advanced too quickly, ruining his intended ambush and allowing the soldiers to pour a withering fire onto the Lakota positions. A midday blizzard made it impossible for either side to see more than a few feet, thereby ending the inconclusive clash. Even though Miles claimed a victory, both sides pulled back, Miles to his Tongue River garrison that was resupplied all winter by overland wagon trains from Bismarck, and Crazy Horse to his village that had less food and ammunition than when he had started. Once again, the army relied on the surplus of the nation while the Lakota had only the subsistence of the northern plains during winter.

The militants' last chance for solidarity came during late January when Sitting Bull and Crazy Horse temporarily joined forces. Even as they counseled together about the next moves, the large village (nearly as large as the last summer's encampment at the Little Bighorn) found the hunting insufficient to feed so many people. Sitting Bull preferred to go north to Canada, to "Grandmother's Country" where the police were honest and the plains still held herds of buffalo. Crazy Horse may have considered this, but ultimately he decided against leaving the land he considered home. "My friend," he said to Sitting Bull, "the soldiers are everywhere; the Indians are getting scattered, so that soldiers can capture or kill them all. This is the end. All the time the soldiers will keep hunting us down. Some day I shall be killed. Well, all right. I am going south to get mine!" Sitting Bull quietly replied, "I do not wish to die yet."[25]

Even as they talked, hungry and fearful Lakota left the large camp in small groups for better hunting or to surrender at the agencies. The *akicitas* could no longer contain first the trickle and then the flood of those departing. The Lakota alliance that had defeated Custer in the summer of 1876 had been held together on the basis of an abundance that allowed great displays of generosity, one of the Lakota's cardinal virtues; now six months later they struggled to feed themselves. They also grew weary of what one warrior called "damn soldiers everywhere." Another elaborated on this reason for turning himself in at the agency: "I am tired of being always on the watch for troops. My desire is to get my family where they can sleep without being continually in the expectation of an attack."[26]

Crazy Horse was already deeply troubled by the growing defections and especially by what he viewed as the collapse of tribal unity evidenced by the disloyal behavior of the Lakota and Cheyenne who scouted for Crook. As more and more families left for the agencies, he became more aloof than ever. Always known for his solitary ways, this winter Crazy Horse spent weeks at a time away from camp hunting, scouting, fasting, and praying for a vision that would show him the way to protect his people and their land. Once Black Elk's family came upon Crazy Horse and his wife camped alone out in the hills. Crazy Horse told them, "It is for the good of my people that I am out alone. Out there I am making plans—nothing but good plans—for the good of my people . . . This country is ours, therefore I am doing this."[27]

Even in this difficult situation, Indian diplomacy helped to gain concessions that made surrender more palatable. Among the Lakota, Spotted Tail—still widely respected even though he had been living at the agency for many years—took the initiative by serving as a peace envoy from General Crook. Crook first wanted to send Spotted Tail to the militant nomads with a demand for unconditional surrender, but Spotted Tail refused. Only after Crook agreed to support an agency for the northern Lakota in their own territory and to allow some flexibility in the surrender of their horses did Spotted Tail agree to travel north to coax the militants into surrendering at the agency. In March Spotted Tail reached the camp of his nephew Crazy Horse with Crook's offer. Crazy Horse was out in the hills praying, fasting, and sweating for a vision that did not come this time. He sent word that he would agree to whatever the people decided, and they were inclined to surrender. As one Lakota summarized, "You see all the people here are in rags, they all need clothing, we might as well go in."[28]

Indian diplomacy also played a crucial role for the Cheyenne in bringing the war to an end. Miles had captured Sweet Taste Woman, the sister-in-law of Ice and a respected elder, after which she agreed to serve as his peace envoy to initiate negotiations with the Cheyenne. Exhausted from the human costs of war, Sweet Taste Woman saw an opportunity to bring peace to her people. She took presents and promises—especially Miles's concession that they would be given a permanent place to live in their homeland—to her Cheyenne relatives and initiated discussions that resulted in peaceable surrender of most of the Cheyenne. Two Moons, once a militant ally of Crazy Horse, reasoned, "We have had enough troubles. More soldiers come to us each time. The white people are moving in like ants and covering the whole country. If you go on fighting we may lose our land and be prisoners, but if we surrender we might get to keep some of it."[29]

Throughout the spring Lakota and Cheyenne families and bands surrendered, and on May 6, 1877, Crazy Horse led a procession of nine hundred people and two thousand ponies to the Red Cloud agency in Nebraska. To symbolize the end of his wartime leadership, he gave his war bonnet and war shirt to Red Cloud. Then he shook hands with Crook's subordinate, Lieutenant William P. Clark, using his left hand, explaining, "I shake with this hand because my heart is on this side; I want this peace to last forever."[30] Officers at the agency, expecting to witness a defeated people coming in to surrender, instead heard Crazy Horse's procession proudly singing their "Song of Peace." Meanwhile, sometime during this same week, Sitting Bull and his following of 135 lodges crossed the Medicine Line into Canada.

The Perils of Peace

A curious paradox of history is that sometimes more evidence leads to less certainty about what actually happened. Nowhere is this truer than in the last four months of Crazy Horse's life, where evidence and contradictions abound. There is more documentation for these last four months of his life than for the thirty-seven years that preceded them, yet it was in these four months that controversies swirled, accounts differed, and Crazy Horse the man who fought for his people started to become Crazy Horse the legendary "mystic warrior of the plains."

When Crazy Horse surrendered, General Crook made two promises to him that he either could not or would not keep. He promised first to support Crazy Horse's request for a permanent agency in the northern Lakota country, the region where most of the fighting had occurred. Crook's second promise was to allow Crazy Horse's camp to leave the agency for a forty-day buffalo hunt later that summer. Crook also planned a trip to Washington, D.C., for Crazy Horse and other Lakota leaders, expecting that the usual display of the immense power of the United States would impress upon them the futility of any further resistance. The trip would also be a chance for Crazy Horse to meet the new Great White Father, President Hayes, for further discussions of the location of the agency. Crazy Horse began the summer in a cheerful mood, hoping for a Sun Dance that would reunite his divided people, a leisurely buffalo hunt, and then a visit and negotiations that would lead to his main goal: a legally recognized place for his people in their own land. According to one account, Crazy Horse was even learning to eat with a fork in order to impress his *wasichu* hosts with his refined table manners.

Crazy Horse's disposition became troubled in August as Crook failed to deliver on either of his promises. Hearing rumors that Sitting Bull was coming back from Canada, Crook denied permission for the buffalo hunt because he feared that Crazy Horse would take the opportunity to reunite with Sitting Bull and reignite the Great Sioux War. Crook delayed any decision about the location of an agency for the northern Lakota, but in reality this decision was not his to make. Up the chain of command, Generals Sheridan and Sherman had already decided against a northern agency, leaving Crook in the awkward position of having made a promise that he was now ordered to break. In response, Crazy Horse cancelled his participation in the upcoming delegation to Washington, D.C., insisting that the whites fulfill at least one promise as a precondition for his participation in diplomacy. To make matters worse, Red Cloud and other Lakota leaders grew intensely jealous of the attention given to Crazy Horse and spread rumors to white authorities that he was leaving the agency, going back to war, or plotting to kill officers. For his part, Crazy Horse feared repeated whisperings that he might be arrested and hanged as revenge for his leadership role in the battle against Custer.

In this climate of suspicion, any remaining goodwill vanished when the Nez Perces crossed the Continental Divide through Yellowstone National Park and spilled out onto the plains, defeating or eluding every force the army threw at them. In preparing to fight the Nez Perces should they come his way, Crook tried to enlist two hundred or more Lakota as Indian allies for the fight. On August 31 when Lieutenant Clark proposed to Crazy Horse that he enlist and lead this fighting force, Crazy Horse rejected the idea. He had given up his warrior ways, he insisted, and was committed to peace. Touch the Clouds, Crazy Horse's 7-foot friend, told Clark that the government was jerking Crazy Horse in different directions, "like a horse with a bit in its mouth." As the debate grew heated, Crazy Horse reluctantly agreed to do as Clark asked. "We are tired of war; we came in for peace, but now that the Great Father asks our help, we will go north and fight until there is not a Nez Perce left." For reasons that remain mysterious, Frank Grouard, the translator, rendered the last phrase "until not a *white man* is left."[31] Historians differ about how serious this mistranslation was and whether or not others in the room might have corrected it. Even without this mistranslation, the meeting included enough angry speeches to fuel the suspicion growing in Clark's mind that Crazy Horse intended to flee the agency and resume the war.

When General Crook heard about this meeting, he considered arresting Crazy Horse but decided to meet with him first. At this point another unexplainable event intervened. As Crook prepared to leave, a Lakota man named Women's Dress told him that at the planned meeting Crazy Horse intended to stab Crook, kill his officers, and lead his people north to freedom. The fact that no one knows the motives of Women's Dress or the source of his information has fed conspiracy theories ever since, but at the time it was enough to make Crook hesitate. Even though he was not sure whether or not to believe this story, he decided to arrest Crazy Horse. The next day a force of four hundred cavalry and five hundred Lakota allies (a larger force than Custer commanded) set out to find and arrest Crazy Horse.

If Crazy Horse was the great war chief of the Oglala, why would so many of his own Sioux people be willing to participate in his arrest? Simple envy was part of the reason, as there were other Lakota leaders, notably Red Cloud, who resented the attention the whites gave to Crazy Horse. Still other Lakota leaders noted that Crazy Horse had not attended council meetings lately and was more reclusive than ever. Some complained of his "dictatorial manners, and disregard for the comfort of his people."[32] These smaller complaints were in the context of the great fear among Lakota that the government would remove them to agencies along the Missouri River, or even worse, to Indian Territory. Many of the five hundred Lakota who rode to arrest Crazy Horse were no doubt afraid that an uprising, or even further so-called intransigence on the part of Crazy Horse, would lead to the entire tribe being punished with removal from their homeland. The times called for diplomacy, not war, they reasoned, and their interests were better served if a war leader were not so prominent.

When the arrest force arrived at Crazy Horse's camp, they found that he had already left for Spotted Tail's agency, 40 miles away. Far from starting a war, he simply hoped to escape the climate of suspicion that prevailed at the Red Cloud agency. He explained that he had come to his uncle's agency "to get away from the trouble there." He told a group of officers that "he should like to keep his country" and complained, "They have misunderstood me and misinterpreted me" at Red Cloud's agency. "My brain is in a whirl. I want to do what is right," he concluded.[33] Jesse Lee, the Indian agent, sympathized with Crazy Horse and promised him safety and a chance to explain his case to the commander at nearby Fort Robinson. Once there, however, the commander refused to meet with Crazy Horse and ordered him taken to the guardhouse. Crazy Horse did not know this, but the military high command had issued orders for his arrest and transportation east, probably to a prison in Florida.

Surrounded by soldiers and warriors, Crazy Horse walked through the fort's crowded parade grounds and into the doorway of the guardhouse. Not until he saw the prison bars and leg irons did Crazy Horse realize that he was under arrest and would be confined as a prisoner. Crazy Horse wrenched free from his captors and pulled a knife from his waistband as Little Big Man jumped on his back to hold him. Slashing Little Big Man's hand and forearm, Crazy Horse broke free and rushed for the doorway. "Kill the son of a bitch! Kill the son of a bitch!" shouted Lieutenant Kensington, the officer in charge of the arrest. Some Lakota in the courtyard echoed, "Kill him! Kill him!" As Crazy Horse neared the door, a guardhouse sentry met him with a bayonet thrust that pierced his side and went deep into his kidneys. The great war chief of the Lakota sank down and sighed, "Let me go; you've got me hurt now."

When guards began to move the mortally wounded man back to the guardhouse, Touch the Clouds intervened, "Don't take him in the Guard House, he is a Chief." They took him instead to the office of the post adjutant where Crazy Horse refused a cot and spent his dying hours on the floor with Touch the Clouds, the post doctor, and a few friends. When Crazy Horse's father, Worm, arrived, he said, "Son, I am here." The dying son replied, "Father, it is no use to depend on me; I am going to die," as his father and friends wept. Late that night, Crazy Horse died. Touch the Clouds lifted the blanket over his face, gently touched his friend's breast, and mourned, "It is good. He has looked for death, and it has come."[34] Several days later his family placed Crazy Horse's body in a secret resting place somewhere in the hills at the head of Wounded Knee Creek.

About the same time that Crazy Horse surrendered in May, Sitting Bull led 135 lodges across the international border into the safe haven of Canada. Major James M. Walsh of the Royal Canadian Mounted Police rode out with an escort of six soldiers to greet the famous Sioux leader. That afternoon Walsh met in council with Sitting Bull and other chiefs to tell them they were now in the land of the Great White Mother. After listening to Sitting Bull's recitation of the injustices inflicted upon his people by the Americans,

Walsh assured the Lakota that they would have the protection of the law in Canada, but they would also be required to obey the laws and specifically they could not use Canada as a safe haven for staging raids south of the border. Over time Walsh and Sitting Bull talked often and gained a deep mutual respect and even friendship. Walsh seemed to empathize with Sitting Bull's lament, "Once I was rich, but the Americans stole it all in the Black Hills. I have come to remain with the White Mother's children."[35]

For two years Sitting Bull and his northern nomads appeared to have found a home on the plains of western Canada. Buffalo herds were still plentiful and white settlement was still far to the east. Walsh agreed with Sitting Bull on the need for the Lakota to have access to trade goods, especially ammunition for the hunt. Traders eagerly accepted buffalo robes and even some Seventh Cavalry horses taken in the Custer fight in exchange for their manufactured goods. The peaceful and relatively abundant Lakota life attracted more refugees from the agencies, especially in the fall of 1877 when the government forced the Sioux to move from the agencies in western Nebraska to locations along the Missouri River. Already alienated by Crazy Horse's death, perhaps a thousand or more of his followers slipped away and headed north to Sitting Bull. Anxious to prevent Sitting Bull from gaining too much power as the locus of continuing resistance, President Hayes sent a commission to plead with the Lakota leaders to return to the United States. Sitting Bull reluctantly attended but refused to shake hands or smoke the peace pipe with the commissioners. After listening politely to their offer, Sitting Bull responded with a long speech that began, "We did not give you our country, you took it from us," and ended, "You come here to tell lies, but we don't want to hear them."[36]

By 1879, however, events conspired to make life difficult for the Lakota in Canadian exile. The buffalo herds grew smaller as hide hunters in Montana decimated the herds there, while the Canadian tribes—Blackfoot, Cree, and Assiniboine—all competed with the Lakota for the dwindling numbers. Dependent on the buffalo for both food and trade, the Lakota now faced hunger and poverty and began slipping back to the agencies. To make matters worse, the winter of 1879–80 was the fiercest yet on the Canadian Plains, so that Lakota first in a trickle and then in a steady stream left their Canadian refuge to return to their relatives in the United States. Gradually, Sitting Bull realized that he too would have to surrender. In the summer of 1881 he led two hundred followers—all that remained of the thousands who once allied with him—to Fort Buford, the garrison that he once had longed to eliminate from his country. When he met the fort's commander, he handed his rifle to his son, Crow Foot, who then gave it to the commander. "I wish it to be remembered that I was the last man of my tribe to surrender my rifle. This boy has given it to you, and now he wants to know how he is going to make a living." At the occasion of his surrender, Sitting Bull composed a song that spoke eloquently to his tragic transformation, "A warrior / I have been / Now / It is all over / A hard time / I have."[37]

In a single generation Plains Indians had gone from being a strong and free people in their own land to becoming dependent wards of the federal government living on reservations that were a fraction of their former land base. Although they had lost control of their own destiny, they had not lost all hope of shaping their future. Defeated and often demoralized, they still struggled to maintain a measure of tribal autonomy in the restricted confines of the reservation. The next threat to this autonomy came now not from the military but from the humanitarian reformers who claimed to be "friends of the Indian." These reformers sincerely believed that forced assimilation was the only alternative to extinction and therefore proceeded with plans to erase tribal identities and spread among the Indians the blessings of American civilization, Christianity, and capitalism. As Commissioner of Indian Affairs Thomas Jefferson Morgan explained, "It has become the settled policy of the Government to break up reservations, destroy tribal relations, settle Indians upon their own homesteads, incorporate them into the national life, and deal with them not as nations or tribes or bands, but as individual citizens. The American Indian is to become the Indian American."[38] Such a dramatic alteration of tribal identity into the national melting pot could not occur so easily, as Mark Twain knew when he ridiculed this effort with characteristic wit, "The time has come," he wrote, "when blood-curdling cruelty has become unnecessary. Inflict soap and a spelling book on every Indian that ravages the plains and let them die."[39] After a quarter century of warfare that had the goal of systematically impoverishing Plains Indians, now the goal was to rebuild them in the white man's image.

In the face of this cultural assault, the Lakota turned to their history to find new ways of turning reservations into homelands. Even on the reservation, Sitting Bull remained the symbol of resistance, often wearing a patch of red buffalo hair on the side of his head as an emblem of White Buffalo Calf Woman and the special relationship she signified between the Sioux and the buffalo. Just as *Wakan Tanka* had taken care of the people in the past, he insisted, so the story of the White Buffalo Calf Woman lived in the present to suggest new cultural possibilities. "You must not think that the Great Spirit does not watch me as closely as he watches you," Sitting Bull explained to a reporter. "He put me on these prairies, and he has permitted me to thrive with them. I know that he is watching me, and he will never leave me to starve. When the buffalo are gone he will give me something else."[40]

The exact shape of this new buffalo remained to be seen. According to the terms of the treaties of 1868 and 1876, the government was supposed to supply clothing, food, housing, schools, and farm implements for everyone on the reservation. Yet these annuities required by treaty obligations proved problematic; rather than providing the Lakota with the subsistence to which they were legally entitled, the annuities became the source of continuing dispute. Annuities were often of inferior quality and insufficient amount to meet the treaty obligations. The food supply was scarce enough to leave people hungry, while the dearth of clothes and blankets left some cold during the long plains winters. Sometimes Indian agents withheld food or clothes in order to compel obedience with assimilationist policies such as requiring children to attend schools or prohibiting adults from attending traditional dances. The Lakota preferred to receive their beef annuity in the form of live cattle delivered in a style that came to be a festive occasion. In an adaptation of the communal buffalo hunt, Lakota men shot cattle from horseback and then women came to dress the carcasses and prepare a feast. In festivities that must have felt familiar, the community gathered around the fires, ate meat in abundance, and gossiped and smoked away the hours. Indian agents deplored this method of distributing cattle because, in their view, it perpetuated savage customs and preserved tribal habits of life. They insisted that cattle should be killed and butchered first and then distributed to Lakota individuals as processed cuts of beef. The Lakota struggled throughout the 1880s to maintain autonomy and community, even if it was in small ways. For instance, they continued to use their word for buffalo hunt to designate the special day when their treaty-required cattle shipments arrived.

Struggles also persisted as Indian agents attempted to break the Lakota of their communal, nomadic hunting economy and replace it with individually owned farms. They urged the Lakota to build widely scattered cabins and settle on family farms, following the social pattern of white homesteaders on the plains. The Lakota often lived in log houses during the winter but returned to their tipis in the summer months, allowing them to move for summer hunts or communal events. Instead of building isolated farmsteads, they preferred to cluster their cabins together along the river bottoms, keeping the extended family group, the *tiospaye*, together as they continued to hunt deer, pronghorn antelope, and other small game. Many Lakota learned to plant subsistence gardens of oats, corn, squash, and melons, and some raised chickens and turkeys. Other Lakota used their familiarity with horses to take up cattle ranching, but rather than build up their herds in the manner of expectant capitalists, they slaughtered surplus cattle for communal feasts that strengthened the kinship ties of the *tiospaye* and met the needs of hungry relatives. Even Sitting Bull settled in a cabin with relatives nearby and over time established a herd of twenty horses and forty-five cattle, along with eighty chickens and fields of oats, corn, and potatoes.

A central front in the assault on tribal integrity was education. Many reformers saw assimilation through education as the humane alternative to extinction. The difference between civilized and savage societies, these humanitarian reformers believed, was not biological but cultural. Richard Henry Pratt, the leader of the movement for Indian education, believed in the Jeffersonian ideal of human equality and that all people had the intellectual capacity to develop as rational creatures. Indians were not an inferior race but rather were trapped in a backward culture. "It is a great mistake," Pratt asserted in a challenge to the racism of his day, "to think that the Indian is born an inevitable savage. He is born blank, like the rest of us." The key, then, was to change the environment of Indian children by removing them from their culture at an early age. This became the basis for the system of removing Indian children, sometimes forcibly, from their reservations and taking them to boarding schools far away. As Pratt famously said, it was necessary to "kill the Indian" in order to "save the man."[41] Modeling his methods on the Hampton Institute's industrial education for freed slaves in the South, Pratt started the Carlisle Boarding School for Indians and began the boarding school experiment that left scars on Indian identities throughout the twentieth century.

Some Lakota children who attended boarding schools tried to turn the attack on their culture into a means of preserving their identity. Luther Standing Bear, for example, understood his decision to attend Pratt's Carlisle Indian School as a modern way to undertake a warrior's journey. Remembering that his father had told him how a warrior risks death for the good of the people, Standing Bear decided to risk the uncertain future of boarding school in the hope of gaining power to help his people. "This chance to go East would prove that I was brave," Standing Bear recalled. Like many other Indian students, Standing Bear developed a profoundly ambivalent relationship with the boarding school experience. He was mortified after the initial traumatic experience of having his long hair cut short. Feeling stripped of his cultural identity, Standing Bear feared that he would no longer be an Indian, "but would be an imitation of a white man."[42] But like some other students, he enjoyed the pleasures of reading and writing in English and learned to appreciate the power that writing could bring. As an adult, he wrote an autobiography and several other books that have communicated his view of Lakota culture to a wider world. Contrary to Pratt's intentions, Standing Bear's Carlisle education became the means of preservation, not assimilation; on his modern warrior journey he had saved himself by preserving the Indian. Other Sioux leaders realized that literacy could prove valuable in dealing with the government and that the next generation of educated Lakota leaders might be useful in restoring the government's treaty obligations and even recovering stolen land. Once again Sitting Bull, in a conversation with a missionary, articulated a Lakota position that spoke for many: "I want you to teach my people to read and write but they must not become white people in their ways."[43]

Of all of the contested areas of reservation life, none was more crucial than the struggle over land. The Sioux wars began in 1854 as a struggle over land, and the effort to dispossess the Sioux continued into the reservation years and ultimately led to the last great tragedy of the Sioux wars. The instrument of dispossession in this case was legislation rather than military action, but the results were just as devastating. The principle that guided the government's intentions for Indian lands passed Congress in 1887 as the General Allotment Act sponsored by Massachusetts senator Henry L. Dawes. The act called for the division of reservation lands into 160-acre family homesteads, with the excess land opened to homesteading by other settlers. Congressional support for the Dawes Act came from two sources: reformers who believed that only by transforming tribal lands into individual family farmsteads could the Indians survive, and land-hungry westerners who sought access to Indian lands. Under the Sioux Act of 1888, the Great Sioux Reservation established in the 1868 Fort Laramie Treaty would be carved into six separate reservations with enough land for allotment into individual homesteads for the Sioux. The remaining nine million acres would be opened to settlers, a delightful prospect for promoters of the Dakota Territory. Because the 1868 Treaty required the signatures of three-fourths of adult males before any change could take place, the government sent a commission headed by Richard Henry Pratt to cajole the reluctant Lakota into signing. Almost all of the Lakota rejected Pratt's entreaties, forcing Pratt to leave the reservation bitter and with no new agreement.

Undeterred, Congress tried again the next year with yet one more attack on the Lakota land base that had been established by the 1868 Fort Laramie Treaty. Just as in the Black Hills swindle of 1876 that dramatically shrank the Lakota territory, so in 1889 a commission led by a sympathetic white leader used a combination of manipulations, threats, and bribes to force the Lakota into giving up more of their land. This time their old adversary General George Crook led the commission. Crook was well known as an Indian fighter but as one who displayed some sympathy for his opponents and advocated a humanitarian understanding of their situation. Just as Crook had made promises he could not keep in 1877, now he again made concessions that he did not have the power to enforce. Crook had promised that rations would be protected and that Lakota would have first consideration in choosing their land allotments. Contrary to this and beyond Crook's control, rations were cut by nearly 25 percent, and reservation land was opened to white claims before surveys could provide for the claims of Lakota already living there.

In early 1890 the Great Sioux Reservation, which had once covered all of western South Dakota, was carved into five smaller reservations that together constituted about one-half of the original reservation. The remaining half was opened for sale to homesteaders at bargain prices, with the proceeds going to compensate the Lakota for their lost land. Those who had signed Crook's document felt betrayed by what appeared to them as yet one more instance of government treachery. American Horse signed believing "I have done what is best for my people," but after the promises were broken he said it was as if "you struck us in the face." Another Lakota veteran of wars, commissions, and land deals said simply, "They made us many promises, more than I can remember, but they never kept but one; they promised to take our land and they took it."[44]

At the same time as their leaders protested the injustice of this latest land cession and the unilateral cut in rations, the Sioux struggled to maintain their spirituality in the presence of Catholic and Protestant missionaries determined to convert them to the Christian gospel. A persistent missionary effort was to eliminate traditional Lakota dances, particularly the Sun Dance, which they saw as especially "heathenish." In one instance, the Oglala Red Dog pleaded to Lieutenant John Bourke for a sympathetic understanding of the Sun Dance, "My friend, this is the way we have been raised. Do not think this is strange. All men are different. Our grandfathers taught us to do this." Rejecting this call to traditional values, Bourke responded by asserting the superiority of Christianity, at least in technological terms, "Your religion brought you the buffalo, ours brought us locomotives and talking wires."[45]

Christian missionaries met with mixed results on the Standing Rock reservation, where the old war chiefs Gall and Sitting Bull demonstrated the range of responses. Gall became friends with Philip Deloria, a Sioux convert who had become an Episcopalian. Some of Gall's family converted, and eventually the old warrior himself sought communion. When offered the wine, he drank the entire chalice and remarked to his friend Deloria, "Now I see why you wanted me to become a Christian. I feel so nice and warm and happy. Why didn't you tell me that Christians did this every Sunday . . . I would have joined your church years ago."[46] In contrast, Sitting Bull remained skeptical of Christianity, arguing that "Whitemen say it is not right for Indians to worship the skulls of buffaloes who gave us the meat of their bodies, but that we should worship the pictures and statues of Whitemen who never gave our ancestors anything." When pushed to choose between Protestants and Catholics, Sitting Bull, who throughout his life maintained a steadfast disapproval of alcohol, stated that he preferred Catholics because the priests "drink all of the wine themselves and do not give it to members of the church."[47] As crosses became an increasingly common public symbol on Standing Rock reservation, Sitting Bull placed a prayer tree outside his house with a buffalo skull attached to it.

In this variety of religious expressions competing to make meaning for a dispossessed people, the Lakota heard rumors of a new Indian messiah who offered a spiritual solution to their powerless situation. Delegates traveled to Nevada where they met a Paiute holy man named Wovoka who had received a vision of the apocalypse. God had showed him a new world with all the dead Indians and buffalo restored and all of the white people gone. This old world was tired, Wovoka told them, and would soon be washed away with a deep layer of water and mud that would obliterate all of the white people. From this mud would grow a new world filled with lush grass, clear water, and abundant herds of buffalo and ponies. All Indians killed by disease and wars would come back to life, families would be restored, and the oppressed would live in perfect peace and happiness. To hasten this coming new age, Wovoka urged his followers to perform a version of the circle dance that came to be known as the Ghost Dance.

Many elements of the Ghost Dance fit well with Lakota religious traditions. The idea of a world restored through moral reformation had indigenous as well as Christian antecedents, and Lakota told many stories of how buffalo came from inside the earth to this world. One Lakota understanding of the scarcity of buffalo during the 1880s was that the buffalo had gone back into the earth and were waiting for a Lakota spiritual regeneration before returning to the surface. Another familiar element was the dance itself, which had many similarities to the Sun Dance. Notably, Sun Dancers performed until pain and exhaustion caused them to fall into a trance and receive a vision that would guide the people. In the Ghost Dance people also fell into a trance and had visions, although significantly women participated in the Ghost Dance and had visions and therefore moral authority to guide the people. The Ghost Dance was different, however, in that Wovoka instructed his followers to hold hands in a circle, as one dancer remembered, "bringing back the sacred hoop—to feel, holding on to the hand of your brother and sister, the rebirth of Indian unity, feel it with your flesh, through your skin."[48]

While the Ghost Dance represented a kind of spiritual resistance to the government policies of assimilation, it ironically borrowed from the very culture that it imagined destroying. Many Indians saw Wovoka as a messiah figure; the Lakota ambassador Kicking Bear claimed "to have spoken to Christ, who is again upon the earth." Many dancers fell into a trance, which for Lakota would have been familiar from the Sun Dance but also resembled the experience of some varieties of evangelical revivalism. American flags flew above Ghost Dance prayer trees; Sunday became the Ghost Dance Sabbath, and dancers spread the word to other reservations in English, the language of the conqueror now being the common language among the various Indian tribes. In a larger sense, the notion that spiritual power would overcome the unjust powers of this earth and usher in a utopia, and that this utopia will only be available to the oppressed peoples of this world, was entirely familiar to the Christian tradition. This synthesis of religious traditions was not entirely new. As one missionary said of her converts in a revival that preceded the Ghost Dance, "They tell various stories, but so much of the Bible is mixed in that it is hard to separate the old legend from new truths."[49]

This creative blend of Christian and Indian beliefs spread rapidly but un-evenly through the Lakota reservations. Support for the dance was strongest among Sitting Bull's Hunkpapa at Standing Rock and among the Oglala at Pine Ridge, the bastions of opposition to the white cultural assault. It was not clear how much faith Sitting Bull placed in the Ghost Dance, but his home became a center of the dancing and Sitting Bull supported it if for no other reason than it put the "civilization project" on hold. For the same rea-son, because it threatened the progress of assimilation activities, the agent at Sitting Bull's Standing Rock reservation, James McLaughlin, opposed it. He had long been looking for a chance to arrest and remove the stubborn chief who was such an obstacle to his civilizing efforts. With schools closed, crops abandoned, and churches empty because of the Ghost Dance, Sitting Bull took some satisfaction in the spiritual revival while McLaughlin saw it as an opportunity to get rid of the symbol of resistance to his paternalistic assimila-tion plans.

While some whites on the reservation interpreted the Ghost Dance as a religious revival that would fade with time, others worried that it marked the beginning of a new Lakota uprising. Red Cloud predicted that it would "disappear as snow before the heat of the sun," but still the army worried that "frenzy and fanaticism" might lead to "acts of violence."[50] As had happened many times during the Sioux wars, Americans became terrified because they confused a challenge to government authority, which the Ghost Dance move-ment was, with a threat to the lives of white Americans, which the Ghost Dance movement was not. When Pine Ridge Indian agent Daniel Royer, so incompetent that the Lakota nicknamed him "Young Man Afraid of His In-dians," issued an order for the dances to stop, Lakota continued to dance in open defiance. Frightened at the prospect of losing all control, Royer sent a letter to his superiors at the Bureau of Indian Affairs, exaggerating the dan-gers of the situation and informing them that the only remedy was military control. On November 20 Miles ordered five thousand soldiers to occupy the Pine Ridge and Rosebud reservations, making this one of the largest military operations since the Civil War.

The military occupation elevated the fear among the Lakota and hysteria among the whites and so provoked the violence that Miles hoped to avoid. Troops on the reservation ignited still fresh memories of army attacks on vil-lages, so many Ghost Dancers moved away to a rugged badlands plateau of the Pine Ridge reservation known as the Stronghold or "Place of Shelter." Atop a high plateau with only one entrance, the Stronghold made a wonderful spot to defend but certainly was no launching spot for an offensive campaign. The Lakota also added to the Ghost Dance a ceremonial shirt that they believed would make them bulletproof. Even if the Ghost Shirt was defensive only, it gave great confidence to Lakota men and may have made them more willing to risk open confrontation. Newspaper "war" correspondents, including Frederic Remington, hurried to Pine Ridge, anxious to report the impending battle and feeding the rumors that it might happen. Agent McLaughlin at Standing Rock, not wanting to miss the chance to rid himself of his main opponent, ordered the agency's Indian police force to arrest Sitting Bull.

On December 15, just before dawn, the heavily armed Indian police knocked on the door of Sitting Bull's cabin. He awoke, invited them in, dressed himself, and started to leave with them as his supporters gathered around his cabin. Catch-the-Bear, one of Sitting Bull's main supporters, shouted, "Just as we had expected all the time. You think you are going to take him. You shall not!" Sitting Bull's young son, Crow Foot, watched his father dragged out the door and suddenly pleaded, "You always called yourself a brave chief. Now you are allowing yourself to be taken by the Indian police." The father listened to his son, paused, then softly announced, "Then I shall not go."[51] Sitting Bull continued to hesitate as police cajoled and prodded him to move when suddenly Catch-the-Bear pulled his Winchester rifle from under his blanket and shot one of the police. As the policeman fell, he turned and shot Sitting Bull in the chest while Red Tomahawk, the policeman directly behind Sitting Bull, shot him point blank in the head. More shooting erupted as Lakota police and Lakota followers of Sitting Bull battled in close quarters. Mixed with the gunfire was the wailing cry of grief from Sitting Bull's two wives. Fourteen Lakota, including Crow Foot, died that morning. More than that, the architect of the coalition that killed Custer, the symbol of resistance to white cultural and military imperialism, found death at the hands of his own people. In a larger sense, however, U.S. policy and the agents who implemented it were to blame for creating the conditions of Sitting Bull's death, for he had committed no crime and was guilty only of standing as a symbol of resistance to Agent McLaughlin's program of civilization.

After Sitting Bull's death, the army's focus for eliminating the perceived threat of the Ghost Dance turned to Big Foot, who General Miles considered as one of the most threatening of the chiefs. Big Foot had once been prominent in the Ghost Dance but had by this time lost his faith in the movement. He had been invited to the Stronghold not to dance but to exercise his well-known diplomatic abilities to keep the peace. Not knowing this, and thinking that Big Foot was planning to reinforce the dancers, Miles sent out patrols with orders to detain Big Foot and his Miniconjou. On December 28, about 30 miles from the Pine Ridge agency, the Seventh Cavalry intercepted Big Foot and his band of 350 Lakota. Big Foot, stricken with pneumonia, persuaded the Seventh Cavalry of his peaceful intentions and pronounced his willingness to go in army custody to the agency. They camped together near Wounded Knee Creek that night, during which Colonel James Forsyth arrived with reinforcements. In the morning Forsyth surrounded the Lakota and placed two Hotchkiss guns on hills overlooking the field of Lakota tipis. Forsyth's force of over 500 soldiers then proceeded to disarm the 350 Lakota, of whom 230 were women and children.

During the disarmament, confusion led to a melee that led to a massacre. The Lakota voluntarily turned in many guns, but officers suspected correctly that there were more guns in hiding. Yellow Bird, a holy man, performed a Ghost Dance around the soldiers and chanted reminders to the Lakota that their shirts would protect them from bullets. When the soldiers heard this translated for them, they interpreted it as an incitement to resistance. Nerves were tense as soldiers searched for guns hidden in tipis or in individuals' clothing. As soldiers grabbed a rifle from a deaf man, his rifle fired into the air. Yellow Bird threw a handful of dirt into the air, symbolizing the cataclysmic renewal of the earth that Wovoka had promised, and both sides opened fire at close range. Once again, the violence that no one wanted had erupted.

For a few minutes there was fierce close-range fighting as men grappled, shot, stabbed, and clubbed each other. Big Foot rose up from his bed to see the fight and was quickly gunned down in a volley of shots. As the two sides separated, the Hotchkiss guns commenced their deadly work, firing as many as fifty rounds per minute into the Indian encampment. Yellow Bird hid in a tipi and sniped at soldiers until the tipi caught fire and burned him inside. Many women and children sought safety in a nearby ravine where some men joined them as others returned fire as best they could. Mounted soldiers chased the fleeing Lakota as they ran and hid in the ravine. The anthropologist of the Ghost Dance, James Mooney, reported, "The pursuit was simply a massacre, where fleeing women, with infants in their arms, were shot down after resistance had ceased."[52] Some bodies were found miles away from the camp, in the fetal position and with powder burns indicating that they were shot at close range. In less than an hour of shooting, the army lost 25 killed and 29 wounded while the Lakota lost at least 150 dead and another 50 wounded. An unknown number of other Lakota, perhaps as many as one hundred more, died as they sought safety away from camp while a blizzard moved in that afternoon, covering the ground with snow and sending the temperature below zero.

Historians and contemporaries alike have wondered to what extent the massacre could be explained as revenge for Custer's defeat. This was, after all, Custer's old regiment, the Seventh Cavalry, gunning down the Sioux, some of whom had fought at the Little Bighorn. Five of the eight troop commanders and eleven of the nineteen total officers at Wounded Knee fought with Custer. Some participants remembered hearing cries of "Remember Custer" shouted during the battle, and at least one scout recalls an officer saying "We've got our revenge now" during the shooting.[53]

Black Elk, who had taken his first scalp at the Little Bighorn and would later become one of the Lakota's most famous leaders in the twentieth century, was at the Pine Ridge agency when the shooting started and, with many others, rode to the sound of gunfire. When they arrived, he recalled, "what we saw was terrible. Dead and wounded women and children and little babies were scattered all along there where they had been trying to run away. The soldiers had followed along the gulch, as they ran, and murdered them in there. Sometimes they were in heaps because they had huddled together, and some were scattered all along." Later, Black Elk added, "There was a big blizzard, and it grew very cold. The snow drifted deep in the crooked gulch, and it was one long grave of butchered women and children and babies, who had never done any harm and were only trying to run away." But in this last act of violence of the Indian wars, this tragic massacre that punctuated the nation's conquest of native peoples, more than individuals died. According to one version of his words, Black Elk recognized "something else died there in the bloody mud, and was buried in the blizzard. A people's dream died there . . . The nation's hoop is broken and scattered. There is no center any longer, and the sacred tree is dead."[54]

In the immediate aftermath of the Wounded Knee massacre, the Lakota united in rage as four thousand gathered north of the Pine Ridge agency. General Miles mixed diplomacy and force to defuse the situation by sending offers of peace with promises of good treatment even while his overwhelming force moved slowly closer to the Lakota encampment. As the Lakota became convinced that Wounded Knee was not part of a planned slaughter, and as they realized again the futility of resisting the superior numbers and firepower of the army, they began to surrender as they had in 1877, in small family groups and bands. Finally, on January 15, 1891, the Ghost Dance evangelist Kicking Bear surrendered, giving his rifle to General Miles just as he had done in 1877. One week later, General Miles reviewed the troops in a formal ceremony marking the end of hostilities. "It was the grandest demonstration by the army ever seen in the West," one correspondent wrote, and when it was over "the sullen and suspicious" Lakota "were still standing like statues on the crest of the hills."[55] What to the correspondent was a mere stereotype must have been experienced very differently from the Lakota's point of view. During the review ceremony the band played Custer's old favorite, "Garry Owen." Perhaps the Lakota were remembering a hot, dusty day on the Greasy Grass River when they had heard that song before.

As Wovoka knew, in every ending lies the possibility of a new beginning. When the leaders of the Ghost Dance surrendered on January 15, 1891, they expected a jail term or worse. The sentence turned out to be a surprisingly light term of six months, but even that was shortened. By spring the Ghost Dance leaders were released from prison to become members of Buffalo Bill Cody's Wild West show on its European tour. The transformation from shaman to showman was under way.

Another new beginning came on New Year's Day of 1891, three days after the slaughter at Wounded Knee, when seventy-five Oglala led by Dr. Charles Eastman went to the killing fields to search for survivors. Eastman, a Santee Sioux who attended Carlisle Boarding School and Dartmouth College and received his medical degree from Boston University, served as the agency physician. Lakota wailed in grief at the sight of the bodies, some caked in blood, others frozen into contorted positions as if stopped in mid-action. Miraculously, Eastman found five adults and two children who survived the carnage and the three days of blizzard that followed. One of the survivors was only four months old, found under a pile of snow lying next to her dead mother. The baby was wrapped in a blanket, with a cap on her head that was embroidered with beadwork in the pattern of the American flag. "All of this," Eastman lamented, "was a severe ordeal for one who had so lately put all his faith in the Christian love and lofty ideals of the white man."[56] Yet persevere Eastman did, and during the twentieth century he became a leading Sioux intellectual, one of those who found in the tragedy of the Indian wars not only death but the spark of new life for his people.

Black Elk also found new hope for his people in the aftermath of Wounded Knee. Although he is most famous for his sentiment that the "nation's hoop is broken," his life reflected anything but hopelessness. After Wounded Knee, he was baptized into the Catholic Church and searched for spiritual unity in the Christian and Lakota traditions that he hoped would revitalize his people. He struggled to use his "spirit powers" to "bring my people out of the black road into the red road." This road would combine the Christian God with the *Wakan Tanka*, the Great Mystery, to find a spiritual way for the people not just to survive but also to prosper. In his words to John Neihardt, his white interviewer, "what I really wanted to do is for us to make that tree bloom. On this tree we shall prosper. Therefore my children and yours are relative-like and therefore we shall go back into the hoop and here we'll cooperate and stand as one."[57]

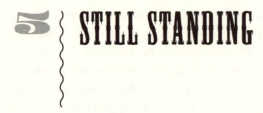

5 { STILL STANDING

It has the power of endless argument, one of the world's battles destined to
be fought forever. NORMAN MACLEAN

IN EARLY June of 1876, as the army was still moving its forces into
position for what would become Custer's final battle, Buffalo Bill Cody announced to an audience in Wilmington, Delaware, that he was leaving the
stage in order to take a role in the Great Sioux War. For several years Cody
had alternated periods of acting in the East with episodes of adventure in the
West, each time renewing the authenticity of his credentials. The Great Sioux
War offered an irresistible opportunity for Cody to enhance his reputation as
a genuine adventure hero even as he performed a real service as a scout for
the army. At General Crook's request, Cody joined the Fifth Cavalry and was
with them in southern Wyoming on July 7 when they learned the news of
Custer's defeat. Cody instantly perceived that the nation had in Custer a new
martyr, a figure who would stand in death as a symbol inspiring the nation's
destiny to conquer the West.

Ten days later Cody had the opportunity to link himself permanently with
the nation's most recent battlefield hero. As the Fifth Cavalry moved north
to join Crook, Colonel Wesley Merritt, now commanding the Fifth, received
word that a large group of Cheyenne warriors had left the reservation and
were on their way to join Sitting Bull's camp. Riding hard and fast, Merritt's
Fifth Cavalry intercepted the eight hundred Cheyenne on July 17 and forced
them to return to the reservation. Cody provided the day's most dramatic
event when he met a lone Cheyenne warrior named Yellow Hair in a fight

whose details are still sketchy. As the two met each other—unexpectedly some sources say—they both fired and missed. Cody's bullet killed Yellow Hair's horse even as Cody's horse stepped in a prairie dog hole and collapsed. Quickly, Cody pulled himself from his fallen horse, knelt, and fired at the charging Cheyenne, this time making sure to hit his target. Cody ran to Yellow Hair's dead body and, as he told it, "scientifically scalped him in about five seconds." Then, as the Fifth Cavalry rode to the scene in pursuit of other Cheyenne warriors, Cody raised his war trophy and shouted, *"The first scalp for Custer!"*[1]

In the coming months and years, Cody transformed this actual historical event—a small part in a minor skirmish—into a vital scene in the popular understanding of the mythic West. Anticipating an encounter worthy of the stage, Cody had dressed for battle that day not in his buckskins but in his theatre garb, "a Mexican costume of black velvet, slashed with scarlet and trimmed with silver buttons and lace."[2] He kept the trophies earned from this fight, including Yellow Hair's warbonnet, shield, gun, and the scalp itself, and sent them east for display. In years to come, Yellow Hair's scalp became Cody's badge of authenticity and a possession so valued that Cody kept the severed hair in the private safe in his railcar. By autumn Cody was touring eastern cities, inventing the Wild West each night to thrilled audiences. "The Red Right Hand; or, The First Scalp for Custer," in which Cody's exploit was portrayed as a duel to the death, became a signature act for his shows. Despite the narrative embellishments, Cody added authenticity by dressing in the same black velvet costume and displaying the actual trophies from his real fight, including Yellow Hair's scalp. When Indian sympathizers in Boston banned the scalping scene as barbaric, this merely fanned the sensationalism and the show's popularity increased. Cody had staged the original event, or at least the first telling of it, so carefully that the theatrical version was realistic, just as the original event was theatrical.

It is a commonplace that fiction imitates reality, but this went further. Cody framed real-life events so that they could be performed on stage, just as he incorporated uniforms and artifacts in his stage performances. The real was staged, and the staged was real. This claim of authenticity gave him a clear advantage over rival showmen and helped make his version of the western experience the most influential in the nation and in Europe. In Buffalo Bill's show, the historical blended seamlessly into the mythical because every scene in the story had a real component, however contrived the original might have been. Buffalo Bill's autobiography enhanced his reputation for authenticity even as it embellished his life's story. In that version, Yellow Hair (whom Cody promoted to war chief for purposes of the story) initiated the duel by taunting Cody, "I know you, *Pa-he-haska*; if you want to fight, come ahead and fight me." The duel with Yellow Hair was settled not with bullets but with a more dramatic knife fight, making the final scalping more in keeping. Never mind that the added elements could not have been true. Cody did not have any previous experience that would have allowed these Cheyenne to recognize him, and, in fact, he did not speak Cheyenne to have understood such a taunt. Nevertheless, this story, along with a woodcut of Cody holding Yellow Hair's scalp and warbonnet in his raised hand, became the climax of his autobiography. A print of this woodcut, with Cody standing over the dead Indian with a knife in one hand and a bloody scalp in the other, became for years the most widely recognized icon of the Wild West show.[3]

His autobiography and each performance of the Wild West show closely linked Cody to Custer, the heroic defender of American conquest in the West. Although Cody had only limited acquaintance with the living Custer, on the stage he closely linked himself with the mythological hero of the "last stand." By "scientifically" taking the "first scalp for Custer," Cody established a persona as Custer's avenging angel who adopted the ferocity of the Indians without fully crossing over into savagery. Cody hitched his horse to Custer's, and together they rode into the nation's mythological consciousness. Every night and on every stage, Cody helped Americans believe that Custer died a noble death, that his "last stand" was a sacrifice that breathed new meaning into the nation's frontier destiny. In Custer's case, the myths did not rise as embellishments to the historical story; rather, the mythological version so fully saturated the actual historical events that it is hard to imagine one without the other.

Interpreting History, Inventing Myth

Custer's luck abandoned him on June 25, 1876, on the hills above the Little Bighorn River, but only in the literal sense. For the purposes of mythology, Custer retained his luck for a remarkably long and vigorous afterlife. The place of his death, on a river whose very name suggests paradox, and the timing of his death, as the nation struggled in its centennial year to reconcile industrial progress with republican ideals, ensured that the charisma and controversy that had marked his life would follow him in death. As a famous Indian fighter, he symbolized both nostalgia and progress, both the longing for the purity of earlier times when individualism reigned supreme and the ambition for material advancement. Custer's life was a tribute to the colorful individual and paradoxically to the power of the undifferentiated masses that filled the ranks of the army. The "Fighting Seventh" was widely regarded as the nation's elite Indian fighters not because of the abilities of its soldiers but because of the reputation of its leader, just as large corporations emerged at the time not, it was thought, because of the skill of the workers but because of the efficiency and leadership imposed by management. In an age of Carnegie and Rockefeller, Custer represented the power of the army machine, still led by the indestructible and invaluable individual. His spectacular death meant that all that had followed him in life would be magnified in his mythical afterlife.

The contours of the mythical Custer assumed their outline within weeks of his death, although the exact shape of the myth would take decades to fill out and would demonstrate a remarkable ability to morph into novel forms. Almost universally, the first response to the news of Custer's demise was stunned disbelief. More than a century later, many students of the battle still work from the premise that Custer could lose the battle not because the Indians won it, but only because something went wrong. They search the battlefield records for evidence of jammed weapons, flawed decisions, faulty intelligence, or alcohol-induced cowardice. Then as now, the essential enigma remains: how could the "Fighting Seventh," the proud representatives of an emerging world power, lose to a band of "savages" who lived in tipis and followed the buffalo? People experienced a deep longing to know what really happened, and all sorts of answers rushed to fill the void. Even as people filled the historical gap with mythological answers, they expressed a certainty that Custer had resisted bravely and so died a sacrificial death that ennobled his country and the cause of western expansion.

The mythmaking began in General Terry's initial battlefield reports. Two days after the battle, with a hillside of corpses fresh in his memory, General Terry composed the first written version of Custer's defeat in the form of a report to his commanding officer, General Philip Sheridan. He explained, in a passive voice that assigned no blame, how "a great disaster overtook General Custer and the troops under his command." Terry narrated the events of Custer's pursuit and attack of the Sioux and Cheyenne village, as he understood it, with details of the movements of the troops under Major Reno and Captain Benteen who had survived the hilltop siege. Then he added the elements of the story that have created intrigue and caused debate ever since. "Of the movements of General Custer and the five companies under his command scarcely anything is known," Terry wrote, "for no officer or soldier who accompanied him has yet been found alive." Yet, despite this lack of survivors to testify, Terry concluded, "there is abundant evidence that a gallant resistance was offered by the troops" as they were "beset on all sides by overpowering numbers." Here in this brief report, written two days after the battle, were the themes that later generations would elaborate on in great detail: the mystery of Custer's troop movements and intentions, combined with the paradoxical certainty that Custer died a brave death fighting heroically against swarming hordes of Indians. Five days later Terry wrote a second report, intended to be read only by Sheridan and Sherman, that defended his own plan and blamed Custer for ignoring orders and rushing to attack before Gibbon's and Terry's forces were in place. "Had the attack been deferred," Terry wrote self-servingly, "I cannot doubt that we should have been successful."[4] Thus, within one week of the battle, Terry narrated a factual account as far as he could, transformed the incomplete history of a lost battle into the myth of a last stand, and finally revised that history to assign blame and account for defeat.

The first reports of the battle to reach the East, however, came not from official army channels but from journalists. Based on scanty factual details carried overland by scouts and then telegraphed eastward, newspapers told a lurid story of how Custer and his men had all been killed. "MASSACRE," screamed the headline of the *Bismarck Tribune*, and the title stuck. Lack of evidence did not stop the paper from adding sensationally that the dead were mutilated and "victims captured alive and tortured in a most fiendish manner."[5] General Sherman, attending the nation's Centennial Exhibition in Philadelphia, was busy explaining to a reporter that these early reports were typical frontier rumors not to be believed. "It seems almost too terrible to be entirely true. It must be exaggerated," he explained. "I cannot believe that Custer and his command would be swept away. I don't think there were enough Indians there to do it like that."[6] Moments later he received a telegram with news from Terry confirming Custer's death. The unthinkable was true after all. For two days the telegraph operator in Bismarck maintained a marathon session of sending details of the battle eastward through the wires, but reporters simply invented as necessary to fill in its mythological shape. In an ironic twist, Terry's second report reached Sheridan and Sherman before the first one, and then it was accidentally given to the press. In the chaos of emerging and conflicting stories, the public and the generals learned at almost the same time that Custer was both a hero and perhaps a bungler. The public arguments, fueled more by acrimony than information, were about to begin.

The *New York Herald*, an expansionist Democratic newspaper whose editors fancied Custer and had earlier dubbed him the "Boy General with the Golden Locks," now cast his death in heroic terms. In a battle description drawn straight from the imagination, the *Herald* placed the battle in a familiar cultural heritage:

> In that mad charge up the narrow ravine, with the rocks above raining down lead upon the fated three hundred, with fire spouting from every bush ahead, with the wild, swarming horsemen circling along the heights like shrieking vultures waiting for the moment to sweep down and finish the bloody tale, every form, from private to general, rises to heroic size . . . They died as grandly as Homer's demigods . . . "Theirs not to reason why / Theirs but to do or die." Success was beyond their grasp so they died— to a man.[7]

In this brief space the newspaper described the battle using the fictional elements of a western adventure story, elevated the Seventh Cavalry to ancient Greek demigods, compared their downfall to the "fated three hundred" Spartans who gave their lives protecting their home from Persian invaders, characterized the Indians as less than human predatory animals, and alluded to Alfred, Lord Tennyson's "Charge of the Light Brigade." In a later editorial, the *Herald* described Custer as a medieval knight of Christendom, whose "name will be respected whenever chivalry is applauded and civilization battles against barbarism." Just in case anyone missed the point, another editorial compared Custer's "hill of death" to Golgotha, the hill where Jesus was crucified.[8]

Journalists were also quick to use Custer's death to further their political agendas. The *Herald*, a long-time opponent of the Grant administration, argued that the "peace policy of General Grant" had killed Custer because it "feeds, clothes, and takes care of their noncombatant force while the men are killing our troops." It also ranted against "That nest of thieves, the Indian Bureau, with its thieving agents and favorites as Indian traders, and its mock humanity and pretence of piety—that is what killed Custer."[9] The *Herald* also linked Custer's war against the "savage" Indians with the nation's struggle to establish control over the nation's other "dangerous classes," notably Southern blacks and immigrants. For the editors at this New York City newspaper, Custer's death represented a lesson in the folly of placating "savages" of all sorts, be they Indians, freed blacks, or foreign workers. The political meaning of the Little Bighorn, the paper insisted, was that the "dangerous classes" must be managed with a firm hand of military discipline rather than the soft philanthropy of well-intentioned idealism. For their part, Southern newspapers agreed that Grant was to blame for the debacle and urged the government to relieve its troops of Reconstruction duty in the South in order to send them west to face the Indian menace. Western newspapers welcomed the call for additional troops and called for revenge against Custer's killers. In response, the aging abolitionist Wendell Phillips queried, "What kind of a war is it, where if we kill the enemy it is death; if he kills us it is a massacre?"[10]

Custer's military reputation had been controversial in life, and it remained so in his afterlife. Colonel Samuel Sturgis, the commanding officer of the Seventh Cavalry whose son was among those who died at the Little Bighorn, described Custer as "a brave man, but also a very selfish man" who was "insanely ambitious of glory" as well as "tyrannical with no regard for the soldiers under him." Based on Terry's second report, Sturgis charged that Custer "made his attack recklessly, earlier by thirty-six hours than he should have done, and with men tired out from forced marches." Other officers privately seconded Sturgis's opinion, believing that Custer had disobeyed orders, rushed into combat without proper reconnaissance, and sacrificed the lives of his solders for the sake of his own vain pride. The harshest judgment of all came from the nation's general-in-chief, President Grant, who confided in a newspaper interview, "I regard Custer's massacre as a sacrifice of troops, brought on by Custer himself, that was wholly unnecessary—wholly unnecessary." Custer was not without friends in the military, however, as demonstrated by Custer's West Point friend and Civil War opponent General Thomas Rosser, who excused Custer from responsibility and instead blamed Major Reno, who, Rosser charged, "took to the hills, and abandoned Custer and his gallant comrades to their fate."[11] Here in the summer of 1876 were the central claims for arguments that would occupy military historians and battlefield buffs for over a century.

While the military arguments kindled a certain kind of fire that would keep Custer's reputation burning, charred perhaps but still creating both heat and light, other mythmakers ensured that the nation's need for heroes in a centennial year would produce nothing less than Custer as a martyr for Manifest Destiny. As the nation pondered whether industrial progress might erode the republican values of a simpler age, Custer symbolized the persistence of the old values of courage, duty, and self-sacrifice into the present. "Long after this generation has passed away," the *New York Herald* predicted, "the name of Custer and the story of his deeds will be fresh in men's memories. The story that comes to us today with so much horror, with so much pathos, will become a part of our national life."[12] In Custer's hometown of Monroe, Michigan, with the grieving Elizabeth Custer in attendance, the minister preached a sermon locating Armstrong in the pantheon of ancient, biblical, and modern heroes whose "countrymen will vindicate his honor." As the Spartans at Thermopylae or the Texans at the Alamo, Custer had courageously resisted the multitudes of bloodthirsty barbarians who stood in opposition to the long progress of civilization from ancient Greece to its highest form in the shape of the American republic.[13]

Poets joined the rush to place Custer in the nation's procession of heroes. Within hours of reading about the Little Bighorn, Walt Whitman composed "Death-Sonnet for Custer" and rushed it to the *New York Tribune* for publication. With poetic disregard for factual accuracy, the poet of American democracy invented a heroic picture of "the tawny hair flowing in battle" while "bearing a bright sword in thy hand," even though Custer had cut his hair for this campaign and the sabers had long been left behind. But details mattered less than Whitman's ability to capture the national mood that longed for assurances that self-sacrifice and duty to country still survived in an era of selfish materialism. "Desperate and glorious, aye in defeat most desperate, most glorious," Whitman wrote of Custer, "Leaving behind thee a memory sweet to soldiers, / Thou yieldest up thyself." In Whitman's poetry, Custer represented in an almost Christlike way the highest value of Christian suffering for the sake of national redemption. John Greenleaf Whittier, Henry Wadsworth Longfellow, and over 150 lesser-known poets joined in penning tributes to Custer, making the Little Bighorn one of the most enduring historical images in popular American poetry.

The same visual appeal of the heroic warrior making his "last stand" that made Custer popular in poetry also made him irresistible for painters and illustrators, who produced no less than two thousand depictions of Custer's final moments. As with the poets, imagination and national yearning for heroes filled in for factual accuracy. Part of the appeal of the subject might have been the fact that there were no survivors among Custer's men and therefore no one who could limit an artist's style by insisting on an accurate portrayal. The most critically acclaimed painting was John Mulvaney's *Custer's Last Rally*, completed in 1881 after two years of research. Painted in oil on a 20-by-11-foot canvas, the painting created considerable interest as it toured the nation's art galleries. The most famous comment came from Walt Whitman, who studied the painting for an hour while it was on display in New York and then described what he saw as "painfully real." Custer and his officers, Whitman said, stood "in full finish and detail, life-size" while facing "swarms upon swarms of savage Sioux, in their war-bonnets, frantic, mostly on ponies, driving through the background, through the smoke, like a hurricane of demons." There was, he concluded, "nothing in the books like it, nothing in Homer, nothing in Shakespeare; more grim and sublime than either, all native, all our own, and all a fact." The painting represented, Whitman claimed, an "artistic expression for our land and people" that exemplified a moment in American history that stood out as unique in the history of nations.[14]

The most widely reproduced painting of Custer, however, may in some ways have an even better claim to representing vintage American values. In 1895 the Anheuser-Busch brewing company commissioned Otto Becker to make a lithograph copy of an older painting by Cassilly Adams entitled *Custer's Last Fight*. The resulting lithograph, perhaps the most influential image of Custer's last moments, featured Custer in the center of the frame, sword held high, surrounded by a landscape of chaos and corpses, standing ready to strike the first Indian who might approach. The brewing company issued two hundred thousand copies of the lithograph and distributed them to saloons across the country to promote Budweiser beer. Although art critics considered it hopelessly lowbrow and historians denigrated it for its many liberties with the facts, the Becker lithograph entered popular culture as a nostalgic picture of manly defiance in the face of overwhelming odds, an image that held irresistible appeal in the masculine world of the saloon. So important was this image of Custer that Budweiser has been called "the beer that made the Seventh famous."[15] There was a certain irony in the teetotaling Custer being used to sell beer, but it was an irony that Custer might have appreciated. After all, he always did have an eye out for ways to make a little money.

The first person to elevate Custer's life story to mythical status was the dime novelist Frederick Whitaker. A fervent admirer of Custer during his life, Whitaker immediately recognized Custer's death as an opportunity to present a hero's story to the public. After securing Libbie Custer's blessing, he cranked out in six months *A Complete Life of Gen. George A. Custer*, the first major biography of the martyred hero. The 648-page turgid tome included many falsehoods taken from newspaper reports, as well as large sections copied directly from Custer's *My Life on the Plains*. Glaring inaccuracies aside, the book became source material for subsequent writers of history, boys' adventure stories, and other popular publications of the Custer myth. Whitaker's Custer was part James Fenimore Cooper's frontier protagonist and part Horatio Alger's rags-to-riches hero. Like Cooper's characters, Whitaker's Custer was impatient with his formal schooling but learned wisdom and morality from the school of nature on the frontier. He identified with his Indian antagonists; indeed, Whitaker wrote that as a boy Custer's senses were "as sharp as those of an Indian even then." The story of Custer as a western hero was also, Whitaker claimed, "the life of a great man, one of the few really great men that America has produced." He began "at the foot of the social ladder" and "rose to the top" because of his "wonderful capacity for hard and energetic work, and a rapidity of intuition which is seldom found apart from military genius of the highest order."[16]

For all of its obvious fictional elements, *A Complete Life of Gen. George A. Custer* became the standard that established the contours of the story for years to follow. One popular history in the Whitaker mold described Custer's last moments as follows: "He is the last to succumb to death, and dies, too, with the glory of accomplished duty in his conscience and the benediction of a grateful country on his head." Whitaker's narrative also established a series of villains who were responsible for Custer's death. In a pattern that proved influential for decades, Whitaker blamed Grant for abusing his authority by his mean-spirited punishment of Custer, Benteen for disobeying orders by not returning hastily at Custer's request, and Reno for cowardice by abandoning the fight on the valley floor. Reno, upset at what he considered this aspersion on his character, asked for an official court of enquiry to clear his name. The court's tepid conclusion that Reno made mistakes but bore no official guilt for his role in the battle satisfied no one and left Whitaker's accusations to stand for generations of historical sleuths to debate.

Whitaker's most important fiction for the Custer myth was his description of the last stand. As Custer was about to be "overwhelmed," the Crow scout Curly found him and offered him a way to escape. Custer rejected the offer, wrote Whitaker, because he knew that death with his "little band of heroes" was "worth the lives of all the general officers in the world . . . He weighed, in that brief moment of reflection, all the consequences to America of the lesson of life and the lesson of heroic death, and he chose death." In choosing a redemptive death, Whitaker's Custer became a Christlike figure who died in order to give new meaning to American values. Whitaker's Custer, "the brave cavalier, the Christian soldier," suffered a death redeemed only by the greater cause of American Manifest Destiny.[17] It was perhaps only a matter of time until Indians inverted this mythological notion into a bumper sticker and the title of Vine Deloria's classic 1969 manifesto, *Custer Died for Your Sins.*

Hovering over all of this mythmaking in the first generation after the Little Bighorn was the sprightly figure of Elizabeth Custer, the grieving widow of the Boy General. Only thirty-four years old when her husband died, she spent the remaining fifty-seven years of her life dedicated to cultivating the image of her "husband as he should be known." Widely admired for her beauty, charm, and modesty, Libbie Custer came to personify the Victorian ideal of feminine loyalty. She assisted Frederick Whitaker with his hagiographic biography of her husband, and in return he wrote of her relationship with the famous general, "Finding him good, she left him perfect, and her sweet and gracious influence can be traced in all his after life." Behind the scenes the grieving widow used her influence to encourage writers to portray her husband in a positive light, while in public she authored three books that silenced his critics and elevated his claim to greatness. Her direct and modest style gave a voice of integrity to their life together that one reviewer called the true "Custer memorial" and another cited as an example of "noble Christian manhood and womanhood." Although she never visited the battlefield where her husband died, she supported the monument there and advocated for establishing a museum on the spot, something that did not happen until after her death.

While she lived, she shaped the public memory of her husband and inhibited those who might criticize the nation's favorite Indian fighter. One insider observed that Elizabeth was "so beloved in the army" that "by a sort of common consent" any of Custer's "misdeeds were not given much publicity." Other participants and would-be historians of the battle held Libbie in such high regard that they refused to state publicly their private criticisms of the hero of the Little Bighorn. Theodore Goldin, a soldier who served with Major Reno at the Little Bighorn, wrote in 1928, fifty-two years after the battle, that "every man's heart bled" for the still grieving widow and that "alone" was "responsible for the suppression of a lot of matters that may throw a clearer light on the campaign." Whatever truth there was to this informal conspiracy of polite silence, Libbie had the last word by outliving almost all of the Seventh Cavalry battle veterans. If they had secrets, those secrets died when they did. In 1933, four days shy of her ninety-first birthday, Elizabeth Custer died. But in the many decades after her husband's death she fulfilled her life's ambition, to ensure that "tradition and history will be so mingled that no one will be able to separate them."[18]

Staging Indians, Becoming Americans

Custer was not the only person who grew larger in death than he had been in life. Mythological symmetry demanded that Custer have a worthy adversary, that the agent of civilization in the West should have a foe who symbolized the savage opposition to progress. In the fancies of the white imagination, the legend of Sitting Bull grew to fill that need. White authorities had always wanted a single head chief who could speak for all of the Sioux; after the Little Bighorn, Sitting Bull came to embody for the dominant culture all that was savage and all that was noble in Lakota culture. In the immediate aftermath of the battle, the public vilified Sitting Bull as the mastermind of Custer's destruction. Searching for explanations as to how a band of primitive Indians could defeat a modern army, newspapers fabricated stories that "racial renegades" must have in some way assisted the Lakota alliance. One story told how French-Canadian Jesuits had educated Sitting Bull, including special training in Napoleonic tactics. For some he became the "Sioux Napoleon."[19] Others claimed that white frontiersmen who had married into Indian society, the so-called squaw men, had advised the Lakota in military tactics. One popular variation of this story asserted that ex-Confederate outlaws became Sitting Bull's special military advisors. Another rumor insisted that Sitting Bull was the disguise for a disgruntled student who had left West Point in disgrace and vowed revenge. The only common thread was a steadfast refusal to believe that Lakota and Cheyenne warriors had defeated the "Fighting Seventh," the regiment with the reputation as army's premier Indian fighters.

In time, as the furies of vengeance faded along with the unfounded rumors, mainstream society began to idealize Sitting Bull less for his military prowess and more as a prime exemplar of indigenous nobility. From his Canadian exile, Sitting Bull began to intuit the possibilities of exploiting American society's curiosity about his role in Custer's defeat and the public fascination with the Plains Indians as the last of the "noble savages." Interviewed by journalists looking for clues to Custer's defeat, Sitting Bull disavowed any personal knowledge of Custer and downplayed his role in the battle. Reporters who traveled to Canada to interview Sitting Bull fed the growing impression that his name was synonymous with Lakota resistance, and that Sitting Bull stood as the single repository of Indian cultural stereotypes just as Custer symbolized the heroism of white society. In his most expansive interview, Sitting Bull addressed the perception that he had killed Custer. "It is a lie," he said. "We did not go outside of our own country to seek them. They came to us, on our own land and would surely have trampled down and slain our women and children."[20]

By the time Sitting Bull returned from Canada, some Lakota were already experimenting with the possibilities of profiting from the white society's fascination with Indian culture. Throughout the western frontier, soldiers and civilians had often flocked to watch Indians perform traditional dances. When the Seventh Cavalry returned from their battle on the Washita, the entire fort turned out to watch as Custer's Osage scouts performed a scalp dance late into the night. For years the major break from the monotony of life at remote outposts such as Fort Laramie or Fort Robinson was the opportunity to attend the spectacle of Plains Indian dancing. In 1874 a group of Lakota dancers charged admission at a Nebraska event, and by 1877 some Lakota who had only months before fought against the army were now charging white photographers six dollars each for taking their picture.

As Cody recruited Lakota performers beginning in 1877, he became aware that their presence lent credibility to his reputation for authenticity, and they quickly became the main attraction for his show. But even as the Lakota drew crowds, they also refused to perform humiliating roles, forcing Cody to reinterpret his own exploits as Indian fighter. Instead of highlighting his Indian-killing ways, Cody began to emphasize stories with a different plot line:

noble Indians who only wanted to protect their lands but were victimized by villainous Indian agents and a few "bad Indians," usually played on the stage by white actors. By the middle of the 1880s, Cody presented a more respectful attitude toward Indians. "In nine times out of ten," Cody announced, "where there is trouble between white men and Indians, it will be found that the white man is responsible." By 1885, the year when Sitting Bull performed with the Wild West show, Cody almost seemed to have changed loyalties about which side was right in the 1876 centennial campaign. When once he had claimed to have taken "the first scalp for Custer," now he described the war as a justifiable defense of Lakota homelands: "Their lands were invaded by the gold seekers, and when the U.S. government failed to protect them they thought it was time to do it themselves."[21]

Yet even as Lakota actors forced plot lines to twist in their favor, the central theme of Cody's show remained racial conflict—the inevitable conquest of "savage" societies by white civilization. For years his signature act was "Attack on Settler's Cabin," featuring an apparently vicious assault on an innocent white family by bloodthirsty Indians (played by white actors). Night after night only the timely arrival of Buffalo Bill himself saved the white woman from the dreaded fate of Indian captivity. Cody's ambivalence about the place of Indians in America's westward advance was widely shared in many factions of society. The irony in Cody's case was that his story was about the ineluctable march of American civilization westward, which most Americans believed would necessitate the end of Indian societies. Yet what gave Cody's stage story its punch, its drawing power, was the very real presence of precisely the same Indians who were supposed to be disappearing. And the Indian who did the most to legitimate Buffalo Bill's version of the Wild West, the one who made his show more authentic than rival shows, was the most famous Indian of them all.

Sitting Bull had explored his stage potential before he met Cody. Upon his return from Canada in 1881, his captors took him to Bismarck, where he was greeted as something of a celebrity. The great war chief dined at the best hotel in town and smiled as he tasted ice cream for the first time. Journalists requested an interview with him, and crowds followed him around town. While in Canada he had learned to write his name, and now he signed autographs, charging a dollar for men but free for women. In 1883 the man who had made war against the construction of the railroad through his homeland now rode the train to Bismarck to appear at the head of an Indian delegation in a parade. Again he sold autographs, this time for up to two dollars each. Sitting Bull also agreed with Bismarck photographer Orlando Goff to sit for two photographs for the fee of 50 dollars. Although he did not like the results—he said the lighting made his face look too white—he did demonstrate a shrewd understanding of the value of his image.

The following year Sitting Bull visited St. Paul, Minnesota, where the newspaper called him the "most famous Indian now alive."[22] In the state from which his Santee relatives had been driven two decades earlier, he sold autographs, gave interviews, and generated remarkable interest as he toured the sights of the Twin Cities. A St. Paul hotel operator and showman approached Sitting Bull's Indian agent, James McLaughlin, about the prospect of sending Sitting Bull on a tour of eastern cities. Giving a whole new meaning to the term "Indian agent," McLaughlin agreed to allow Sitting Bull to go on tour because he recognized, "There is money to be made in this if properly managed."[23] Sitting Bull agreed to the trip when he was told that he would visit major cities and get to meet with the president. Accompanied by his wives and five other Lakota, as well as an interpreter and a manager, the "Sitting Bull Combination" toured eastern cities in the fall of 1884. In New York the show drew six thousand people on the first day and packed the house for two weeks. On stage Sitting Bull lectured while the other Lakota cooked and smoked, all wearing their traditional clothing. After Sitting Bull spoke, the interpreter translated Sitting Bull's speech for the audience.

One evening in Philadelphia Luther Standing Bear, a Lakota youth who was studying at the nearby Carlisle School, attended the program. He thought it fanciful to see the newspaper advertise the show as presenting "the Indian who killed Custer," for Standing Bear knew what had happened at the Little Bighorn. Fluent in English and Lakota, he listened carefully as Sitting Bull explained Lakota customs and expressed a desire to see his children educated and living in peace with the whites. Standing Bear was naturally quite astonished when the "translator" then narrated a lurid tale of Sitting Bull's actions during the "Custer massacre" when the Lakota "had swooped down on Custer and wiped his soldiers all out." As Standing Bear remembered, the translator "told so many lies that I had to smile."[24] After the show when Standing Bear told Sitting Bull of the translator's trick, Sitting Bull abruptly ended that phase of his experience in mutual cultural tourism.

Less than a year later, however, Sitting Bull joined Buffalo Bill, and together they made the Wild West show the most popular entertainment of the

day. In the early 1880s, as Cody put together the elements for his grand spectacle that eventually required over fifty railroad cars for over four hundred
employees and the horses, buffalo, elk, and equipment that traveled with the
show, he wrote to his business partner, "I am going to try hard to get Sitting
Bull. If we can manage to get him our lasting fortune is made."[25] Standing
Rock Indian agent McLaughlin was reluctant to let Sitting Bull leave the reservation this time, but he relented when General Sherman approved of the
trip: "Sitting Bull is a humbug but has a popular fame on which he has a
natural right to 'bank.' "[26] The standard wage for performers in Cody's show
was twenty-five dollars per month, but Sitting Bull negotiated a contract
that paid him fifty dollars per week, as well as a signing bonus of 125 dollars
paid in advance. The contract also specified that he retained exclusive rights
to sell his own photographs and autographs. Sitting Bull became the main
attraction for the Wild West show in 1885 and came to regard Cody as his
friend. With the program calling him the "Napoleon of the Indian Race," Sitting Bull's name usually appeared just below Cody's in the show's publicity.
He did not act in any of the show's dramatic productions, but merely rode
into the arena, appearing for the audience as the personification of the stoic
Indian, the defeated but still noble savage. After the show he greeted visitors, talked while they ate barbecue at special events, and sold his autograph
and photos. He even sold his pipe bag several times, apparently being sure to
always have a spare. He became special friends with Annie Oakley, who he
dubbed "Little Sure Shot" and adopted into his family. One popular publicity
poster showed a photo of him shaking hands with Cody above the caption
"Foes in '76, Friends in '85."[27]

As much as Sitting Bull seemed to like elements of the show business life,
he remained unimpressed with the society he encountered in eastern cities.
When he wandered city streets to meet people and view the sights, he usually received a polite reception, yet the perception that he was the "killer of
Custer" remained near the surface. When a reporter asked him "if he ever
had any regret for his share in the Custer massacre," Sitting Bull shot back, "I
did not murder Custer; it was a fight in open day. He would have killed me if
he could. I have answered to my people for the dead on my side, let Custer's
friends answer to his people for the dead on his side."[28] Although whites often thought that visiting eastern cities would impress Plains Indians with the
superiority of American society, Sitting Bull learned instead new criticisms of
the society he had resisted for so long. Whites had long judged Indian society

for treating women as mere worker drones, but Sitting Bull mocked white society for its treatment of women. "The Whitemen loved their whores more than their wives," he argued, because they "dressed them better" and treated them with more affection. He also rebuked whites for being "so odored with whiskey" that it will take "hundreds of years before the winds and storms will purify" the white soul so that people "in the other life can endure the smell of it there."[29]

Most of all, Sitting Bull criticized American society for the way it valued money. "The eagle sits upon money," he noted, "and money rules over the people."[30] Another time Sitting Bull remarked, "The white man knows how to make everything, but he does not know how to distribute it."[31] Despite all of his earnings during his time with the Wild West show, he returned home without much money. He simply could not understand how a wealthy society could allow its children to live in poverty, and he could not say no to the many children on the streets who asked him for money. When he returned to Standing Rock, he sponsored feasts and dispersed the rest among the needy in his tribe. By the end of the winter he had no money left. Sitting Bull's Lakota culture had taught him that a chief does not accumulate wealth but redistributes it, and Sitting Bull was more interested in giving away money to enhance his status as chief than in building up his own fortune. Agent McLaughlin refused to allow Sitting Bull to participate again in Cody's show, claiming that he did not make "good use of the money he thus earns, but on the contrary spends it extravagantly among the Indians to perpetuate baneful influences," that is, to resist McLaughlin's assimilation program.[32] Show business had taught Sitting Bull how to make money in white society, but he was never a capitalist; he merely wanted to disperse the income as he would have dispersed ponies or surplus from the hunt in previous times—to bolster his status and enhance the welfare of the people.

Beginning in 1877 Cody's shows concluded *The Drama of Civilization* with a stirring re-enactment of "Custer's Last Stand." In many years Cody could truthfully advertise that "Custer's Last Stand" included actual Lakota battle participants, a claim that bolstered the appearance of authenticity in the show. Set against the backdrop of a large painting of the Little Bighorn valley, Custer's troops set off in search of Indians. When a scout discovers Sitting Bull's village, the bugle announces the soldiers' charge while the Indians prepare an ambush. Waving his sword, Custer "rides down upon the Indian village like a cyclone." As he and his men are surrounded, the Indians overwhelm them in ferocious combat. Finally, "Custer is the last man killed, and he dies after performing prodigies of valor." After a brief silence that allowed the audience to have the field of carnage fixed in memory, Cody rode into the arena as the words "Too Late" were projected onto the background.[33]

Despite its historical inaccuracies, reviewers praised the scene for its authenticity. Cody was hundreds of miles away and could have done nothing to help Custer in any case. There was no ambush, nor any evidence identifying who was the last man killed. Nevertheless, Cody's nightly portrayals of "Custer's Last Stand" helped to make this battle the most frequently reproduced scene in American history, and Cody's version became the visual standard for artists, historians, and moviemakers for years to come. "Those who had 'been thar' said it was a faithful representation," one critic wrote, while another found "Custer's Last Stand" so realistic that from the grandstands one could imagine "that he was on the plains within eyeshot of the spot where Gen. Custer made his last charge . . . It was a scene long to be remembered, so vividly were the minutest details portrayed of the slaughter of those brave men who were with Custer in his last charge."[34] Ironically, it was the presence of Lakota who had actually helped to kill Custer that allowed white audiences to feel as if they were watching the real thing.

In arriving on the scene only barely "too late," Cody helped to hitch his star to the glowing memory of Custer. Cody's earlier performance of his duel with Yellow Hair, in which he takes "the first scalp for Custer," had established him as the first avenger of the martyred hero. Now this performance portrayed Cody as Custer's near savior, his first mourner, and almost his successor. To make the connection clearer, Cody wore his hair, beard, and mustache to look like Custer and began wearing clothes—fringed buckskin jacket, high boots, and broad-brimmed hat—to mimic the popular image of Custer's appearance. After the battle of the Washita, Custer had altered his appearance to take on the persona of the frontier scout; now the most famous of the frontier scouts returned the favor as he fashioned himself in the image of Custer. While the show was in New York City, Elizabeth Custer frequented the backstage rehearsals of "Custer's Last Stand" and attended the show numerous times. In her book *Tenting on the Plains*, she approved of the observation that Buffalo Bill appeared as the near-perfect image of General Custer in battle. Libbie Custer also wrote Cody, thanking him for the performance that did so much "to keep my husband's memory green. You have done so much to make him an idol among the children and young people." The Wild West show, she believed, was important for "teaching the youth the history of our country, where the noble officers, soldiers, and scouts sacrificed so much for the sake of our native land."[35]

With this kind of praise, one must wonder what the natives thought about participating in a show that praised Custer as a hero defending his "native land" and wove a narrative of national greatness that featured the actual natives of that land primarily in the roles of savage opponents. *The Drama of Civilization* performed in the Wild West show, for instance, featured Indians in the first epoch as a part of nature reinforcing the "noble savage" stereotype, while in the last scene it portrayed shrieking savages who slaughtered the brave Custer. Paternalistic reformers who pushed the assimilation agenda generally opposed the Wild West show on the grounds that the roles given to the Lakota merely perpetuated stereotypes of Indians as primitives, delayed assimilation, and exposed Indians to the seamy show business side of American society. Chauncey Yellow Robe, a Carlisle-educated Lakota who was sympathetic to the assimilationist goals of the humanitarian reformers, thought that the Wild West shows were "degrading, demoralizing, and degenerating."[36] Were these "Show Indians" mere victims of show business exploitation, hapless caricatures of the proud people who had defeated Custer?

In truth, employment in Cody's Wild West show offered many advantages to the Lakota. In a time when the reservation was a place of confinement, when Lakota needed permission from their agent to leave the reservation, working for Cody offered unparalleled mobility. Show Indians traveled in eastern cities and even Europe, roaming the streets freely during nonworking hours. For these Lakota, this was a measure of personal freedom simply not available on the reservation. In addition, working with the Wild West show offered economic opportunities not found on the reservation. Cody paid the Lakota at the same rate as his other performers, twenty-five dollars per month for men and fifteen per month for women, far more than they could make in any job on the reservation. For two decades the Wild West show employed from seventy-five to one hundred Lakota each year. Although this was a small fraction of the overall population, the income from these jobs may have represented one of the largest sources of income for the reservation during these lean years.

The Lakota who participated in Cody's show thought of themselves not as victims but as entrepreneurs, seeking out opportunities not only to profit but also to express their curiosity and to claim an Indian-American identity. After his education at Carlisle Indian School, Luther Standing Bear worked for Cody as an interpreter, eager for the money as well as the chance to travel the world. In several cases Standing Bear protected other Lakota from being mistreated and "fixed things to our satisfaction." According to Standing Bear, Cody asserted in one dispute, "My Indians are the principal feature of this show, and they are the one people I will not allow to be misused or neglected."[37] Another Lakota explained that working in Cody's show provided culturally meaningful employment. "We were raised on horseback," he said, and "that is the reason we want to work for" Cody's Wild West show. Furthermore, he claimed for Indians the right "to work at any place and earn money," the same "privilege" that "white man" enjoyed—"any kind of work he wants." Many Lakota appreciated Cody for providing this equal opportunity and equal treatment. Kicking Bear, imprisoned for his role as a leader of the Ghost Dance, expressed great gratitude when Cody provided employment for the prisoners. "For six weeks I have been a dead man," he enthused when Cody arrived, "now that I see you, I am alive again."[38]

Working with Cody's Wild West show, Lakota who had lived through the Little Bighorn visited London, toured Europe, and began to glimpse a role for themselves as American Indians in a global culture. Black Elk joined in order to satisfy his curiosity about the larger world: "I wanted to see the great water, the great world and the ways of the white men." In London he performed with others in a private showing for Queen Victoria's Golden Jubilee celebrating her fifty-year reign. After the show, the Queen requested the opportunity to meet all of the Indian performers, who for her and many of her British subjects were the most interesting actors in the show. According to Black Elk, "She did not care much about seeing the white men in the show. She only shook hands with the Indians." Later, this Little Bighorn veteran got separated from Cody's show, toured Europe with the rival Mexican Joe's Wild West show, and settled in Paris with his "girl friend" and her family. Eventually he caught up with the original Wild West show where Cody arranged for him to receive bonus pay and travel home.[39] Although most Lakota, like Black Elk, were happy to return home, a few joined other shows and stayed in Europe. Luther Standing Bear wrote that he was "sorry to leave London because I had been given a chance to see many wonderful sights." American Horse expressed the mixture of wonder and disorientation that many felt: "I see so much that is wonderful and strange that I feel a wish to sometimes go out in the forest and cover my head with a blanket, so that I can see no more and have a chance to think over what I have seen."[40]

American Horse's ambivalence was certainly understandable. On the one hand, the Lakota were hired to represent the past, acting out on stage roles that were not merely performing but in some sense were intended to be daily reliving the actual past. The roles continued after hours as audience members were invited to visit with the Lakota in their camp as they socialized, cooked, and played games. They were a twenty-four-hour-a-day living ethnographic exhibit, always performing under the gaze of white eyes. On the other hand, many Lakota eagerly embraced the excitement of urban modernity. They wandered European cities like any tourist, marveling at the sites and buying trinkets (even as they sold Lakota beadwork and artifacts to Europeans). They rode bicycles, drove cars, climbed the Eiffel Tower, played Ping-Pong, and met the Pope. Once an English soldier approached Rocky Bear, a veteran Wild West performer, and attempted conversation about the rainy weather in Pidgin English, "How! Heavy wet." Rocky Bear responded in his best British accent, "Yes, it's rawther nawsty, me boy." While in Barcelona, Cody's advance agent arranged for a group of Lakota to have their picture taken in front of a statue of Christopher Columbus. One member of the group was heard mumbling, "It was a damn bad day for us when he discovered America."[41]

The Lakota's embrace of modern culture, even in ironic jests, suggested that they were demonstrating an alternative path to assimilation. During a time when conceptions of race and national identity were remarkably fluid, when Italians and Irish were not considered "white" until after they left Europe,[42] many Lakota learned to see themselves as Indian-Americans while in Europe. As the Columbus jest indicated, Lakota in Europe thought of themselves not just in terms of their own tribe (who were hundreds of miles and several centuries away from Columbus or his descendents) but as representatives of all of the indigenous inhabitants of the continent. But they were not only Indians; they were Americans as well. Rocky Bear, who knew enough to use an English accent to mock a condescending British soldier, also commented, "The more I see of other countries, the more I like America." His reasons included his experience that it was in America where his Indian identity was most respected. Contrary to the visions of reformers such as Pratt, who thought that Indians would have to lose their Indian identity in order to become Americans, these Indians in Europe were becoming American precisely because they were Indian. Their boss, Buffalo Bill Cody, recognized as much on several occasions. He spoke publicly on behalf of the rights held by "these Indians, as Americans," and in Berlin he defended their rights as "original Americans" against the injustices of a government who had made them "wanderers in their home land." Even Mark Twain characterized the Wild West show, headlined by its Lakota participants, as "purely and distinctively American."[43]

The contradictions of being both Indian and American were on full display in Chicago in 1893 at the World's Columbian Exposition. At the center of the exposition was a large White City built for the occasion from wood and plaster and signifying the triumph of American technological progress. Along the Midway leading to the White City were a series of reconstructed scenes of village life from "primitive" peoples around the world, all suggesting the historical evolution toward the modern American ideal. Celebrating the four-hundredth anniversary of Columbus's first voyage (one year late), the exposition proclaimed a heroic version of western civilization's rise to global domination. Excluded from the exposition itself, Cody's Wild West show set up just beyond the official grounds and sold more than three million tickets in 1893. As the Lakota came in view during the opening ceremonies, the band struck up "My Country 'Tis of Thee" as crowds cheered the Indians, who were the show's biggest attraction. Yet even if Indians were the favorite performers, the overall theme of the Wild West show was entirely consistent with the triumphalist history of the Columbian Exposition. A large banner at the Wild West show had at one end a picture of Columbus with the caption "Pilot of the Ocean, the First Pioneer" and at the other a likeness of Cody with the words "Pilot of the Prairie, the Last Pioneer."[44]

Cody's narrative of American expansion played to the crowds, but there was a competing narrative expounded in Chicago that summer. Across the way from the Wild West show, a handful of history professors listened to a series of academic papers about the meaning of America. The last paper of the day was Frederick Jackson Turner's "The Significance of the Frontier in American History," which was virtually ignored at the conference but over time became one of the most influential essays ever written about American history. Turner himself did not make it to the Wild West show because he was too busy editing his essay at the last minute, but at least one of Turner's future colleagues skipped the academic lectures for the entertainment of Cody's show. Although the academic historians were busy distinguishing their professional understanding of history from the mere amateur ideas found in popular culture, anyone paying attention would have noticed in Cody's show an interpretation of American history that both paralleled and competed with Turner's. They both looked to the frontier as the central stage of American history, with Turner claiming that the frontier was where Americans developed their distinctive habits of democracy, individualism, and pragmatism. Both also explained American greatness with a compelling national narrative that was based more on the power of symbols than on the quality of evidence. For Turner, the icons of the frontier were the log cabin, the axe, and the plow; the central character was the frontier farmer who carved a rude but democratic, egalitarian civilization out of the wilderness. In Turner's frontier, the continent began as a wilderness, sparsely inhabited, and largely a huge reservoir of vacant land. Native people were marginalized at best and often simply absent from his famous frontier thesis.

Across town Cody was telling a different frontier story that amused, educated, and entertained the masses. In addition to *The Drama of Civilization*, Cody added "Custer's Last Stand" to the program halfway through the summer. If Turner's frontier was the farmers' struggle to wrest a society from a vacant continent, Cody's version of American history appeared like one long Indian war. While Turner's history relied on images of log cabins and covered wagons, Cody's program featured "The Rifle as an Aid to Civilization," claiming that the "bullet is the pioneer of civilization," for without it "America would not be today in possession of a free and unified country, and mighty in our strength."[45] In Cody's popular culture version, weapons were the icons and Indians were central characters, but they often appeared as the enemies of the nation, the opponents of progress. Cody's history presented what one historian has called an "inverted conquest" in which Indians were the aggressors and whites the victims. In Cody's stories, whites settled, protected, and occasionally retaliated, while Indians attacked, assaulted, and occasionally murdered. The conquerors assumed the role of victims, and those whose land was taken became aggressors. In this narrative, the Battle of the Little Bighorn assumed a pivotal role. Interpreted as "Custer's Last Stand," it established the image of savage Indians relentlessly attacking white heroes, of Custer standing on a lonely hilltop, sword in hand, dying a martyr's death.[46]

For both Turner and Cody, the frontier ended in 1890, although for different reasons. Turner's frontier closed when the Census Bureau announced that year the end of a continuous line of settlement spreading west, while Cody's frontier ended with the final violent clash of the Indian wars at Wounded Knee. Yet both interpretations of history proved influential for decades to come. Turner's career developed along with the growth of the profession of history as a leading discipline in American universities, and his ideas about the frontier, including the relative absence of Indians, dominated academic interpretations of American history for much of the next century. Cody's career developed in parallel fashion along with the growth of the entertainment industry in America, from the mass spectacle of the Wild West shows to the big screen of cinema. Cody himself attempted to make the transition, but his movies never had the popularity or the commercial success of his show. But thanks to Cody, at least in part, Indian wars became a familiar part of cinematic "westerns," and Indians attacking cabins, stagecoaches, and the cavalry have become cliché. And whether Custer dies a hero, as portrayed by Errol Flynn in the 1942 classic *They Died with Their Boots On*, or as a villain, as imagined in the 1972 film *Little Big Man*, he always dies waving his sword on a lonely hilltop, surrounded by hordes of swarming Indians, exactly as Cody would have it.

Sacred Ground, Contested Meaning

A crucial part of the ennoblement of Custer was to make sacred the place of his death. Making meaning out of Custer's defeat required not only the conquest of the "hostile" Indians but also the taming of an uncontrolled landscape. In the first months and years after the battle, visitors to the site expressed shock at the bodily remains strewn around the field. The hastily dug graves had not provided much protection, and visitors noted with disgust that rain had eroded the graves and predatory animals had feasted on the exposed flesh. The image was an almost hellish scene of corpses rising from the ground and wild beasts (wolves, coyotes, and wild Indians were mentioned) roaming the earth. Libbie Custer requested that her husband's remains be removed from this gruesome place for a proper burial at West Point, and military tradition favored providing permanent resting places for all of the officers. In May 1877 General Sheridan sent his brother, Lieutenant Colonel Michael Sheridan, to the battlefield to exhume the bodies of Custer and any other officers who could be identified for proper burials elsewhere, as well as to bury the skeletal remains of all other bodies. By the time General Sheridan and his entourage arrived in July, the battlefield was considerably sanitized.

One of many highly fictionalized versions of "Custer's Last Stand." Despite the historical inaccuracies, images such as this one helped establish the heroic image of Custer nobly defending himself from hordes of savages. Photo from the July 1926 cover of *Antiquarian* magazine. Courtesy Denver Public Library.

The general "found all the graves nicely raised as in cemeteries inside civilization"[47] and recommended that the area be designated as a national cemetery. He also became the first of many who walked the hills and valleys of the battlefield in an attempt to reconstruct the causes of Custer's defeat. The Lakota battle veterans who accompanied him and the evidence of the landscape confirmed for Sheridan his belief that Custer's fatal mistake had been to divide his forces. The combined force under Custer, Sheridan was convinced, could have defeated the Indians or at least held its own in defense.

The battlefield took its first crucial steps toward becoming holy ground in the next few years. In 1879 the War Department established the Custer Battlefield National Cemetery, and two years later it erected a granite obelisk on the hilltop that became known as Last Stand Hill. The monument, promoters argued, should be made of granite and "massive and heavy enough to remain for ages where placed—a landmark of the conflict between civilization and barbarism."[48] The result was 6 feet wide at the base and almost 12 feet tall, with the names of 261 soldiers and scouts who died there engraved into the stone. Carved in Massachusetts, the 18-ton obelisk was shipped in three pieces through the Great Lakes, carried by train to Bismarck, then by steamship up the Yellowstone River, and finally hauled by sledge to the Little Bighorn. Placed on top of the hill where Custer died, the monument commanded the surrounding landscape and became a symbol of victory in defeat, a towering reminder of the power of what "civilization" could bring to this distant western country. It has also served as a focal point for the many who came, as Sheridan did, to walk the sacred battlefield in search of answers.

The answers one received, of course, depended on the questions one asked, as became clear in 1886 on the tenth anniversary of the battle. In late June, on and around the date of the battle, about one thousand people gathered near the battlefield to commemorate the anniversary and tour the field. Battle veterans, including Crow, Lakota, and army, wandered the grounds and compared stories about what had happened at that spot ten years earlier. The most famous meeting was between Captain Edward S. Godfrey and the Hunkpapa leader Gall. Godfrey and many newspaper reporters hoped that Gall would explain the precise movements of soldiers and warriors on the battlefield. This was the first time, but hardly the last, that whites turned to Indian testimony for answers to the military question that burned in some quarters of white society, but that Indians rarely asked: How did the Indians win? Godfrey hoped that Indian survivors could explain the precise story of Custer's defeat in tactical terms, that is, that they could unlock the military mystery that would explain how a modern nation's most famous Indian fighter could actually have lost to the supposedly inferior forces. The alleged primitives believed that an obvious answer, requiring no great military expertise, was at hand. To them Custer's defeat was not a mystery, but rather the obvious outcome of attacking a superior force.

In September of that year Sitting Bull and one hundred Lakota visited their old enemies, the Crow, and provided a different meaning for the battlefield. In two weeks of visiting, feasting, and reminiscing, the Lakota toured the field of their greatest victory and saw in it reasons for united Indian resistance to government assimilationist policies. From the top of what the whites called Last Stand Hill, Sitting Bull claimed a different meaning for the sacred ground. "Look at that monument. That marks the work of our people," he declared. The battleground provided an ongoing reminder, Sitting Bull argued, that the white government ultimately respected the Lakota strategy of resistance rather than the Crow path of accommodation. Specifically, Sitting Bull urged Crow leaders to resist the government's plans for the individual allotment of tribal lands. As one Crow agent concluded, Sitting Bull's visit "was mainly for the purpose of inducing the Crows to take common action in opposition" to allotment and the control of government Indian agents.[49] Thus, Sitting Bull was the first, but hardly the last, to find on the battlefield a sacred symbol of pan-Indian identity and common opposition to white cultural onslaught. For Sitting Bull, the question was not what can this landscape tell us about how Custer lost, but rather how can this special place remind us of our strength as a people. After all, the same hilltop that the whites called Last Stand Hill was where Sitting Bull had prayed to *Wakan Tanka* asking for protection, "We want to live. Guard us against all misfortunes or calamities." In the valley of the Little Bighorn there were layers of historical meaning, stories on top of stories all trying to reach the surface.

Thirty years later, on the fortieth anniversary of the battle and the eve of U.S. entry into World War I, battle veterans and six thousand spectators met at the Little Bighorn to recognize a spirit of "Peace and Reconciliation." Near the Custer monument, Godfrey (now a general) met with former Crow scout White Man Runs Him and a contingent of Northern Cheyenne led by the aged Two Moons. Standing in his automobile, Godfrey read a message from Elizabeth Custer followed by his own comments, including a description of how the field appeared in the aftermath of the battle when the area had been a "wilderness without civilized habitation" compared to the present "land of peace and plenty." Two Moons, who might have thought that he lived in a land of peace and plenty before the wars against the whites, followed with his own words, "Forty years ago we had a fight here with Custer. I came to fight Custer. We wiped him from the face of the earth. But now we are brothers under the same flag."[50] Any conflict seemed buried safely in the past, with the present dedicated to honoring the heroes from all sides without any mention of the reasons that impelled them to fight. After the speeches, the participants shook hands, a contingent of Spanish-American War veterans fired a salute, and the Crow Indian school band played "Garry Owen." That afternoon the Crow rodeo entertained the crowds, and by evening trains took most of the spectators back to Billings, the nearest city. Other spectators drove away in the three hundred automobiles that were present at the ceremonies, driving along the newly named Custer Battlefield Highway that stretched from Iowa to Glacier National Park. Such machines in the once-remote valley of the Little Bighorn symbolized the break with the past and marked the area as a new focus of commercial tourism.

When war came to the United States in 1917, Indians eagerly joined the "war to end all wars." While Indians had fought alongside white Americans in every conflict since the Revolution, tribe and region had limited previous participation to a small proportion of the overall native population. This time, however, Indian participation was widespread. By 1918 there were nearly twelve thousand Indians in uniform, about half of them volunteers. Overall, about 25 to 30 percent of adult Indian males enlisted, nearly double the national average of 15 percent. Although they did not fight in segregated units as African-Americans were forced to do, Indians did often stick together in their units and were often characterized according to stereotypical views that transformed their alleged savage traits into virtues. Because they were deemed to be stealthy, for instance, Indians were often assigned as scouts or messengers. But clearly many Indians embraced fighting in a modern army as a connection with their warrior past and sought to prove themselves by seeking out dangerous action, as if striving to be merely equal with white soldiers was a sign of limited ambition. Not surprisingly, then, Indian casualties in the U.S. Army during World War I were five times as high as white soldiers. One Sioux from South Dakota explained, "The men wanted to go; the women ordered us to go. No good Indian would run away from a fight. We knew that the life of America depended on its men, and we are Americans." At the Standing Rock reservation, an enlistment ceremony included references to "Custer's last fight" and calls from aging veterans of that and other fights against the United States to join in fighting for their country. When Indian casualties came home for burial, the community often grieved with songs and rituals drawn from older cultural patterns they had followed for centuries.[51]

After World War I, however, the cultural patterns that had been forged in intertribal warfare or in war against the Americans now bent toward greater participation within the American political community. Participation in the war decreased tribal identities in favor of a pan-Indian identity, increased political mobilization, and most of all led to the widespread identification with the flag as a symbol of American Indian loyalty. One Sioux soldier stated, "Whatever may have happened in the past is over now. We are Americans, loyal Americans." The national press praised Indian soldiers for putting aside old grievances and fighting for the flag "as valiantly as their hostile fathers fought against it." Indians were "the original exponent of the thing we're fighting for—American liberty," one newspaper wrote, while another added that the "oldest American" was quite naturally the "incarnation of democracy and freedom." Chauncey Yellow Robe, a leading Lakota member of the pan-Indian advocacy organization known as the Society of American Indians, noted that Indians had fought for liberty since the Revolution and called for "one American flag for all, one flag and one God."[52] Along with increased patriotism came calls for Indian unity and a greater recognition of Indian rights, especially the most basic right of citizenship. One year after the war, Congress granted citizenship to all Indian veterans of World War I, and in 1924 Congress extended citizenship to all American Indians, finally allowing them to vote in the country for which they had fought and died.

All of these modern themes were evident in 1926 for the fiftieth-anniversary celebration of the battle, the grandest celebration of them all. Conceived in part by regional boosters hoping to promote tourism, the three-day event featured a theme of peace and reconciliation. Nearly fifty thousand spectators attended, some arriving in special trains from Billings or Sheridan and others driving on the Custer Battlefield Highway. Film star William S. Hart came with his friend and movie sidekick, Luther Standing Bear, while 250 men of the Seventh Cavalry arrived by train from Texas. Battle veterans included over eighty Lakota and Cheyenne, as well as a handful of those who had ridden with Custer. The many tourists were not disappointed with the entertaining spectacle: airplanes demonstrated loops and dives over the battlefield while offering rides for sale, afternoon rodeos and Indian dances drew large crowds, and a thousand-dollar fireworks display concluded the ceremonies.

Along with the entertainment were spectacles designed to exhibit the theme of reconciliation. On June 25, with fifty thousand people watching, the Seventh Cavalry approached Last Stand Hill from the south while a large group of Sioux and Cheyenne riders approached from the north. When they met, the crowd hushed as Custer scout White Man Runs Him took out a peace pipe, held it to the sky, and presented it to Sioux leader White Bull. General Godfrey then gave an American flag to White Bull, who offered a blanket to Godfrey. After more exchange of gifts, the two lines rode off the hill in pairs of army and Indian, side by side. The next day presented another drama of reconciliation when the remains of an unknown soldier—unexpectedly dug up by a road-building crew—were buried along with a hatchet in a demonstration of "our common citizenship and everlasting peace."

Despite the emphasis on modernity, the past could not be buried quite so easily. In a speech during the "burial of the hatchet" ceremony, a spokesman for Indian War Veterans noted "the benefits derived from Indian Wars on the frontier," most especially the possibility that "a young lady may mount her pony and ride all over this country in safety." Although Indians had suffered from "grievous wrongs," the speaker admitted, the overall course of Manifest Destiny meant that the Indian wars were part of "the struggle of the white civilization for supremacy, possession, development, and culture, as against savagery and barbaric nature." During the same ceremony, the Hunkpapa leader Red Tomahawk spoke not of the inevitability of dispossession but of specific treaty violations that caused the Indian wars. "I have honored and respected all the treaties you ever signed with me," he said through an interpreter, "but time and again, you have broken those treaties with me." The 1868 Fort Laramie Treaty, he remarked, "was the last treaty that was signed before the Custer battle," and pointing to the Custer monument on Last Stand Hill, he concluded, "you see the results of unkept words on the top of the hill."[53] Only three years before this ceremony, the Sioux nation had filed a lawsuit against the United States government to recover ownership of the Black Hills. Lakota in a post–World War I era might shake the hand of friendship with army counterparts and recognize a common citizenship, but they also claimed a militant identity that flowed from their interpretation of the history that rose from the ground on the battlefield of their greatest victory.

The most important storyteller at the fiftieth-anniversary celebration, however, was not a speaker but the cameras from Universal Pictures, on scene to record authentic Indian moments and a reenactment of a charge by the Seventh Cavalry. Although the ceremonies did not include a full battle reenactment, there had been many such reenactments in the past. They provided a visual spectacle that combined education and entertainment in a package that harkened back to Buffalo Bill's Wild West show, but they also were sensitive to the contested meanings of the Little Bighorn. The first recorded reenactment occurred at the 1877 Sun Dance, one year after the battle, when Crazy Horse organized a mock fight between the agency Indians, representing Custer, and the Lakota who had actually been at the previous year's battle. As could happen with reenactments, the blows were often more real than pretend. A 1902 reenactment in Sheridan, Wyoming, between one thousand Crow and the Wyoming National Guard erupted into a full-scale brawl when a Crow leader attempted to take the cavalry's flag from a "dead" guardsman. Suddenly, as the event organizer described it, "Every guardsman came to life and slugged the nearest Crow. It was a knock-down and drag-out all over these hills."[54] The film footage from reenactments allowed filmmakers in these early years to claim that their epics about Custer's last fight featured Indians from the original battle as well as the actual scenery. Just like Cody's show, the films had value because they were authentic: these were not actors but the real thing.

During the first half of the century, these Indians fought and lost a battle to control the representation of their own Indian identity. After working in the Wild West show, Luther Standing Bear realized the power of cultural representation and moved to Hollywood as the best-known member of a small group of Lakota who tried to influence film images of Indians. "I met many people who were interested in learning the truth in regard to the Indians," he wrote, and aspired "to do more for my own race off the reservation than to remain there under the iron rule of the white agent."[55] But as movies developed, entertainment came to matter more than authenticity. Movies about the Little Bighorn or the Indian wars became increasingly focused on the character of Custer and less concerned with presenting an image of Indians as Standing Bear had hoped.

The most notable examples of this were the two films that many cultural critics regard as the best Custer films of all, *They Died with Their Boots On* and *Fort Apache*. The first of these paired Errol Flynn as the swashbuckling Custer with Olivia de Havilland as Elizabeth Custer, making it the only Custer movie to give the romantic relationship between the two a central place in developing the character of Custer. Elizabeth's books about her husband shape the narrative so that the movie is truly a version of Custer as Libbie wanted her husband to be remembered. Indians are mere background as unscrupulous capitalists betray them and steal the Black Hills. Custer, in an act of sacrificial courage that stands in marked contrast to the seedy corruption of the society around him, rides knowingly to his death performing his duty as a soldier, but with his final wish being that the Indians should have the Black Hills restored to them. The final scene of Custer (Flynn) fighting alone on the hillside against vast numbers of faceless Indians presents the most memorable of all images of Custer's Last Stand, an image shaped by the Wild West show and Otto Becker's famous Budweiser lithograph of the great individual standing against the crowd. Released in November 1941, the film provided a theme of martial courage standing heroically against corrupt capitalism that must have appealed to a nation emerging from depression and one month away from war. The Little Bighorn was Custer's story, with Indians reduced to anonymous props in the background.

The same tendency was true of John Ford's *Fort Apache*, released two years after the end of World War II. Ford fictionalized the Custer story, moving the location from Montana to Monument Valley and changing the names of characters, thus creating a fictional space in which to explore a higher truth than mere literal recitation of events. Ford's Custer character, Lieutenant Colonel Thursday, begins as an egomaniacal martinet who disdains the men in his command and underestimates the enemy Apache Indians. His mistakes lead to the annihilation of his command, and, in a plot device that goes back to Frederick Whittaker, Thursday refuses the chance to escape and instead dies with his troops. If only he had heeded the advice of Captain York (John Wayne), Thursday and his men would have lived. The final scene, however, is not the last stand but a later conversation between York (Wayne) and reporters, a clue that Ford's real point is not about the actual battle but about how the hero is remembered. York, who had been at odds with Thursday throughout the film, tells the reporters what the movie viewers know is not true, "No man died more gallantly, nor won more honor for his regiment." Thus, *Fort Apache* challenged viewers in the wake of World War II to believe in heroic myths of military courage even when there was evidence that they were not true. Ford thought that the heroic ideal, even if not true, was "good for the country" and claimed about Custer, "A legend is more interesting than the actual facts."[56] But even the fictionalized Little Bighorn was Custer's story, the nation's parable about the importance of heroes, while Indians were honorable but marginalized, stoic stereotypes playing bit roles. The movies transformed their greatest victory into the spiritual triumph of the military hero they defeated.

Even as Hollywood became the most influential interpreter of popular history and lifted the Custer story into a timeless and placeless myth, events in the studio inadvertently led to a renewed emphasis on the specific ground of the Little Bighorn and an enlarged role for the Indian players in the battle. During the filming of *They Died with Their Boots On*, Joseph Medicine Crow, a descendent of Custer's Crow scout White Man Runs Him, was in Los Angeles studying for his master's degree in anthropology at the University of Southern California. Answering an advertisement for Indian extras, Medicine Crow reported to the Warner lot only to learn that the film was about Custer. When the studio learned of his personal connection to the Little Bighorn, it assigned him to help in writing the script. When a producer asked Medicine Crow what he thought of Custer, he replied, "My grandfather always said Custer was very foolish. He didn't listen to them [the Crow scouts]. He didn't wait for the other columns to arrive." In a decision that showed how much the pretense of realism had lost to the romance of myth, the producer fired Medicine Crow on the spot. As he headed to the door, Medicine Crow offered a critique and made a promise, "You people here in Hollywood, you mess up good stories, and that is what you are doing here . . . But someday I'm going to write my own Custer story and tell it like it was."[57]

His chance came decades later when the Crow tribe and the nearby town of Hardin, Montana, decided to bring Custer back to life for a reenactment. Motivated by the desire to promote tourism, the town and the tribe began sponsoring an annual event based on a script written by Medicine Crow. Beginning with Lewis and Clark, the narrative structure adopted a larger historical frame for the battle, which gave it ample time to display Plains Indian cultural life. According to *Newsweek*, "What made the Custer re-enactment special was that the battle of the Little Bighorn unfolded entirely from the Indian's point of view."[58] The Hardin pageant was not so much about Custer as it was about Sitting Bull, and the climax of the story was not the final battle but Sitting Bull's earlier Sun Dance. But the "Indian point of view" was clearly from a late twentieth-century Indian perspective. The event was an act of cultural tourism intended to provide a cooperative endeavor for the badly divided communities of Crow tribe and white town. The script was written by a Crow, starred a Lakota chief, and began with a rodeo-like rendition of "The Star Spangled Banner." It was no surprise that Medicine Crow, a combat veteran of World War II, closed the two-hour spectacle by stating that the Little Bighorn "has brought dignity to the red man" and that "We—red man and white man—live in a united fortress of democracy—the United States of America."[59] So it is that every year on the fields outside of Hardin,

15 miles from the Little Bighorn, the grandson of Custer's scout brings the hero back to life, only to marginalize him from the narrative of Manifest Destiny, bring dignity to the Indian point of view, and declare allegiance to the country and the flag that his grandfather fought for and Sitting Bull fought against—all in the name of civic boosterism and national unity.

The Hardin reenactment of Custer's Last Stand began in 1964, just as America was becoming ensnarled in a war that would do much to change the way Americans thought about the Indian wars. In some ways World War II had changed the way Americans viewed Custer, making his last battle appear incompetent and inconsequential in light of the scale of twentieth-century total warfare. The name of Custer had become a byword for vainglorious failure in an age of modern military heroes such as Eisenhower or MacArthur. The planning and execution of large-scale assaults such as D day or Inchon made Custer's failed attack seem both amateurish and irrelevant. Vietnam, however, brought renewed attention to Custer not so much as a failure, but as a symbol of overbearing arrogance in pursuit of misguided national interest. Two books captured the new mood: Vine Deloria's 1969 bestseller *Custer Died for Your Sins: An American Indian Manifesto* and Dee Brown's 1970 history of the Indian wars, *Bury My Heart at Wounded Knee*. Despite the title, Deloria's declaration had little to say about Custer, aside from pointing out that he was the most popular subject of jokes in Indian country. The title did help to make Custer's name synonymous with the unjust treatment of Indians. Brown's book reinforced this sense of grievance against America's historical treatment of Indians precisely at the time when American presumptions of Manifest Destiny in Southeast Asia were under bitter attack. The link to Custer was clear in the words of a graffiti artist in Vietnam: "We'll bring peace to this land if we have to kill them all. CUSTER."[60]

Once again Hollywood provided a pop culture version of this new image of Custer in a popular 1970 movie, *Little Big Man*. Based loosely on Thomas Berger's novel of the same name, with some parts filmed on site near the Little Bighorn Battlefield, the film played on traditional elements of the Custer story—the hypothetical sole white survivor, Custer arrogance, and Indian nobility—to portray the Indian wars as an earlier version of American imperialism. Narrated by a white captive (Dustin Hoffman) who comes to realize the superiority of Cheyenne culture against the movie's satirical critique of the foibles of white society, Custer appears as a preening egomaniac, while his attack at Washita looks suspiciously like Vietnam's My Lai massacre. As the antihero, Custer still dies alone on the hillside, but this time in the middle of a mindless rant that includes the phrase, "Take no prisoners." The brightest spot of the movie, which was nominated for an Academy Award, was the performance of Dan George, a Salish Indian from Vancouver, as a contemplative, warm-hearted Cheyenne chief. George's success sparked a return of native roles for cinema, proving that Indian actors could develop individual character and present indigenous culture in a positive light, exactly as Luther Standing Bear had hoped at the beginning of the century.

This renewed cultural awareness included a more militant political activism on behalf of Indian rights. The best known of the new Indian rights groups was the American Indian Movement (AIM), which agitated against historical and contemporary mistreatment of Indian people and specialized in events that garnered national publicity for the cause. AIM organized the occupation of symbolic sights such as Alcatraz Island in 1969 and Wounded Knee in 1973, effectively bringing national attention to their cause. As 1976 and the Little Bighorn centennial approached, AIM set its sights on changing the way the Custer story was told. The Custer Centennial Committee, sponsored largely by Custer buffs and civic boosters, hoped to stage a repeat of the successful fiftieth-anniversary celebration in 1926, only this time with twice as many visitors. Fearing violence from AIM or other groups, the National Park Service scaled back expectations and hoped to manage a small-scale event that provided an evenhanded treatment of the battle. As the ceremony began, over one hundred Indians led by Russell Means of AIM arrived with chants and drumbeats and carrying an upside-down American flag, the symbol of American ideals gone astray. The speeches continued amidst an uneasy truce, but the hijacked ceremony left a bitter taste in the mouths of many Custerphiles and a longing for more representation in the official Little Bighorn story in the minds of many Indian activists.

In 1988 Means and others returned to the battlefield and upped the symbolic ante, this time placing a steel plaque near the granite Custer monument "In honor of the Indian Patriots who fought and defeated" Custer's Seventh Cavalry on that spot. The Indian defense was, according to the plaque, "to save our women and children from mass murder" and to preserve "rights to our Homelands, Treaties, and Sovereignty." As a crowd gathered, Means addressed them, "You remove our monument, and we'll remove yours." Adopting an explicitly confrontational stance, Means went on to suggest that the 1881 Custer monument was as welcome on Indian land as a "Hitler national monument" would be in Jerusalem.[61] Yet the complexity of the historical context was bound to give multiple meanings to the rhetoric of Indian patriotism and the defense of homelands. After all, Indian patriots were also American patriots, fighting and dying for their nation in greater numbers than their white counterparts during the wars of the twentieth century. Likewise, the question of whose homeland this was could have more than one answer. For Means and the AIM activists, Custer's attack on June 25, 1876, stood for all European and American conquests of native peoples since Columbus, but underneath that story was the Crow Indian memory that their Indian ancestors were, on that fateful day, defending their homes against Lakota intruders. After all, the battle occurred on Crow land and the battlefield is surrounded by Crow reservation.

EPILOGUE

CONTESTS OVER the meaning of the sacred battleground have continued until the present. In 1991 Congress changed the official name from Custer Battlefield National Monument to Little Bighorn Battlefield National Monument, recognizing that the place was home not only to Custer's story but to many Indian stories as well. Some argued that the name change was yet another example of "politically correct" revisionist history, a "national guilt movement" to "appease" the nation's "collective conscience." U.S. Representative Ben Nighthorse Campbell, Democrat from Colorado and a member of the Northern Cheyenne tribe, countered that the name change was simply "a matter of writing history the way it should have been written in the first place."[1]

During the 1990s, the battlefield had two Indian superintendents, including Gerard Baker, who cultivated ties between the monument and various tribes. In 1996 he allowed a dawn ceremony in which young Indian men "counted coup" in the Custer memorial, which for many Custer aficionados was an act of sacrilege. Also during this decade, the Park Service began to place red grave markers at the place of known Indian fatalities on the battlefield, matching the white stones that mark the place where cavalrymen fell. The Park Service also hired many Indians as seasonal summer interpretive rangers, who expanded the selection of programming from mere military history to a range of cultural stories, including life in an Indian village and the ways of a Plains warrior. By the end of the decade superintendent Neil Mangum reported, "the park is telling a balanced story—that is, from a multicultural perspective."[2]

The most dramatic event in the struggle of Indians to take back the meaning of the Little Bighorn was the construction of an Indian memorial, authorized in 1991 and completed in 2003, designed to honor the Indians who fought in the battle and to complement the memorial to Custer and the dead cavalrymen that has stood at the top of Last Stand Hill since 1881. In many ways, however, the Indian Memorial appears as the opposite of the Custer monument. Built into the side of the hill on the same ridge, the Indian Memorial is a circular structure that fits unobtrusively into the earth. If the Custer obelisk looks like a miniature version of the Washington Monument, then the Indian Memorial appears as a small-scale imitation of the Vietnam Veterans Memorial, with dark stone panels set into the earth memorializing Indian leaders and their tribes. In one direction the view looks through a wire silhouette sculpture of three warriors on horseback, while the opposite view peers through a "spirit gate" (to allow the spirits of dead warriors to pass through) that frames a view of the Custer obelisk perched on the skyline of Last Stand Hill. According to Ernie LaPointe, a descendent of Sitting Bull, the Indian Memorial was "a long overdue memorial to the victors." Emmanuel Red Bear, who includes both Sitting Bull and Crazy Horse in his lineage, remarked about the monument, "There will never be a day when everything will be made up to us, but coming back here is like a healing to us."[3]

In the first decade of the twenty-first century, the battle of the Little Bighorn did not fade further into the distant past but rather came to speak more directly to contemporary concerns. Twenty-first-century wars in Iraq and Afghanistan continued a trend since Vietnam of American wars that had more in common with the Indian wars of the nineteenth century than the total warfare of the mid-twentieth century. Cultural historian Richard Slotkin called Vietnam "our last great Indian war," a claim that appears incomplete only in the sense that Vietnam was only the first of recent counterinsurgency wars that adopted the rhetoric of Indian fighting. From the jungles of Southeast Asia to the deserts of Baghdad, American soldiers have referred to treacherous and hostile landscapes as "Indian country" and have sometimes considered Third World peoples as inferior beings. More commonly, as Robert Kaplan reports, "In a world in which mass infantry invasions are becoming politically and diplomatically prohibitive—even as dirty little struggles proliferate, featuring small clusters of combatants hiding out in Third World slums—the American military is back to the days of fighting Indians."[4]

The great irony in this, of course, is that many of those uniformed Americans making forays into "Indian country" are themselves Indians. As in earlier wars, American Indians continue to serve their country in disproportionately high numbers. Even in the widely unpopular American war in Iraq, Indians continue to volunteer at a higher per capita rate than any other racial or ethnic group. Many of those volunteers claim this as a way of embracing their warrior heritage, but it also might be for some a culturally sanctioned avenue of escape from the poverty and unemployment of the reservation. Whatever the motives—and Indians would certainly not be the only Americans with mixed motives for serving in the armed forces—native cultures do provide a framework for understanding a warrior as a tradition of service to the people in defense of homes and families. On the Crow, Northern Cheyenne, and Sioux reservations, there are active soldiers and recent veterans who proudly trace their ancestry to those who fought at the Little Bighorn. Like their forefathers, many pray for guidance in a sweat lodge, perform in the Sun Dance for healing, and return home to the acclamation of their communities. For those who do not return, the tribal community offers a familiar way of making meaning out of the loss, performing funeral and burial rituals that connect the recently deceased with the heroes of the nineteenth-century wars against the Americans. As one Lakota combat veteran from Vietnam whose son recently returned from Iraq noted, "In 1876, the Lakota Sioux took that flag from Custer. So that flag is ours, too."[5]

Little wonder, then, that the dedication ceremony for the Indian Memorial at the Little Bighorn Battlefield began with a rousing rendition of Lee Greenwood's "God Bless the U.S.A.," better known by its chorus "I'm proud to be an American." The battlefield has become a place that expresses the nation's hopes for an inclusive multicultural history, a place where Indians speak to whites about their shared American history, and a place where visitors can buy tee shirts with an image of armed Apache warriors and the slogan "Homeland Security: Fighting Terrorism Since 1492." Multiple overlapping and complicated loyalties flow from a place where a multiracial force attacked a village that believed it was merely defending itself and where defeat was transformed into spiritual victory.

Most of all, the Little Bighorn Battlefield stands as a reminder of our deeply conflicted understanding of American history. On the one hand, many Americans tend to view our historical conquest of the West as inevitable, as a demographically if not divinely mandated march of democratic progress. This view of history admits to the abuse and mistreatment of natives along the way, but it cannot genuinely imagine any significant alternative to the way things turned out. The story of Custer's last stand fits in this version of history as an image of American conquest as primarily defensive, merely protecting innocent pioneers from savage attack. On the other hand, however, Indian voices at the Little Bighorn speak not of ineluctable destiny but of specific decisions, individual choices, treaties made and broken, and possibilities left unexplored. In this view the Indian wars were not a regrettable but inevitable by-product of the march of progress, but the calculated result of specific individual and national choices. The Little Bighorn calls us not only to understand what happened in our history but also to imagine how things might have worked out differently. The stories that walk the ground at the Little Bighorn Battlefield tell us not only what we have been but what we might become.

ACKNOWLEDGMENTS

ALTHOUGH WRITING is a solitary task, I was never alone while working on this book. Every day as I sat at the kitchen table in my small apartment, scores of scholars, teachers, students, and friends joined me in my daily labors. Decades ago, first around campfires in the Uinta Mountains and then in classrooms at Earlham College, Professor Doug Steeples sparked my interest in western history, demonstrating that narrative history and rigorous analysis were not only compatible but often inseparable. My historical sensibilities owe a great deal to the late Bob Southard, also at Earlham College, and to professors and colleagues at the University of North Carolina at Chapel Hill, especially Otis Graham and William Leuchtenburg. Although my interests have strayed from the topics I studied with them, many years later they continue to shape my understanding of the craft of writing and the discipline of history. Although none of these professors should be held responsible for this book, all of them helped make it possible.

My thanks to the many students and colleagues at Rocky Mountain College who over the years have fed my intellectual curiosity and honed my teaching. There is nothing quite like an early morning class full of sleepy students to sort out what is, and what is not, interesting to a general audience. My thanks especially to Professor of Anthropology Ron Cochran, who invited me to team-teach a course about the Little Bighorn. I continue to learn much from him, about teaching and anthropology, and I appreciate his reading a portion of the manuscript and improving it with his insights. I am also grateful to Academic Vice President Anthony Piltz, who approved my request for a year's leave from teaching so that I had time to write. Thanks to Brian McDivitt, Alison Palser, Jordan Jackson, and Jordan Whiteman for reading and commenting on portions of the manuscript. Several friends showed me the courtesy of reading the manuscript and the even greater kindness of suggesting ways to improve it. Bev Ross, Sig Ross, Tom Lyman, and Kevin Brusteun all deserve credit for helping me to think carefully and to write clearly.

A book like this rests on the work of a community of scholars; the footnotes can only begin to express my indebtedness to the many historians who have spent years working on the Little Bighorn and its context. Especially influential in my thinking about Plains Indian wars has been the work of Robert Utley, Jerome Greene, Elliott West, Jeffrey Ostler, Raymond DeMaille, and Gary Anderson. I would also like to thank the good people at the Johns Hopkins University Press for expressing interest in this project at an early stage and supporting it wholeheartedly throughout. Special appreciation to Senior Acquisitions Editor Robert J. Brugger and Witness to History Series Editor Peter Charles Hoffer for their unfailing guidance, as well as to an anonymous reader from the Press who sharpened the analysis and improved the narrative. Copy editor Jeremy Horsefield saved the manuscript from many errors and infelicities.

Most of all, I would like to thank my wife, Danell Jones. It is commonplace for authors to thank spouses, but in my case it is especially true that this book would not exist without her love, support, and inspiration. She helped me to think through the project from the beginning, paid the bills while I took a leave from teaching in order to write, listened patiently and critically as I talked my way through the story, and edited every word in the manuscript, some of it two or three times. She brought her analytical mind to questions of scholarship and her writer's eye to the craft of narrative. This book has more style because she is my writing partner, just as my life has more grace because she is my life partner.

NOTES

PROLOGUE

Epigraph: Lieutenant James H. Bradley, *The March of the Montana Column: Prelude to the Custer Disaster* (Norman: University of Oklahoma Press, 1961), 154.

1. Bradley, *March of the Montana Column*, 153–55.

2. Quoted in James Donovan, *A Terrible Glory: Custer and the Little Bighorn—The Last Great Battle of the American West* (New York: Little, Brown, 2008), 310.

3. Donovan, *Terrible Glory*, 308; Godfrey quoted in William A. Graham, *The Custer Myth: A Source Book of Custeriana* (New York: Bonanza Books, 1953), 365.

4. Kingsley M. Bray, *Crazy Horse: A Lakota Life* (Norman: University of Oklahoma Press, 2006), 235; Raymond J. DeMallie, ed., *The Sixth Grandfather: Black Elk's Teachings as Given to John G. Neihardt* (Lincoln: University of Nebraska Press, 1984), 197.

CHAPTER ONE: The Pen, the Pipe, and the Gun

Epigraph: Kingsley M. Bray, *Crazy Horse: A Lakota Life* (Norman: University of Oklahoma Press, 2006), 350.

1. George E. Hyde, *Red Cloud's Folk* (Norman: University of Oklahoma Press, 1937), 72.

2. R. Eli Paul, *Blue Water Creek and the First Sioux War, 1854–1856* (Norman: University of Oklahoma Press, 2004), 19.

3. Ibid., 20.

4. Gary Moulton, ed., *The Definitive Journals of Lewis and Clark*, vol. 3 (Lincoln: University of Nebraska Press, 1987), 111–30.

5. Anthony F. C. Wallace, *Jefferson and the Indians: The Tragic Fate of the First Americans* (Cambridge, MA: Harvard University Press, 1999), 223.

6. Anders Stephanson, *Manifest Destiny: American Expansion and the Empire of Right* (New York: Hill and Wang, 1995), 42, 44.

7. Quoted in Robert A. Trennert Jr., *Alternative to Extinction: Federal Indian Policy and the Beginnings of the Reservation System* (Philadelphia: Temple University Press, 1975), 153.

8. Robert M. Utley, *The Indian Frontier of the American West, 1846–1890* (Albuquerque: University of New Mexico Press, 1984), 61.

9. Jeffrey Ostler, *The Plains Sioux and U.S. Colonialism from Lewis and Clark to Wounded Knee* (Cambridge: Cambridge University Press, 2004), 41.

10. Bray, *Crazy Horse*, 34.

11. Paul, *Blue Water Creek*, 90.

12. Ibid., 95.

13. Robert M. Utley, *The Lance and the Shield: The Life and Times of Sitting Bull* (New York: Ballantine Books, 1994), 46–48.

14. Elliott West, *The Contested Plains: Indians, Goldseekers, and the Rush to Colorado* (Lawrence: University Press of Kansas, 1998), 1–6; Thom Hatch, *Black Kettle: The Cheyenne Chief Who Sought Peace but Found War* (Hoboken, NJ: John Wiley & Sons, 2004), 48–61.

15. Ostler, *Plains Sioux*, 42.

16. Bray, *Crazy Horse*, 59.

17. Utley, *Indian Frontier*, 76.

18. Thom Hatch, *The Blue, the Gray, and the Red: Indian Campaigns of the Civil War* (Mechanicsburg, PA: Stackpole Books, 2003), 103; see also Micheal Clodfelter, *The Dakota War: The United States Army versus the Sioux, 1862–1865* (Jefferson, NC: McFarland, 1998), 23–61.

19. Clodfelter, *Dakota War*, 61.

20. Sarah F. Wakefield, *Six Weeks in the Sioux Teepees: A Narrative of Indian Captivity*, ed. June Namias (Norman: University of Oklahoma Press, 1997, originally published 1863), 62–69.

21. Clodfelter, *Dakota War*, 160–61.

22. Clodfelter, *Dakota War*, 166–75.

23. Clodfelter, *Dakota War*, 180, 185–86; see also Utley, *Lance and Shield*, 58–59.

24. Fanny Kelly, *Narrative of My Captivity among the Sioux Indians* (repr., New York: Corinth Books, 1962), 77–78, 210; Utley, *Lance and Shield*, 63.

25. James H. Bradley, *March of the Montana Column: A Prelude to the Custer Disaster* (Norman: University of Oklahoma Press, 1961).

26. Charles A. Bryant and Abel B. Murch, *A History of the Great Massacre by the Sioux Indians in Minnesota* (Cincinnati: Ricky and Carroll, 1864), quoted in Roy W. Meyer, *History of the Santee Sioux: United States Indian Policy on Trial* (Lincoln: University of Nebraska Press, 1967), 116.

27. Ostler, *Plains Sioux*, 44.

28. Hatch, *The Blue, the Gray, and the Red*, 191–92.

29. West, *Contested Plains*, 187.

30. George E. Hyde, *Life of George Bent: Written from His Letters* (repr., Norman: University of Oklahoma Press, 1983), 127.

31. Hatch, *Black Kettle*, 101.

32. Ibid., 117–18.

33. Jerome Greene and Douglas D. Scott, *Finding Sand Creek: History, Archaeology, and the 1864 Massacre Site* (Norman: University of Oklahoma Press, 2004), 9.

34. Stan Hoig, *The Sand Creek Massacre* (Norman: University of Oklahoma Press, 1961), 112.

35. Ibid., 142–43.

36. Jerome A. Greene, *Washita: The U.S. Army and the Southern Cheyennes, 1867–1879* (Norman: University of Oklahoma Press, 2004), 142–43.

37. Hoig, *Sand Creek Massacre,* 179.

38. Utley, *Indian Frontier,* 86–92; Greene and Scott, *Finding Sand Creek,* chap. 1.

39. Greene, *Washita,* 24.

40. Katie Kane, "Nits Make Lice: Drogheda, Sand Creek, and the Poetics of Colonial Extermination," *Cultural Critique* 42 (spring 1999), 81–103. Other reported uses of the phrase come from Tennessee, California, and, as seen earlier, from Winnebago Indians in Minnesota. This suggests a wider and earlier use of the phrase.

41. Greene and Scott, *Finding Sand Creek,* 21.

42. Utley, *Indian Frontier,* 102.

43. Bray, *Crazy Horse,* 76, 79, 83.

44. Dee Brown, *Bury My Heart at Wounded Knee: An Indian History of the American West* (New York: Holt, Rinehart and Winston, 1970), 105.

45. Robert M. Utley and Wilcomb E. Washburn, *Indian Wars* (Boston: Houghton Mifflin, 1977), 213.

46. James C. Olson, *Red Cloud and the Sioux Problem* (Lincoln: University of Nebraska Press, 1965), 52.

47. Francis Paul Prucha, *American Indian Policy in Crisis: Christian Reformers and the American Indian, 1865–1900* (Norman: University of Oklahoma Press, 1976), 21.

48. Ostler, *Plains Sioux,* 48.

49. Utley, *Indian Frontier,* 118.

50. Ostler, *Plains Sioux,* 50.

51. Ibid., 49–51.

CHAPTER TWO: War and Peace . . . and War

Epigraph: Louise Barnett, *Touched by Fire: The Life, Death, and Mythic Afterlife of George Armstrong Custer* (Lincoln: University of Nebraska Press, 1996), 147.

1. Robert M. Utley, *Cavalier in Buckskin: George Armstrong Custer and the Western Military Frontier,* rev. ed. (Norman: University of Oklahoma Press, 2001), 14, 16.

2. Ibid., 22–23, 34.

3. Ibid., 27.

4. Ibid., 33–34; Marguerite Merington, ed., *The Custer Story: The Life and Intimate Letters of George A. Custer and His Wife Elizabeth* (Lincoln: University of Nebraska Press, 1987), 62.

5. Brian W. Dippie, "Custer: The Indian Fighter," *The Custer Reader,* ed. Paul Andrew Hutton (Lincoln: University of Nebraska Press, 1992), 105.

6. Dippie, "Custer: The Indian Fighter," 103.

7. Utley, *Cavalier in Buckskin*, 50.

8. Ibid., 52.

9. Stan Hoig, *The Battle of the Washita* (New York: Doubleday, 1976), 37.

10. John W. Bailey, "Civilization the Military Way," *The Military and Conflict between Cultures: Soldiers at the Interface*, ed. James C. Bradford (College Station: Texas A&M University Press, 1997), 115.

11. Paul Andrew Hutton, *Phil Sheridan and His Army* (Lincoln: University of Nebraska Press, 1985), 180, 196.

12. Jerome A. Greene, *Washita: The U.S. Army and the Southern Cheyennes, 1867–1869* (Norman: University of Oklahoma Press, 2004), 31.

13. Lance Janda, "Shutting the Gates of Mercy: The American Origins of Total War, 1860–1880," *Journal of American Military History* 59, no. 1 (January 1995): 7–26.

14. Barnett, *Touched by Fire*, 179; Bailey, "Civilization the Military Way," 109.

15. Janda, "Shutting the Gates of Mercy," 7–26.

16. Utley, *Cavalier in Buckskin*, 61.

17. General George Armstrong Custer, *My Life on the Plains* (repr., Norman: University of Oklahoma Press, 1962), 49.

18. Greene, *Washita*, 72.

19. Ibid., 97, 99–100.

20. Utley, *Cavalier in Buckskin*, 65.

21. Barnett, *Touched by Fire*, 156.

22. Richard G. Hardorff, *Washita Memories: Eyewitness Views of Custer's Attack on Black Kettle's Village* (Norman: University of Oklahoma Press, 2006), 206, 208, 333.

23. Utley, *Cavalier in Buckskin*, 67–68.

24. Ibid., 68; Hardorff, *Washita Memories*, 20.

25. Utley, *Cavalier in Buckskin*, 68.

26. Custer's Official Report, November 28, 1868, reprinted in Hardorff, *Washita Memories*, 61–65.

27. Custer, *My Life on the Plains*, 249.

28. Utley, *Cavalier in Buckskin*, 70.

29. Hardorff, *Washita Memories*, 28.

30. Greene, *Washita*, 164–65; Hardorff, *Washita Memories*, 29.

31. Greene, *Washita*, 164–66; Hardorff, *Washita Memories*, 29; Thom Hatch, *Black Kettle: The Cheyenne Chief Who Sought Peace but Found War* (Hoboken, NJ: John Wiley & Sons, 2004), 255–58.

32. Hardorff, *Washita Memories*, 305, 336.

33. Greene, *Washita*, 163.

34. Custer, *My Life on the Plains*, 22, 21.

35. William Temple Hornaday, *The Extermination of the American Bison* (Washington, DC: Smithsonian Institution Press, 2002; originally published 1889), 214.

36. Barnett, *Touched by Fire*, 218; Robert Wooster, *The Military and United States*

Indian Policy, 1865–1903 (Lincoln: University of Nebraska Press, 1988), 171; David D. Smits, "The Frontier Army and the Destruction of the Buffalo: 1865–1883," *Western Historical Quarterly* 25 (Autumn 1994): 330, 337, 338.

37. Richard Slotkin, *The Fatal Environment: The Myth of the Frontier in the Age of Industrialization, 1800–1890* (Norman: University of Oklahoma Press, 1985), 408.

38. Greene, *Washita*, 180; Utley, *Cavalier in Buckskin*, 73.

39. Custer, *My Life on the Plains*, 282.

40. Hardorff, *Washita Memories*, 230–31; Utley, *Cavalier in Buckskin*, 107.

41. Robert M. Utley, *The Indian Frontier of the American West, 1846–1890* (Albuquerque: University of New Mexico Press, 1984), 129.

42. Francis Paul Prucha, *American Indian Policy in Crisis: Christian Reformers and the Indian, 1865–1900* (Norman: University of Oklahoma Press, 1976), 25.

43. Heather Cox Richardson, *West from Appomattox: The Reconstruction of America after the Civil War* (New Haven, CT: Yale University Press, 2007), 115.

44. Clyde A. Milner II, *With Good Intentions: Quaker Work among the Pawnees, Otos, and Omahas in the 1870s* (Lincoln: University of Nebraska Press, 1982), 5; Utley, *Indian Frontier*, 130.

45. Catherine Price, *The Oglala People, 1841–1879: A Political History* (Lincoln: University of Nebraska Press, 1996), 89, 90.

46. George Hyde, *Spotted Tail's Folk: A History of the Brule People* (Norman: University of Oklahoma Press, 1961), 174.

47. Hyde, *Spotted Tail's Folk*, 177–78.

48. James C. Olsen, *Red Cloud and the Sioux Problem* (Lincoln: University of Nebraska Press, 1965), 104–5.

49. Ibid., 106.

50. Robert G. Athearn, *William Tecumseh Sherman and the Settlement of the West* (Norman: University of Oklahoma Press, 1956), 286.

51. Olson, *Red Cloud*, 110.

52. Price, *The Oglala People*, 92.

53. Thomas B. Marquis, interpreter, *Wooden Leg: A Warrior Who Fought Custer* (Lincoln: University of Nebraska Press, 1962), 205.

54. Robert M. Utley, *The Lance and the Shield: The Life and Times of Sitting Bull* (New York: Ballantine Books, 1993), 91, 73.

55. Utley, *Cavalier in Buckskin*, 112, 111.

56. Jeffery Ostler, *The Plains Sioux and U.S. Colonialism from Lewis and Clark to Wounded Knee* (Cambridge: Cambridge University Press, 2004), 52.

57. Utley, *Lance and Shield*, 109.

58. Ibid., 111.

59. Utley, *Cavalier in Buckskin*, 117.

60. Ibid., 134.

61. Utley, *Lance and Shield*, 115.

62. Utley, *Cavalier in Buckskin*, 137, 136.

63. Ibid., 137, 140, 147.

64. Kingsley M. Bray, *Crazy Horse: A Lakota Life* (Norman: University of Oklahoma Press, 2006), 189.

65. Ostler, *Plains Sioux*, 61–62.

CHAPTER THREE: Custer's Luck and Sitting Bull's Medicine

Epigraph: Raymond Wilson, *Ohiyesa: Charles Eastman, Santee Sioux* (Urbana: University of Illinois Press, 1983), 137–38.

Epigraph: Paul Andrew Hutton, *Phil Sheridan and His Army* (Lincoln: University of Nebraska Press, 1985), 326.

1. Robert M. Utley, *Cavalier in Buckskin: George Armstrong Custer and the Western Military Frontier*, rev. ed. (Norman: University of Oklahoma Press, 2001), 165.

2. Charles Windolph, *I Fought with Custer: The Story of Sergeant Windolph, Last Survivor of the Battle of the Little Big Horn* (Lincoln: University of Nebraska Press, originally published 1947), 53.

3. Utley, *Cavalier in Buckskin*, 167.

4. John S. Gray, *Centennial Campaign: The Sioux War of 1876* (Norman: University of Oklahoma Press, 1988), 48.

5. Thomas B. Marquis, interpreter, *Wooden Leg: A Warrior Who Fought Custer* (Lincoln: University of Nebraska Press, 1962), 172–74.

6. Kingsley M. Bray, *Crazy Horse: A Lakota Life* (Norman: University of Oklahoma Press, 2006), 199–201.

7. Hutton, *Phil Sheridan*, 186.

8. Ibid., 182–83.

9. Ibid., 128; George Crook, *General George Crook: His Autobiography*, ed. Martin F. Schmitt (Norman: University of Oklahoma Press, 1986), 16, 267; Utley, *Cavalier in Buckskin*, 206.

10. John W. Bailey, "Civilization the Military Way," *The Military and Conflict between Cultures: Soldiers at the Interface*, ed. James C. Bradford (College Station: Texas A&M University Press, 1997), 126.

11. George Armstrong Custer, *My Life on the Plains: Or, Personal Experiences with Indians* (Norman: University of Oklahoma Press, 1977), 26, 22, 13, 148.

12. Utley, *Cavalier in Buckskin*, 158.

13. James Donovan, *A Terrible Glory: Custer and the Little Bighorn—The Last Great Battle of the American West* (New York: Little, Brown, 2008), 122.

14. Louis S. Warren, *Buffalo Bill's America: William Cody and the Wild West Show* (New York: Knopf, 2005), 97.

15. Windolph, *I Fought with Custer*, 3, 4.

16. Plenty-Coups as told to Frank Bird Linderman, *Plenty-Coups, Chief of the Crows*, 2nd ed. (Lincoln: University of Nebraska Press, 2002), 85.

17. Warren, *Buffalo Bill's America*, 97.

18. Marquis, *Wooden Leg*, 179.

19. Ibid., 185.

20. Robert M. Utley, *The Lance and the Shield: The Life and Times of Sitting Bull* (New York: Ballantine Books, 1993), 137, 138.

21. Marquis, *Wooden Leg*, 200.

22. George Bird Grinnell, *The Fighting Cheyennes* (New York: Charles Scribner's Sons, 1915), 324; Thomas W. Dunlay, *Wolves for the Blue Soldiers: Indian Scouts and Auxiliaries with the United States Army, 1860–1890* (Lincoln: University of Nebraska Press, 1987), 116.

23. Gary C. Anderson, *Sitting Bull and the Paradox of Lakota Nationhood* (New York: Pearson Longman, 2007), 100.

24. Anderson, *Sitting Bull*, 42.

25. Donovan, *Terrible Glory*, 151.

26. Anderson, *Sitting Bull*, 101.

27. Utley, *Lance and Shield*, 144.

28. Windolph, *I Fought with Custer*, 79.

29. Donovan, *Terrible Glory*, 143.

30. Ibid., 143.

31. Ibid., 159.

32. Utley, *Cavalier in Buckskin*, 176.

33. Donovan, *Terrible Glory*, 176.

34. Utley, *Cavalier in Buckskin*, 177.

35. Donovan, *Terrible Glory*, 183.

36. Ibid., 195.

37. Ibid., 201.

38. Gray, *Centennial Campaign*, 167.

39. Utley, *Cavalier in Buckskin*, 181.

40. Donovan, *Terrible Glory*, 209.

41. Ibid., 212.

42. Utley, *Cavalier in Buckskin*, 183.

43. Donovan, *Terrible Glory*, 217.

44. Utley, *Cavalier in Buckskin*, 186.

45. Ibid.

46. John G. Neihardt, *Black Elk Speaks: Being the Life Story of a Holy Man of the Oglala Sioux* (Lincoln: University of Nebraska Press, 1988), 105.

47. Richard G. Hardorff, *Indian Views of the Custer Fight* (Norman: University of Oklahoma Press, 2005), 64, 118.

48. Jerome A. Greene, ed., *Lakota and Cheyenne: Indian Views of the Great Sioux War, 1876–1877* (Norman: University of Oklahoma Press, 1994), 42–43.

49. Anderson, *Sitting Bull*, 104; Marquis, *Wooden Leg*, 217; "Interviews with Two Moons," in *Cheyenne Memories of the Custer Fight*, ed. Richard G. Hardorff (Lincoln: University of Nebraska Press, 1995), 101.

50. Bray, *Crazy Horse*, 218; Neihardt, *Black Elk Speaks*, 111.

51. Donovan, *Terrible Glory*, 240–41.

52. Bray, *Crazy Horse*, 220; "Interviews with Two Moons," 101.

53. Marquis, *Wooden Leg*, 221–23.

54. Raymond J. DeMallie, ed., *The Sixth Grandfather: Black Elk's Teachings Given to John G. Neihardt* (Lincoln: University of Nebraska Press, 1984), 183.

55. Utley, *Lance and Shield*, 153.

56. "Interviews with Two Moons," 102; Hardorff, *Indian Views*, 74.

57. John S. Gray, *Custer's Last Campaign: Mitch Boyer and the Little Bighorn Reconstructed* (Lincoln: University of Nebraska Press, 1993), 367.

58. George Armstrong Custer, *My Life on the Plains: Or Personal Experiences with Indians* (repr., Norman: University of Oklahoma, 1962), 327.

59. Richard G. Hardorff, *Lakota Recollections of the Custer Fight: New Sources of Indian-Military History* (Lincoln: University of Nebraska Press, 1991), 54.

60. Greene, *Lakota and Cheyenne*, 45; Robert Taft, "The Pictorial Record of the Old West," in *The Custer Reader*, ed. Paul Andrew Hutton (Lincoln: University of Nebraska Press, 1992), 429.

61. Utley, *Lance and Shield*, 156.

62. Marquis, *Wooden Leg*, 231.

63. Bray, *Crazy Horse*, 228–29.

64. Utley, *Cavalier in Buckskin*, 199.

65. Utley, *Lance and Shield*, 158.

66. Marquis, *Wooden Leg*, 237.

67. Kate Bighead, "She Watched Custer's Last Battle," in *The Custer Reader*, ed. Paul Andrew Hutton (Lincoln: University of Nebraska Press, 1992), 371.

68. Ibid., 376.

69. Louise Barnett, *Touched by Fire: The Life, Death, and Mythic Afterlife of George Armstrong Custer* (Lincoln: University of Nebraska Press, 1996), 292.

70. Windolph, *I Fought with Custer*, 102.

71. Greene, *Lakota and Cheyenne*, 46; Marquis, *Wooden Leg*, 256.

72. Hardorff, *Indian Views*, 122.

73. Greene, *Lakota and Cheyenne*, 46.

74. Hardorff, *Indian Views*, 166, 126.

CHAPTER FOUR: Surrounded

Epigraph: John G. Neihardt, *Black Elk Speaks: Being the Life Story of a Holy Man of the Oglala Sioux* (repr., Lincoln: University of Nebraska Press, 2000), 102.

1. John Gregory Bourke, *On the Border with Crook* (Lincoln: University of Nebraska Press, 1971), 299, 343.

2. John Frederick Finerty, *War-Path and Bivouac* (Norman: University of Oklahoma Press, 1890), 148.

3. Bourke, *On the Border*, 334.

4. Jerome A. Greene, *Slim Buttes, 1876: An Episode of the Great Sioux War* (Norman: University of Oklahoma Press, 1982), 7.

5. Paul Hedren, *We Trailed the Sioux: Enlisted Men Speak on Custer, Crook, and the Great Sioux War* (Mechanicsburg, PA: Stackpole Books, 2003), 34.

6. Hedren, *We Trailed the Sioux*, 51; Charles M. Robinson III, *A Good Year to Die: The Story of the Great Sioux War* (Norman: University of Oklahoma Press, 1995), 244.

7. Greene, *Slim Buttes*, 63; Jerome A. Greene, ed., *Lakota and Cheyenne: Indian Views of the Great Sioux War, 1876–1877* (Norman: University of Oklahoma Press, 2000), 86.

8. Greene, *Lakota and Cheyenne*, 46.

9. Greene, *Slim Buttes*, 115.

10. Bourke, *On the Border*, 374, 375.

11. Greene, *Slim Buttes*, 112–14.

12. Bourke, *On the Border*, 380.

13. Jerome A. Greene, *Yellowstone Command: Colonel Nelson A. Miles and the Great Sioux War, 1876–1877* (Norman: University of Oklahoma Press, 2006), 71.

14. Robert M. Utley, *The Lance and the Shield: The Life and Times of Sitting Bull* (New York: Ballantine Books, 1993), 169.

15. Greene, *Lakota and Cheyenne*, 107; Greene, *Yellowstone Command*, 96.

16. Greene, *Yellowstone Command*, 98, 96.

17. Ibid., 103.

18. Jerome A. Greene, *Morning Star Dawn: The Powder River Expedition and the Northern Cheyennes, 1876* (Norman: University of Oklahoma Press, 2003), 78, 41.

19. Greene, *Lakota and Cheyenne*, 119.

20. Ibid., 114.

21. Greene, *Morning Star Dawn*, 122.

22. Ibid., 139.

23. Ibid., 165.

24. Greene, *Lakota and Cheyenne*, 115.

25. Kingsley M. Bray, *Crazy Horse: A Lakota Life* (Norman: University of Oklahoma Press, 2006), 261.

26. Utley, *Lance and Shield*, 180, 181.

27. Raymond J. DeMallie, ed., *The Sixth Grandfather: Black Elk's Teachings Given to John G. Neihardt* (Lincoln: University of Nebraska Press, 1984), 202.

28. Bray, *Crazy Horse*, 269, 271.

29. Richard G. Hardorff, *Cheyenne Memories of the Custer Fight* (Lincoln: University of Nebraska Press, 1995), 105.

30. Bray, *Crazy Horse*, 282.

31. Ibid., 339–41; see also Mari Sandoz, *Crazy Horse: The Strange Man of the Oglalas* (Lincoln: University of Nebraska Press, 1942), 392.

32. Bray, *Crazy Horse*, 331.

33. Ibid., 369–71.

34. Ibid., 385–90.

35. Gary C. Anderson, *Sitting Bull and the Paradox of Lakota Nationhood* (New York: Pearson Longman, 2007), 124.

36. Ibid., 128.

37. Utley, *Lance and Shield*, 232, 233.

38. Jeffrey Ostler, *The Plains Sioux and U.S. Colonialism from Lewis and Clark to Wounded Knee* (Cambridge: Cambridge University Press, 2004), 194.

39. Robert G. Athearn, *William Tecumseh Sherman and the Settlement of the West* (Norman: University of Oklahoma Press, 1956), 168.

40. Ostler, *Plains Sioux*, 129.

41. Pratt quoted in Clifford E. Trafzer, Jean A. Keller, and Lorene Sisquoc, *Boarding School Blues: Revisiting American Indian Educational Experiences* (Lincoln: University of Nebraska Press, 2006), intro., 1, 13.

42. Luther Standing Bear, *My People the Sioux* (New York: Houghton Mifflin, 1928), 124, 141.

43. Utley, *Lance and Shield*, 269.

44. Ostler, *Plains Sioux*, 238; Utley, *Lance and Shield*, 280.

45. Ostler, *Plains Sioux*, 174.

46. Robert W. Larson, *Gall: Lakota War Chief* (Norman: University of Oklahoma Press, 2007), 190.

47. Anderson, *Sitting Bull*, 165.

48. Ostler, *Plains Sioux*, 265.

49. Anderson, *Sitting Bull*, 172, 177.

50. Ostler, *Plains Sioux*, 291.

51. Anderson, *Sitting Bull*, 186; Utley, *Lance and Shield*, 300–301.

52. James Mooney, *The Ghost Dance Religion and Wounded Knee* (repr., New York: Dover Publications, Inc., 1973), 869.

53. Ostler, *Plains Sioux*, 351.

54. John G. Neihardt, *Black Elk Speaks: Being the Life of a Holy Man of the Oglala Sioux* (Lincoln: University of Nebraska Press, 1988), 270.

55. Robert M. Utley and Wilcomb E. Washburn, *Indian Wars* (New York: Houghton Mifflin, 1987), 301.

56. Charles A. Eastman, *From the Deep Woods to Civilization* (Boston: Little, Brown, 1916), 114.

57. DeMallie, *Sixth Grandfather*, 294.

CHAPTER FIVE: Still Standing

Epigraph: Norman Maclean, *The Norman Maclean Reader*, ed. O. Alan Weltzien (Chicago: University of Chicago Press, 2008), 11.

1. William F. Cody, *The Life of Buffalo Bill* (Hartford, CT: F. E. Bliss, 1879; repr., New York: Time-Life Books, 1982), 344.

2. Charles King, *Campaigning with Crook* (Norman: University of Oklahoma Press, 1964), 38.

3. Cody, *Life of Buffalo Bill*, 343, 345.

4. Both of Terry's reports are quoted at length in Charles M. Robinson III, *A Good*

Year to Die: The Story of the Great Sioux War (Norman: University of Oklahoma Press, 1995), 211, 213.

5. Robert Utley, *Custer and the Great Controversy* (Los Angeles: Westernlore Press, 1962), 37.

6. James Donovan, *A Terrible Glory: Custer and the Little Bighorn—The Last Great Battle of the American West* (New York: Little, Brown, 2008), 320.

7. Robert Utley, *Cavalier in Buckskin: George Armstrong Custer and the Western Military Frontier* (Norman: University of Oklahoma Press, 1988), 5.

8. Richard Slotkin, *The Fatal Environment: The Myth of the Frontier in the Age of Industrialization, 1800–1890* (Norman: University of Oklahoma Press, 1985), 455–58.

9. Utley, *Cavalier in Buckskin*, 5.

10. Slotkin, *Fatal Environment*, 473–76; Utley, *Custer and the Great Controversy*, 41.

11. Utley, *Custer and the Great Controversy*, 44, 45, 47.

12. Brian Dippie, *Custer's Last Stand: Anatomy of an American Myth* (Lincoln: University of Nebraska Press, 1976), 1.

13. Shirley A. Leckie, *Elizabeth Bacon Custer and the Making of a Myth* (Norman: University of Oklahoma Press, 1993), 206.

14. Michael A. Elliott, *Custerology: The Enduring Legacy of the Indian Wars and George Armstrong Custer* (Chicago: University of Chicago Press, 2007), 31–32; Dippie, *Custer's Last Stand*, 49.

15. Dippie, *Custer's Last Stand*, 52.

16. Frederick Whitaker, *A Complete Life of Gen. George A. Custer* (New York: Sheldon, 1876), 1, 8.

17. Utley, *Custer and the Great Controversy*, 123–24, 137; Slotkin, *Fatal Environment*, 510.

18. All Elizabeth Custer quotations from Leckie, *Elizabeth Bacon Custer*, 281, 212, 236–37, 303, 305.

19. Slotkin, *Fatal Environment*, 460.

20. Gary C. Anderson, *Sitting Bull and the Paradox of Lakota Nationhood* (New York: Pearson Longman, 2007), 132.

21. Louis S. Warren, *Buffalo Bill's America: William Cody and the Wild West Show* (New York: Knopf, 2005), 195, 198.

22. Quoted in Anderson, *Sitting Bull*, 156.

23. Robert M. Utley, *The Lance and the Shield: The Life and Times of Sitting Bull* (New York: Ballantine Books, 1993), 264.

24. Luther Standing Bear, *My People the Sioux* (Boston: Houghton Mifflin, 1928), 185.

25. Warren, *Buffalo Bill's America*, 219.

26. Utley, *Lance and Shield*, 264.

27. Ibid.

28. L. G. Moses, *Wild West Shows and the Images of American Indians, 1883–1933* (Albuquerque: University of New Mexico Press, 1996), 28.

29. Ostler, *Plains Sioux*, 214, 215.

30. Ibid., 215.

31. Dan Moos, *Outside America: Race, Ethnicity, and the Role of the American West in National Belonging* (Dartmouth: Dartmouth University Press, 2005), 175.

32. Moses, *Wild West Shows*, 31.

33. Warren, *Buffalo Bill's America*, 269; Moses, *Wild West Shows*, 35.

34. Joy Kasson, *Buffalo Bill's Wild West* (New York: Hill and Wang, 2000), 113, 244.

35. Quoted in Warren, *Buffalo Bill's America*, 274.

36. Quoted in Moses, *Wild West Shows*, 6.

37. Standing Bear, *My People the Sioux*, 258, 261.

38. Quoted in Moses, *Wild West Shows*, 103, 111.

39. Raymond J. DeMallie, ed., *The Sixth Grandfather: Black Elk's Teachings Given to John G. Neihardt* (Lincoln: University of Nebraska Press, 1984), 245, 250, 252.

40. Standing Bear, *My People the Sioux*, 259; Moses, *Wild West Shows*, 33.

41. Philip J. Deloria, *Indians in Unexpected Places* (Lawrence: University Press of Kansas, 2004), 67; Moses, *Wild West Shows*, 85–86.

42. Matthew Frye Jacobson, *Whiteness of a Different Color: European Immigrants and the Alchemy of Race* (Cambridge, MA: Harvard University Press, 1998), especially chap. 2.

43. Moses, *Wild West Shows*, 89, 39; Cody's Berlin interview is quoted in Paul Reddin, *Wild West Shows* (Urbana: University of Illinois Press, 1999), 114; Twain quoted in Warren, *Buffalo Bill's America*, 295.

44. Reddin, *Wild West Shows*, 121.

45. Quoted in Richard Slotkin, *Gunfighter Nation: The Myth of the Frontier in Twentieth Century America* (Norman: University of Oklahoma Press, 1985), 77.

46. For a development of this theme, see Richard White, "Frederick Jackson Turner and Buffalo Bill," in *The Frontier in American Culture*, ed. James R. Grossman (Berkeley: University of California Press, 1994), 7–65.

47. Quoted in Jerome Greene, *Stricken Field: The Little Bighorn since 1876* (Norman: University of Oklahoma Press, 2008), 25.

48. Ibid., 31.

49. Frederick E. Hoxie, *Parading through History: The Making of the Crow Nation in America, 1805–1935* (Cambridge: Cambridge University Press, 1995), 148–49.

50. Greene, *Stricken Field*, 55.

51. Russel Lawrence Barsh, "American Indians in the Great War," *Ethnohistory* 38 (Summer 1991): 3, 276–303.

52. Quotations in Barsh, "American Indians in the Great War," 287, 288, 289.

53. Quotations from Elliott, *Custerology*, 38–39.

54. Dippie, *Custer's Last Stand*, 96.

55. Standing Bear, *My People the Sioux*, 278.

56. Paul Andrew Hutton, "'Correct in Every Detail': General Custer in Hollywood," in *The Custer Reader*, ed. Paul Andrew Hutton (Lincoln: University of Nebraska Press, 1992), 488, 489, 504.

57. Elliott, *Custerology*, 232.

58. Ibid., 233.

59. Ibid., 246.

60. Quoted in Dippie, *Custer's Last Stand*, 140.

61. Elliott, *Custerology*, 41.

Epilogue

1. Michael A. Elliott, *Custerology: The Enduring Legacy of the Indian Wars and George Armstrong Custer* (Chicago: University of Chicago Press, 2007), 43.

2. Jerome Greene, *Stricken Field: The Little Bighorn since 1876* (Norman: University of Oklahoma Press, 2008), 191.

3. Ibid., 237.

4. Richard Slotkin, *Regeneration through Violence: The Mythology of the American Frontier, 1600–1860* (Middletown, CT: Wesleyan University Press, 1973), 562; Robert D. Kaplan, "War on Terrorism: Indian Country," *Wall Street Journal*, September 21, 2004.

5. Quoted in Jim Sheeler, "Wake for an Indian Warrior," *Rocky Mountain News*, January 21, 2006.

SUGGESTED FURTHER READING

More has been written about the Battle of the Little Bighorn than any other battle in American history, with the possible exception of Gettysburg. From this vast library, some books stand out for their clarity, judiciousness, and careful scholarship. For a recent, lively retelling of the battle, see James Donovan, *A Terrible Glory: Custer and the Little Bighorn—The Last Great Battle of the American West* (New York: Little, Brown, 2008). Robert M. Utley's *The Indian Frontier of the American West, 1846–1890* (Albuquerque: University of New Mexico Press, 1984) provides a judicious overview of the larger context of the Indian wars, while Jeffrey Ostler's *The Plains Sioux and U.S. Colonialism from Lewis and Clark to Wounded Knee* (Cambridge: Cambridge University Press, 2004) combines invaluable insight and meticulous research in a detailed account of the struggles of the Sioux during this period. A recent testament to the ongoing significance of the battle in native and nonnative American lives is Michael A. Elliott's *Custerology: The Enduring Legacy of the Indian Wars and George Armstrong Custer* (Chicago: University of Chicago Press, 2007).

Good introductions to the Indian context for the nineteenth-century wars include Royal B. Hassrick, *The Sioux: Life and Customs of a Warrior Society* (Norman: University of Oklahoma, 1964); Guy Gibbon, *The Sioux: The Dakota and Lakota Nations* (Malden, MA: Blackwell Press, 2003); Frederick E. Hoxie, *Parading through History: The Making of the Crow Nation in America, 1805–1935* (Cambridge: Cambridge University Press, 1995); George Bird Grinnell, *The Fighting Cheyennes* (New York: Charles Scribner's Sons, 1915); and Loretta Fowler's helpful overview, *The Columbia Guide to American Indians of the Great Plains* (New York: Columbia University Press, 2003). For a sophisticated treatment of the Cheyenne on the central plains read Elliot West, *The Contested Plains: Indians, Goldseekers, and the Rush to Colorado* (Lawrence: University Press of Kansas, 1998). Frank Secoy's *Changing Military Patterns of the Great Plains Indians* (Lincoln: University of Nebraska Press, 1992) covers the earlier history of intertribal warfare, as do two provocative articles, John C. Ewers, "Intertribal Warfare as the Precursor of Indian-White Warfare on the Northern Great Plains," *Western Historical Quarterly* 6 (October 1975): 397–410; and Richard White, "The Winning of the West: The Expansion of the Western Sioux in the Eighteenth and Nineteenth Centuries," *Journal of American History* 65 (September 1978): 319–43.

For a deeper understanding of Sioux political life before and during the wars, read George E. Hyde's two studies, *Red Cloud's Folk* (Norman: University of Oklahoma Press, 1937) and *Spotted Tail's Folk: A History of the Brule People* (Norman: University of Oklahoma Press, 1961). These should be supplemented with James C. Olson's *Red Cloud and the Sioux Problem* (Lincoln: University of Nebraska Press, 1965) and Catherine Price's *The Oglala People, 1841–1879: A Political History* (Lincoln: University of Nebraska Press, 1996). Charles M. Robinson III's *A Good Year to Die: The Story of the Great Sioux War* (Norman: University of Oklahoma Press, 1995) provides a readable, balanced overview of the topic, while reliable, detailed studies of specific events are found in Micheal Clodfelter's *The Dakota War: The United States Army versus the Sioux, 1862–1865* (Jefferson, NC: McFarland, 1998); Stan Hoig's *The Sand Creek Massacre* (Norman: University of Oklahoma Press, 1961); and many works by Jerome A. Greene, notably *Washita: The U.S. Army and the Southern Cheyennes, 1867–1879* (Norman: University of Oklahoma Press, 2004); *Slim Buttes, 1876: An Episode of the Great Sioux War* (Norman: University of Oklahoma Press, 1982); *Morning Star Dawn: The Powder River Expedition and the Northern Cheyennes, 1876* (Norman: University of Oklahoma Press, 2003); and *Yellowstone Command: Colonel Nelson A. Miles and the Great Sioux War, 1876–1877* (Norman: University of Oklahoma Press, 2006).

Much of the best information about the Little Bighorn and its context is found in several outstanding biographies of key participants. The best recent biographies of the army's protagonist are Robert M. Utley, *Cavalier in Buckskin: George Armstrong Custer and the Western Military Frontier* (Norman: University of Oklahoma Press, 1988, rev. ed. 2001) and Louise Barnett, *Touched by Fire: The Life, Death, and Mythic Afterlife of George Armstrong Custer* (Lincoln: University of Nebraska Press, 1996). Rounding out these interpretations are the various perspectives contained in Paul Andrew Hutton, editor, *The Custer Reader* (Lincoln: University of Nebraska Press, 1992). For two interpretations of the Lakota holy man and war leader Sitting Bull, consult Robert M. Utley, *The Lance and the Shield: The Life and Times of Sitting Bull* (New York: Ballantine Books, 1993); and Gary C. Anderson, *Sitting Bull and the Paradox of Lakota Nationhood* (New York: Pearson Longman, 2007). The recent authoritative biography of the most famous Lakota warrior is Kingley M. Bray's *Crazy Horse: A Lakota Life* (Norman: University of Oklahoma Press, 2006). Some readers may prefer the shorter treatment by Larry McMurtry, *Crazy Horse: A Life* (New York: Penguin, 1999), or the older literary biography by Mari Sandoz, *Crazy Horse: The Strange Man of the Oglalas* (Lincoln: University of Nebraska Press, 1942). Also useful are two biographies of important supporting characters, Robert W. Larson's *Gall: Lakota War Chief* (Norman: University of Oklahoma Press, 2007) and Thom Hatch's *Black Kettle: The Cheyenne Chief Who Sought Peace but Found War* (Hoboken, NJ: John Wiley and Sons, 2004).

Vital to understanding the Seventh Cavalry's movements leading up to and during the battle are two books by John S. Gray, *Centennial Campaign: The Sioux War of 1876* (Norman: University of Oklahoma Press, 1988) and *Custer's Last Campaign: Mitch Boyer and the Little Bighorn Reconsidered* (Lincoln: University of Nebraska Press, 1991). A useful supplement to these is Gregory F. Michno's *Lakota Noon: The Indian Narrative of Custer's Defeat* (Missoula, MT: Mountain Press, 1997). Archaeology has added immensely to recent understandings of troop and Indian movements on the battlefield. The best summary is Richard Allen Fox Jr., *Archaeology, History, and Custer's Last Battle* (Norman: University of Oklahoma Press, 1993); see also Chuck Rankin, editor, *Legacy: New Perspectives on the Battle of the Little Bighorn* (Helena, MT: Montana State Historical Society Press, 1996). For a broader perspective on the Army's view of the Indian wars, consult several astute biographies of the leading generals, including Robert G. Athearn, *William Tecumseh Sherman and the Settlement of the West* (Norman: University of Oklahoma Press, 1956); Paul Andrew Hutton, *Phil Sheridan and His Army* (Lincoln: University of Nebraska Press, 1985); and Charles M. Robinson III, *General Crook and the Western Frontier* (Norman: University of Oklahoma Press, 2001). In *The View from Officers' Row: Army Perceptions of Western Indians* (Tucson: University of Arizona Press, 1990) Sherry Lynn Smith presents a shrewd analysis of the complex ideas military leaders held about their foes. Also important for understanding the army's efforts is Thomas W. Dunlay's *Wolves for the Blue Soldiers: Indian Scouts and Auxiliaries with the United States Army, 1860–1890* (Lincoln: University of Nebraska Press, 1982). Entertaining first-person accounts that round out the diversity of military views include John Gregory Bourke's *On the Border with Crook* (repr., Lincoln: University of Nebraska Press, 1971); Charles King's *Campaigning with Crook* (New York: Harper & Brothers, 1905); Charles Windolph's *I Fought with Custer* (Lincoln: University of Nebraska Press, 1947); James H. Bradley's *March of the Montana Column: Prelude to the Custer Disaster* (Norman: University of Oklahoma Press, 1961); journalist John Frederick Finerty's *War-Path and Bivouac* (Norman: University of Oklahoma Press, 1961); and Paul Hedren's edited collection, *We Trailed the Sioux: Enlisted Men Speak on Custer, Crook, and the Great Sioux War* (Mechanicsburg, PA: Stackpole Books, 2003). No list of first-person accounts could be complete without *My Life on the Plains* (Lincoln: University of Nebraska Press, 1966) by George Armstrong Custer and *Following the Guidon* (New York: Harper & Brothers, 1890) by Elizabeth Bacon Custer.

Indian accounts of the nineteenth-century wars have found a wider audience in recent years. An earlier classic is *Black Elk Speaks: Being the Life Story of a Holy Man of the Oglala Sioux*, as told to John G. Neihardt (Lincoln: University of Nebraska Press, 1932), which should be accompanied by the more accurate but less poetic *The Sixth Grandfather: Black Elk's Teachings as Given to John G. Neihardt* (Lincoln: University of Nebraska Press, 1984), edited by Raymond J. DeMallie. Still useful, if controversial, is Dee Brown's *Bury My Heart at Wounded Knee: An Indian History of the American West* (New York: Henry Holt, 1970). Lakota historian Joseph Marshall III has two books that offer important insights, *The Day the World Ended at Little Bighorn* (New York: Penguin, 2007) and *The Journey of Crazy Horse* (New York: Viking, 2004). A Northern Cheyenne perspective comes from tribal historian John Stands in Timber, *Cheyenne Memories* (New Haven: Yale University Press, 1967), and from the lively first-person account interpreted by Thomas B. Marquis, *Wooden Leg: A Warrior Who Fought Custer* (Lincoln: University of Nebraska Press, 1931). The two best-known Crow narratives are *Plenty-Coups: Chief of the Crows* (Lincoln: University of Nebraska Press, 1930) and *Pretty-shield: Medicine Woman of the Crows* (Lincoln: University of Nebraska Press,

1974), both first-person accounts as told to Frank Bird Linderman. Recently two historians have performed a valuable service by compiling and making available interviews with Indian battle survivors. Richard G. Hardorff has edited *Washita Memories: Eyewitness Views of Custer's Attack on Black Kettle's Village* (Norman: University of Oklahoma Press, 2006); *Cheyenne Memories of the Custer Fight* (Lincoln: University of Nebraska Press, 1995); *Indian Views of the Custer Fight* (Norman: Arthur H. Clark, 2004); and *Lakota Recollections of the Custer Fight* (Lincoln: University of Nebraska Press, 1991). Equally valuable are the compilations of Jerome A. Greene, *Lakota and Cheyenne: Indian Views of the Great Sioux War, 1876–1877* (Norman: University of Oklahoma Press, 1994) and *Battles and Skirmishes of the Great Sioux War, 1876–1877: The Military View* (Norman: University of Oklahoma Press, 1993).

The mythic afterlife of "Custer's Last Stand" has proven a fruitful field for cultural historians. The best biography of the man who interpreted the West for most easterners is Louis Warren's *Buffalo Bill's America: William Cody and the Wild West Show* (New York: Knopf, 2005), which is usefully supplemented by Joy Kasson's *Buffalo Bill's Wild West* (New York: Hill and Wang, 2000) and the autobiography by William F. Cody, *The Life of Buffalo Bill* (New York: Time-Life Books, 1982, originally published 1879). An informative catalog of variations on the Custer myth is Brian Dippie's *Custer's Last Stand: Anatomy of An American Myth* (Lincoln: University of Nebraska Press, 1976), while the role of his wife in enshrining a role for her martyred husband is told by Shirley A. Leckie, *Elizabeth Bacon Custer and the Making of a Myth* (Norman: University of Oklahoma Press, 1993). For more about the representation of Native Americans in the decades after the Little Bighorn, start with L. G. Moses, *Wild West Shows and the Images of American Indians, 1883–1933* (Albuquerque: University of New Mexico Press, 1996); Dan Moos, *Outside America: Race, Ethnicity, and the Role of the American West in National Belonging* (Dartmouth: Dartmouth University Press, 2005); and the delightful destroyer of stereotypes by Philip J. Deloria, *Indians in Unexpected Places* (Lawrence: University Press of Kansas, 2004). Informing all of these treatments of the western myth in American cultural life is the seminal trilogy of Richard Slotkin, *Regeneration through Violence: The Mythology of the American Frontier, 1600–1860* (Middletown, CT: Wesleyan University Press, 1974); *The Fatal Environment: The Myth of the Frontier in the Age of Industrialization, 1800–1890* (New York: HarperCollins, 1992); and *Gunfighter Nation: The Myth of the Frontier in Twentieth Century America* (Norman: University of Oklahoma Press, 1985). Finally, for how this struggle for meaning has played out on the battlefield itself, consult Jerome A. Greene, *Stricken Field: The Little Bighorn since 1876* (Norman: University of Oklahoma Press, 2008).

INDEX

Page numbers in *italics* indicate illustrations.

7-29-10
20